COMPENSATION AND RESTITUTION
TO VICTIMS OF CRIME

PATTERSON SMITH REPRINT SERIES IN
CRIMINOLOGY, LAW ENFORCEMENT, AND SOCIAL PROBLEMS

A listing of publications in the SERIES *will be found at rear of volume*

PUBLICATION NO. 120: PATTERSON SMITH REPRINT SERIES IN
CRIMINOLOGY, LAW ENFORCEMENT, AND SOCIAL PROBLEMS

Compensation and Restitution to Victims of Crime

BY STEPHEN SCHAFER

NORTHEASTERN UNIVERSITY

SECOND EDITION ENLARGED

MONTCLAIR, NEW JERSEY : PATTERSON SMITH : 1970

First edition published under the title "Restitution to Victims of Crime"
Copyright 1960 by Stevens & Sons Limited, London
Second edition published 1970 by special arrangement with
Stephen Schafer
Copyright © 1970 by
Patterson Smith Publishing Corporation
Montclair, New Jersey 07042

The statutes in the Appendix, together with uncodified amend-
ments and footnotes, were compiled by the Southern California
Law Review. *They are reproduced through the courtesy of the*
Southern California Law Review, *to whom grateful acknowl-*
edgment is extended.

SBN 87585–120–7

Library of Congress Catalog Card Number: 74–108237

This book is printed on three-hundred-year acid-free paper.

TO LEX

CONTENTS

Preface to the Second Edition . . . . . . *page* ix
Preface to the First Edition xiii

PART ONE

THE HISTORICAL BACKGROUND

1. THE COMMON PAST OF RESTITUTION AND PUNISHMENT . 3
2. THE DECLINE OF RESTITUTION 8

PART TWO

LEGISLATION OUTSIDE THE UNITED KINGDOM TO 1960

3. AIMS AND METHODS OF THE SURVEY 15
4. WESTERN EUROPE 18
   Belgium 18
   France 21
   Holland 24
5. CENTRAL EUROPE 30
   Austria 30
   Switzerland 31
   German Federal Republic 32
6. NORTHERN EUROPE 41
   Denmark 41
   Finland 43
   Norway 46
   Sweden 50
7. SOUTHERN EUROPE 53
   Italy 53
8. EASTERN EUROPE 56
   Turkey 56
   Greece 57
   Yugoslavia 59
9. NORTH AMERICA 60
   Canada 60
   United States 61
10. CENTRAL AMERICA 66
   Cuba 66
   Dominica 72
   Mexico 74

11. SOUTH AMERICA 76
    Argentina 76
12. MIDDLE EAST 80
    Israel 80
    Persia 83
    Egypt 84
13. FAR EAST 85
    India 85
    Pakistan 87
14. AUSTRALASIA 89
    Australia 89
    New Zealand 92
15. AFRICA 94
    Union of South Africa 94
16. COMMUNIST TERRITORIES 98
    Hungary 98
    Soviet Union 99
17. COMPARATIVE SUMMARY 101

PART THREE

UNITED KINGDOM

18. DEVELOPMENTS TO 1960 111

PART FOUR

PUNISHMENT AND RESTITUTION

19. THE RESTITUTIVE CONCEPT OF PUNISHMENT . . . 117
20. THE PUNITIVE CONCEPT OF RESTITUTION 123
21. THE JUSTIFICATION OF COMPENSATION AND
    CORRECTIONAL RESTITUTION 130

PART FIVE

DEVELOPMENTS IN VICTIM COMPENSATION TO 1970

22. NEW ZEALAND 139
23. UNITED KINGDOM 143
24. UNITED STATES 147

APPENDIX

SURVEY QUESTIONNAIRE 161
UNITED STATES STATUTES 163

Index 209

PREFACE TO THE SECOND EDITION

IT was in London, just past tea-time on the afternoon of May 20, 1958, in the traditional drizzle which clouded the top of Big Ben, when the author of this book entered the lobby of the Home Office, where he was greeted by the "Home Office cat," a friendly guard of the old White-hall building and the only cat on the British civil service payroll. The author had been called in to discuss his six-month-old proposal on vic-tim compensation with an *ad hoc* committee which was chaired by Francis Graham-Harrison, Under Secretary of State for the Home Office, and included Tom Lodge, the Director of Research, Leslie T. Wilkins, who had been instrumental in attracting the author to the problem of compensating victims of crime, and, to use their official language, "others concerned."

In the course of the meeting, in an atmosphere that was one of the kindest the author ever experienced with officials, the committee seemed somewhat surprised by three points that arose: First, no theoretically clear distinction existed between compensation and restitution, and if the former term was generally used to refer to payments by the offender to his victim, this had been a distinction drawn between the two terms in Great Britain only for convenience. Second, a system of compensa-tion to victims of crime (as the term was then understood) had been in operation in Switzerland and Cuba for some time and restitution to vic-tims of crime (as the term was then understood) was a feature of many foreign legal systems. The third and perhaps most striking surprise was that the author of this book, not being accustomed to "think for money," was strongly reluctant to ask for financial aid for his work, prompting the committee to state in the minutes of the meeting that "it appeared from what he [Schafer] said that the research would be quite inexpen-sive." Nonetheless, it should be recorded that subsequently the Home Office generously offered a small grant, which, at the time, was wel-come indeed.

Although the distinction between compensation and restitution re-mained unclear even at the end of this meeting, the author began his investigations and the research was announced in the Home Secretary's White Paper, "Penal Practice in a Changing Society," presented to Par-

ix

liament in February, 1959. Since the writer was informed that the Home
Secretary was interested in both proposals (compensation and restitution to victims of crime), his research and this resulting book attempted
to treat both concepts. The original title of the book, accordingly, was
planned to be *Compensation and Restitution to Victims of Crime;* at
the suggestion of the first publisher, who thought it cumbersome, the
title was shortened to *Restitution to Victims of Crime.* The full title has
been restored to this second edition to reflect the true scope of the work.
Perhaps it is worthy of mention that the distinction between the two
terms is still open to argument, and they are often used interchangeably
although they connote different responsibilities and refer to different
directions from which the satisfaction of the victim and the service of
his interests can best be approached. Compensation is an attempt to
counterbalance the victim's loss resulting from a criminal attack. It represents a sum of money awarded to him for the damage or injury
caused by a crime. It is an indication of the responsibility assumed by
society; it is, in essence, civil or neutral in character and thus represents
a non-criminal goal in a criminal case. Restitution differs in that it allo-
cates the responsibility to the offender. The restoration or reparation of
the victim's position and rights that were damaged or destroyed by the
criminal attack become, in effect, a part of the offender's sentence. It
is a claim for restitutive action to be taken by the criminal and is, in
essence, penal in character and thus represents a correctional goal in a
criminal process. Finally, the procedure of compensation calls for application by the victim for payment by society; restitution calls for the
decision of a criminal court and payment or action by the offender.

The theoretical clarity of the two concepts, however, was really not
relevant to the meritorious consideration of the English Home Office,
which essentially wanted to do justice to the "habitually ignored" victim,
and the fact that some compensation and restitution systems already
did exist in other countries before the Home Office decided upon action
cannot deny the fact that the English efforts were of an innovative and
constructive nature.

The idea of compensating and restituting victims of crime, as we
understand the concept today, had been ineffective as a legislative force
for centuries when, in 1957, Margery Fry, after consulting with Max
Grünhut and others, published her "Justice for Victims" in *The Observer.* This paper, written by the descendant of another English social
reformer, Elizabeth Fry, was so clear a presentation of the merits of

compensation and restitution that gradually other meaningful and powerful voices joined the pleas for "better help" for the victim of crime. The Home Secretary's White Paper of February, 1959, the "Round Table" symposium which appeared in the American *Journal of Public Law* later that year, and another White Paper issued by the Home Secretary in June, 1961, were among the more notable manifestations of this new concern. The interest of the lay and expert public gave the impression that a movement was afoot to reevaluate the offender-victim relationship and that the increasing recognition of the broadened concept of responsibility in such a relationship would have to include the thesis that we cannot deal with crimes and criminals without dealing with the victims. With the questioning of the effectiveness of the laws in force for repairing the harm, injury or other disadvantage caused by crime to the victim the promise was for legislative reexamination of the many legal systems relevant to the problem. The academic forum, always actively in the vanguard, pressed for meaningful solutions.

In a relatively short time the legislative responses did come. In New Zealand the Criminal Injuries Compensation Act brought a victim compensation system into force on January 1, 1964. England's program became effective eight months later. (The delays occasioned by a decade of arduous struggle for public recognition prevented the English victim compensation scheme from becoming the first, chronologically, in a series of modern models that followed. Nonetheless, England will doubtless be remembered as the pioneer in present-day compensation systems.) Subsequently in the United States, California, New York, Massachusetts, Maryland and Hawaii introduced compensation schemes. The so-called Yarborough proposal for federal legislation of victim compensation, which was introduced to the United States Congress in 1965, was reintroduced in 1967 and in 1969 and still awaits legislative response. Senator Yarborough submitted another bill in 1969 for similar legislation for the District of Columbia. During this period Illinois and other states announced plans for compensation systems. In Canada the provinces of Saskatchewan and Newfoundland initiated compensation programs while in Australia, New South Wales and Queensland enacted schemes. Italy is in the process of following these constructive examples, and preparations for a new law seem to be underway in other countries as well.

Many of the efforts that have thus far been made for the victim of crime seem primarily directed at meeting public anger over the rising volume of aggressive crime. It would be hoped that in time an enlightened populace will come to see the merits of a restitutive and compensative scheme based on a more substantive set of values. However, in addition to the numerous "popular" demands for victim compensation there also have appeared numerous articles and essays in professional journals emphasizing the theoretical importance of the issue.

Yet the impression seems to emerge that after an admirable beginning the movement for a modern and efficient system of victim compensation has begun to slacken pace. The overwhelming majority of the American states and most foreign countries still operate without a compensation scheme; most of them do not even contemplate one. Many legislators, lawyers, and even criminologists are habituated to the traditional conceptualization of the responsibility of the offender and appear hesitant to include the victim in any rationale of legislative reform; many laws on the statute books reflect ideas so outdated. Not only is restitution to victims of crime as a correctional device—a refined revival of the medieval idea of "composition"—still missing from most legal systems, but so also is compensation to victims as a restorative instrument—a refined version of civil law damages. It seems that after a heartening reexamination the problem of restitution and compensation to victims of crime may be forgotten again. Certainly the current neglect of the interests of the victim of crime suggests that we temper hope for any rapid global developments which the burgeoning enthusiasm of a decade ago gave promise.

This second edition of *Compensation and Restitution to Victims of Crime* retains the first twenty chapters of the original edition, consisting of Part One, Part Two (retitled), Part Three, and the first two chapters of Part Four. The new material consists of the last chapter of Part Four, the three chapters of Part Five, an Appendix containing relevant United States state and federal bills and statutes, and an Index.

I wish to take this opportunity of expressing my appreciation to the publishers of the second edition for their cooperation in making possible this enlargement of my earlier work.

STEPHEN SCHAFER

Boston
January, 1970

PREFACE TO THE FIRST EDITION

" THE guilty man lodged, fed, clothed, warmed, lighted, entertained, at
the expense of the State in a model cell, issued from it with a sum of
money lawfully earned, has paid his debt to society; he can set his victims
at defiance; but the victim has his consolation; he can think that by taxes
he pays to the Treasury, he has contributed towards the paternal care,
which has guarded the criminal during his stay in prison." [1] These were
the bitter and sarcastic words of Prins, the Belgian, at the Paris Prison
Congress in 1895, when during a discussion of the problem of restitution
to victims of crime, he could no longer contain his indignation at various
practical and theoretical difficulties raised against his proposals on behalf
of the victim.

His was not the first voice claiming recognition and respect for the
victim's injury, and it was by no means the last. Adherents to the classic
criminal law, just as much as modern criminologists, increasingly voiced
their concern; but, in fact, although the legislation of some States has,
in one form or another, accepted the principle of restitution (sometimes
called compensation, damages, etc.) " the unfortunate victim of criminality was habitually ignored " [2] right up to the present time. " Attention
was frequently called to the hardship which ensues to a person, who loses
his property by some criminal act, and who has to be content, if the
offender be brought to justice, with no other satisfaction for his loss
than can be afforded by the punishment of the offender by the State, as
one guilty of a public wrong, but not required to make restitution for
the private loss which his action has caused." [3]

For this reason I was glad to try to comply with the commission of
the Home Office to work on the problem of restitution, which the Italian
Garofalo considered " as one of the most important problems in penal

---

[1] The Paris Prison Congress, 1895, Summary Report (London).
[2] William Tallack, *Reparation to the Injured; and the Rights of the Victims of Crime
to Compensation* (London, 1900), pp. 10–11.
[3] E. Ruggles-Brise, *Report to the Secretary of State for the Home Department on the
Proceedings of the Fifth and Sixth International Penitentiary Congresses* (His
Majesty's Stationery Office, London, 1901), p. 51.

legislation." [4] The problem however, is not simple. It involves several practical and theoretical complications: but these must not be allowed to break the ties, by which the victim, through his injury and loss, is associated with the criminal offence.

This brief work is presented mainly in the service of knowledge: but, in addition to an examination of the legislation of different States, I have attempted to indicate, at least vaguely, my personal conviction as well, which seemed to me not only my right but perhaps also my duty.

I have tried to approach the problem from two angles in an attempt to serve not only the ideas of the victimology but the tasks of the penology as well. Restitution should carry out a mission not only in helping the victim in his present neglected position but, at the same time, in refining the practical concept of punishment. My approach differs from current solutions which are almost confined to the sphere of the civil law; however it also differs from the past solutions in which restitution appeared almost entirely as a criminal retribution.

Without holding such extreme views it does seem to be possible to establish a close relation between crime and its object, and the criminal and his victim. Not pity towards the victim, but appreciation of his claim is needed. Not thirst for revenge against the criminal, but a clearer understanding of his deed would help his reform and rehabilitation. Restitution might give emphasis to the fact that crime construes a relation not only between the criminal and society, but also between the criminal and his victim. The victim is not just simply the cause of the criminal procedure, but has a major part to play in the search for criminal justice.

In this work I try to offer a solution through which restitution may come nearer to the requirements of both victimology and penology. I have no illusion that in these brief lines I have succeeded in solving the problem of restitution to victims of crime. At most I have tried to pave the way, and I can only hope that the comments I have made may help in the search for a solution.

At this point it seems necessary to offer excuses for not having followed the sometimes rather obscure path of dogmatic dissection of

---

[4] Samuel J. Barrows, *The Sixth International Congress: Report of its Proceedings and Conclusions* (Washington, 1903), pp. 22–23.

minutiae. The purpose of this work is to offer a rough but true picture. I am indebted and sincerely grateful to all those (many of whose names are in the footnotes) who so kindly helped me to become acquainted with, or to understand better the relevant legislation of their countries; many of them, indeed, contributed ideas of their own. Similarly, I am grateful to all those who in the course of my work have encouraged me, exchanged ideas, and by their criticism have sharpened my thinking. Among others, I thank first of all the members of the Home Office Research Unit and Dr. M. Grünhut, Reader in Criminology at the University of Oxford. But in the end, of course, the author alone is responsible for any defects in this work.

STEPHEN SCHAFER.

LONDON,
July 1960.

PART ONE

THE HISTORICAL BACKGROUND

1

THE COMMON PAST OF RESTITUTION AND PUNISHMENT

THE title of this chapter does not necessarily involve a *petitio principii*. A common past does not, of course, imply a common present and future, but neither the adherents of restitution nor its opponents can be indifferent to the fact that restitution to victims of crime is an ancient institution, has had an established position in the history of penology, and for a long period was almost inseparably attached to the institution of punishment.

The historical origin of restitution, in a proper sense, the so-called system of " composition," lies in the Middle Ages, and can mainly be found in the Germanic common laws.

Earlier sources do not offer clear information.[1] There are some sporadic references. The death fine in Greece is referred to more than once in Homer[2]; thus, in the 9th Book of the Iliad, Ajax, in reproaching Achilles for not accepting the offer of reparation made to him by Agamemnon, reminds him that even a brother's death may be appeased by a pecuniary fine, and that the murderer, having paid the fine, may remain at home, free among his own people. Not only in the time of the Greeks, but in still earlier ages, when the Mosaic Dispensation was established among the Hebrews, traces of restitution are apparent. " That Dispensation, in its penal department, took special and prominent cognizance of the rights, and claims of the injured person, as against the offender."[3] For injuries both to person and property, restitution or reparation in some form was the chief and often the only element of punishment. Among Semitic nations the death fine was general, and it continued to prevail in the Turkish Empire.[4]

Indian Hinduism required restitution and atonement: he who atones is forgiven. In India, in the Sutra period, the settling of compensation was treated as a royal right: for murder the offender was obliged by the king to compensate the relatives of the deceased or the king or both. In the

---

[1] K. Jordan, " Adhäsionsprozess " in *Rechtslexikon für Juristen aller tentschen Staaten enthaltend die gesamte Rechtswissenschaft,* edited by Weiske (Berlin, 1839), Vol. I, pp. 122–123.

[2] Richard R. Cherry, *Lectures on the Growth of Criminal Law in Ancient Communities* (London, 1890), p. 10.   [3] Tallack, *op. cit.,* pp. 6–7.   [4] Cherry, *op. cit.,* p. 11.

time of Manu, compensation was regarded as a penance : hence it could be given to the priests. Islam also enjoins restitution and atonement.[5]

These sources, as well as, for example, the Law of Moses, which required fourfold restitution for stolen sheep and fivefold for the more useful ox,[6] or the Code of Hammurabi,[7] which was notorious for its deterrent cruelty and in some cases of criminal offences demanded even thirty times the value of the damage caused, suggest that the obligation of payment imposed on the criminal was enforced not in the interests of the victim, but rather for the purpose of increasing the severity of the criminal's punishment. Where the offender against society paid for his crimes with " an eye for an eye, a tooth for a tooth," or in a similar way, he paid as an object of the victim's vengeance, not in compensation for the victim's injury.

In ancient Roman law, in spite of the fairly close relationship between criminal law and civil law, it is not easy to get reliable information concerning the position of restitution in criminal law. Indeed, according to the Law of the Twelve Tables, in the case of theft, the thief, who was not caught in the act of committing the theft, was obliged to pay double the value of the stolen object. In cases where the stolen object was found in the course of a house-search, he was to pay three times the value, or four times the value if he resisted the execution of the house-search. Again he was to pay four times the value of the stolen object if he had taken it by robbery.

In the case of slander also, the insulting person had to pay. The sum to be paid was decided by the magistrate according to the rank of the victim, his relation to the offender, the seriousness of the offence, and the place it was committed. Generally, in case of any *delictum* or *quasi delictum* the offender was obliged to pay damages, and in exceptional cases the specially assessed value of the article damaged or lost as well.

But despite these requirements, the 48th and 49th Books of the Digest (*libri terribiles*) do not contain any clear reference to restitution or compensation. At best, there are some vague passages which indicate a presumption that in certain cases the judge might be competent to consider the civil claim within the scope of the criminal procedure.[8]

---

[5] M. J. Sethna, *Society and the Criminal* (Bombay, 1952), p. 218; M. J. Sethna, *Jurisprudence* (2nd ed., Girgaon-Bombay, 1959), p. 340.
[6] Margery Fry, *Arms of the Law* (London, 1951), p. 124.
[7] About 2200 B.C.
[8] Herman Ortloff, *Der Adhäsionsprozess* (Leipzig, 1864), p. 6; Karl Binding, *Grundriss des Deutschen Strafprozessrecht* (Berlin, 1904), p. 115; Adolf Schönke, *Beiträge zur Lehre vom Adhäsionsprozess* (Berlin and Leipzig, 1935), p. 5.

It was only recognised towards the end of the Middle Ages that the concept of restitution was closely related to that of punishment,[9] and it was temporarily merged in penal law. In several systems, for example under the early American law, a thief, in addition to his punishment, was ordered to return to the injured party three times the value of his stolen goods, or in the case of insolvency, his person was placed at the disposal of the victim for a certain time.[10] In the Germanic common laws a further refinement transformed retaliation into the system of composition, by which even murder could be compounded for between the wrongdoer and the victim or the nearest relative of the slain.[11] The " law of injury " seems to have been ruled by the idea of reciprocity.[12]

The change from vengeful retaliation to composition was part of a natural historical process. As tribes settled down, reaction to injury or loss became less severe. Compensation or composition served to mitigate blood feuds, which, as tribes settled and became more or less stable communities, only caused endless trouble: an injury once committed would start a perpetual vendetta.[13] Composition offered an alternative which was in many ways equally satisfactory to the victim. In Germanic law compensation provided a touch of self-humiliation, which appeased the instinct for revenge felt by the victim.[14]

Composition combined punishment with damages. For that very reason it could not be applied to public crimes, but only to private wrongs[15]; and this was also the reason for its being in the first period of its practice, subject to private compromise. This feature supports the view that the penal law of ancient communities, in which crimes were met by restitution, was not a law of crimes, but a law of torts.[16] The injuring party offered a certain monetary satisfaction or something of economic value to the injured party, and if the latter accepted it, then revenge was satisfied and the " criminal procedure " was complete.

This monetary satisfaction was due entirely to the victim or his

---

9 In German laws the word " punishment " (*Strafe*) first appeared in sources of the fourteenth century: Herman Conrad, *Deutsche Rechtsgeschichte* (Karlsruhe, 1954), Vol. I, p. 69.

10 E. Ruggles-Brise, *op. cit.*, pp. 51–52.

11 Cherry, *op. cit.*, p. 10.

12 Bernhard Rehfeldt, *Die Wurzeln des Rechtes* (Berlin, 1951), p. 11.

13 Harry Elmer Barnes and Negley K. Teeters, *New Horizons in Criminology* (New York, 1944), pp. 400–401.

14 Hans von Hentig, *Punishment, its origin, purpose and psychology* (London, 1937), p. 215.

15 Barnes and Teeters, *op. cit.*, p. 401

16 Irving E. Cohen, " The Integration of Restitution in the Probation Services " (*Journal of Criminal Law and Criminology*, Vol. XXXIV, No. 5, January–February 1944, Chicago), p. 315.

family, and served as a requital of the injury. The amount to be handed over was dependent on the importance and extent of the injury. The Germanic common laws were objective: composition was determined by the effect of the wrongful act, and not by the offender's subjective guilt. The amount of compensation varied according to the nature of the crime and the age, rank, sex and prestige of the injured party: " a free-born man is worth more than a slave, a grown-up more than a child, a man more than a woman, and a person of rank more than a freeman." [17]

It is difficult to mark accurately the start of new developments, since the community already exercised a certain collective control over the extent of compensation. The bridge leading to the emergence of state criminal law had as a support the system of composition, and the settlement of the amount to be paid by periodical tribal assemblies provides an early example of judicial proceedings. Soon afterwards some laws (*leges barbarorum*) stipulated the amount of compensation, concerning which an intricate tariff was elaborated. Every kind of blow or wound given to every kind of person had its price.[18] From the many differences in the amount of damages and the value of the victim, there grew up such a complicated system of regulations, that the earliest codified law of many peoples, particularly that of the Anglo-Saxons, is largely devoted to this subject.[19] Presumably *Friedlosigkeit*, and in other places " outlawry," which represented the consequence of a failure of composition, developed in connection with these tariff regulations. For instance, if the wrongdoer was reluctant to pay or could not pay the necessary sum, he was declared as *friedlos* or " outlaw ": he was to be regarded as ostracised, and anybody might kill him with impunity.[20]

Since that time the influence of state power over composition has gradually increased. The community claimed a share from the compensation given to the victim, and as the central power in a community grew stronger, so its share increased.

" A share is claimed by the community or overlord or king, as a commission for its trouble in bringing about a reconciliation between the

---

[17] Ephraim Emerton, *Introduction to the History of the Middle Ages* (Ginn, 1888), pp. 87–90; Barnes and Teeters, *op. cit.*, p. 401; Edwin H. Sutherland, *Principles of Criminology* (4th ed., Chicago, 1947), p. 345.
[18] Frederick Pollock and Frederic William Maitland, *The History of English Law* (2nd ed., Cambridge, 1898), Vol. II, p. 451.
[19] Barnes and Teeters, *op. cit.*, p. 401.
[20] Pollock and Maitland, *op. cit.*, Vol. II, p. 451; Rustem Vámbéry, *Büntetöjog* (Budapest, 1913), Vol. I, p. 68; Pal Angyal, *A magyar büntetöjog tankönyve* (Budapest, 1920), Vol. I, p. 18.

parties, or, perhaps, as the price payable by the malefactor either for the opportunity which the community secures for him of redeeming his wrong by a money payment, or for the protection which it affords him, after he has satisfied the award, against further retaliation on the part of the man whom he has injured." [21] One part of the composition was due to the victim (*Wergeld, Busse, emenda, lendis*). The other part was due to the community or the king (*Friedensgeld, fredus, gewedde*). [22] In Saxon England, the Wer or payment for homicide and the Bot, the betterment [23] or compensation for injury, existed alongside the Wite or fine paid to the king or overlord.[24]

By this twofold payment the offender could buy back the peace that he had broken. The double nature of the payment shows clearly the close connection between punishment and compensation.[25]

Before long the injured person's right to restitution grew less and less, and, after the dividing of the Frankish Empire by the Treaty of Verdun, was gradually absorbed by the fine which went to the state. One payment again took the place of the double payment, but now the king or overlord took the entire payment. After the ancient system of law, discretionary money penalties took the place of the old wites, while the bot gave way to damages, assessed by a tribunal.[26] As the state monopolised the institution of punishment,[27] so the rights of the injured were slowly separated from the penal law: composition, as the obligation to pay damages, became separated from the criminal law and became a special field in civil law.[28]

---

21 Heinrich Oppenheimer, *The Rationale of Punishment* (London, 1913), pp. 162–163.
22 Karl Binding, *Die Entstehung der öffentlichen Strafe in germanisch-deutschen Recht* (Rektoratsrede, Leipzig, 1908), p. 32; Angyal, *op. cit.*, Vol. I, p. 18.
23 Pollock and Maitland, *op. cit.*, Vol. II, p. 451.
24 Fry, *op. cit.*, p. 32.
25 A. B. Schmidt, *Die Grundsätze über den Schadensersatz in den Volksrechten* (Leipzig, 1885), pp. 9–16; Binding, *op. cit.* (*Entstehung der öffentlichen Strafe*), p. 34.
26 Pollock and Maitland, *op. cit.*, Vol. II, pp. 458–459; L. J. Hobhouse, G. C. Wheeler, N. Ginsberg, *The Material Culture and Social Institutions of the Simpler Peoples* (London, 1915), pp. 86–119.
27 Wolfgang Starke, *Die Entschädigung des Verletzten nach deutschem Recht unter besonderer Berücksichtigung der Wiedergutmachung nach geltendem Strafrecht* (Freiburg, 1959), p. 1.
28 J. Makarewicz, *Einführung in die Philosophie des Strafrechts auf entwicklungs-geschichtlicher Grundlage* (Stuttgart, 1906), p. 269; Rehfeldt, *op. cit.*, p. 17; Conrad, *op. cit.*, pp. 220–221.

2

THE DECLINE OF RESTITUTION

" IT was chiefly owing to the violent greed of feudal barons and mediaeval ecclesiastical powers that the rights of the injured party were gradually infringed upon, and finally, to a large extent, appropriated by these authorities, who exacted a double vengeance, indeed, upon the offender, by forfeiting his property to themselves instead of to his victim, and then punishing him by the dungeon, the torture, the stake or the gibbet. But the original victim of wrong was practically ignored." [1] After the Middle Ages, restitution, kept apart from punishment, seems to have been degraded. The victim became the Cinderella of the criminal law.[2]

The decline in the penological importance of restitution gained theoretical support from the endeavour to find different bases for penal and civil liability. The multitude of theories which distinguished between civil and penal liability showed, generally, two trends. According to the subjective view, penal liability results from the deliberate infringement of law, something with which civil liability cannot be connected, since civil liability results from a less deliberate opposing of the will of the state.[3] According to the objective view, however, penal wrong follows from some kind of direct injury to the victim which exists in itself, quite apart from any statement by the victim, something with which civil illegality cannot be connected, the latter being an indirect injury solely dependent on the victim's statement.[4] Generally speaking, since the disappearance of the period of composition the conventional view is that a crime is an offence against the state, while a tort is an offence against individual rights only.[5]

---

[1] Tallack, op. cit., pp. 11–12.
[2] H. F. Pfenninger, quoted by Thomas Würtenberger, *Uber Rechte und Pflichten des Verletzten im deutschen Adhäsionsprozess* (Festschrift, Prof. Dr. H. F. Pfenninger, Strafprozess und Rechtsstaat) (Zürich, 1956), p. 193.
[3] This theory fails to take into consideration the criminal offences committed by negligence. On the other hand, there are certain kinds of deliberate infringement which give rise to civil liability only.
[4] This theory fails to consider that infringement of the civil law can exist independently of the statement of the victim. On the other hand, *volenti non fit injuria* has some application to criminal law.
[5] Karl Binding, *Normen* (3rd ed., Berlin, 1916), Vol. I, pp. 433–479; Sutherland, op. cit., p. 14.

However that may be, the system of composition only surrendered after a struggle; even after the German Busse-penal-law there are records of victims who, in spite of the common character of the criminal law, claimed besides public punishment indemnification and personal satisfaction as well. The connection between the crime and restitution (*continentia causae*) could fall into decline, but not be completely disregarded, even after the introduction of the procedure of inquisition, where the theoretical and practical distinctions between the demands of penal law and the victim are at their most acute. Court practice in the sixteenth and seventeenth centuries (*Gerichtspraxis des gemeinen Rechts*) made possible the so-called adhesive procedure (*Adhäsionsprozess*), which opened the way for the judge of the criminal case to make a decision, according to his discretion, on the claim of the victim for restitution within the scope of the criminal proceedings.[6] Penal codes of the nineteenth century also seemed to give some support to the idea of restitution in the form of the adhesive procedure, which was enacted in about half the laws of the federal German states. A few years later, however, the situation got worse, and even in the German law of criminal procedure was kept alive only by the force of tradition.[7]

Advocates of restitution, however, were not looking on with folded arms. In 1847 Bonneville de Marsangy outlined a definite plan of reparation[8]; and later on, several international Prison or Penitentiary Congresses enthusiastically advocated re-establishing the rights of victims of crime.

At the International Prison Congress held in Stockholm in 1878, two speakers, Sir George Arney, Chief Justice of New Zealand, and William Tallack, proposed a more general return to the ancient practice of making reparation to the injured.[9] Raffaelo Garofalo raised the question at the International Prison Congress held in Rome in 1885[10]; and the problem was also discussed at the International Prison Congress held at St. Petersburg in 1890. A year later the question was again considered by the International Penal Association at its Congress held at Christiania in 1891. At that Congress the following conclusions were adopted:

---

6 Schönke, *op. cit.*, p. 11: Hans Heinrich Jescheck, " Die Entschädigung der Verletzten nach deutschem Strafrecht " (*Juristenzeitung*, No. 19–20, October 17, 1958, Tübingen), p. 592.
7 Schönke, *op. cit.*, pp. 28–42; Jescheck, *op. cit.*, p. 592.
8 Sutherland, *op. cit.*, p. 576.
9 Tallack, *op. cit.*, p. 3.
10 Barrows, *op. cit.*, p. 23.

(a) modern law does not sufficiently consider the reparation due to injured parties;

(b) in the case of petty offences, time should be given for indemnification; and

(c) prisoners' earnings in prison might be utilised for this end.[11]

At the International Prison Congress held in Paris in 1895, the fifth of a quinquennial series, attended by penologists such as Berenger (France), Bertillon (France), Tarde (France), Vidal (France), Bonneville de Marsangy (France), Krohne (Germany), Mittermaier (Germany), Foinitsky (Russia), Beltrany-Scalia (Italy), Garofalo (Italy), Prins (Belgium), Van Hamel (Holland), Guillaume (Switzerland), and others, the problem of restitution to victims was exhaustively discussed. The problem was one of the questions raised officially on the Agenda. Question 4 of Section I of the Agenda asked: " Is the victim of a delict sufficiently armed by modern law to enable him to obtain indemnity from the man who has injured him?"

At this Congress it was felt that modern laws were particularly weak on this point and, in some respects, the laws in different countries were harder on the victim than the offender.[12] The Italian penologists in particular had long urged that this matter should be discussed, and Garofalo and Pierantoni dealt with it in an impressive manner. It was also the subject of six valuable papers, by Cornet, Flandin, Pascaud, Poet, Prins and Zucker, which insisted that compensation or restitution should be made by offenders to the persons they had injured.[13] The Paris Prison Congress discussed the subject thoroughly, but without arriving at any clear or satisfactory conclusion. For that reason they decided to consider the matter further at the next Congress. The final resolutions of the Paris Congress were similar in principle to those passed in 1891 at Christiania, but it was decided to express no decided conclusion " in the absence of sufficient evidence," and the problem was adjourned to the Brussels Congress five years later.

The question was duly included in the programme of the next Prison Congress, the Sixth International Penitentiary Congress, held at Brussels in 1900. Section I of the First Question was: " What would be, following the order of ideas indicated by the Congress of Paris, the most practical

---

[11] *Mitteilungen der Internationale Kriminalistische Vereinigung* (3 Jahrg., Berlin, 1892), pp. 121, 236, 265, 281.
[12] *Report of the Delegates of the United States to the Fifth International Prison Congress* (Washington, 1896), p. 27.
[13] The Paris Prison Congress, *op. cit.*, pp. 12–13.

means of securing for the victim of a criminal offence the indemnity due him from the delinquent?" [14] On this occasion the problem of restitution was again the subject of exhaustive discussion by the most respected penologists of the time; but the question, which the Paris Congress confessed itself unable to solve, came no nearer to being solved at Brussels.

The *rapporteur* of the question, the Belgian Prins, pressed in vain for a decisive vote on the matter, which, he said, had been discussed in successive Congresses with zeal and almost with passion for fifteen years. At the end of the Brussels Congress the delegates were not able to do more than reaffirm the Paris vote: in favour of a reform of procedure, which would facilitate civil action. [15]

The connection between restitution and punishment has still not been re-established. The theory developed at the end of the Middle Ages that crime is an offence exclusively against the state had severed that connection. The concept of punishment remained untouched by the civil concept of restitution. [16] Even the adhesive procedure [17] was almost reduced to theoretical importance only. It did not, after all, fit with harmony into the changed system. [18] Even where legal systems introduced this or a similar procedure, and thus permitted the victim to claim restitution within the scope of criminal procedure, at the same time they gave the court the right to put aside the decision on the question of restitution, if it considered that civil interests might hinder the effectiveness of penal interests. The institution *Busse*, still found in some legislations, is officially regarded as having no connection with punishment, and as civil indemnification only. [19]

Attention has frequently been called to the fact that the separation

---

[14] *Actes du Congrès Pénitentiaire International de Bruxelles, Août 1900* (Bruxelles et Berne, 1901), Vol. II, pp. 3–153; Barrows, *op. cit.*, p. 19.

[15] E. Ruggles-Brise, *op. cit.*, p. 51.

[16] Starke, *op. cit.*, pp. 1–2.

[17] This term "adhesive" (*Adhäsion*) was first applied in 1788 by Eschenbach (*Von den Einteilungen und Quellen des Criminalprozesses, published in Plitt: Repertorium für das peinliche Recht, 1790* (Vol. II, p. 159)), to embrace the terms "denouncing procedure" (*Denuntiationsprozess*) and "mixed procedure" (*gemischter Prozess*); and has come to denote the connection between the criminal procedure and civil claim for damages (the victim used to declare his joining with the following words: *se processual quoad suum interesse privatum adhaerere velle*).

[18] Alexander Graf zu Dohna, *Die Stellung der Busse im reichsrechtlichen System des Immaterialgüterschutzes* (Berlin, 1902), §§ 1–7.

[19] Starke, *op. cit.*, p. 5; Adolph Schönke-Schroder, *Kommentar zum StGB* (8th ed., Berlin, 1957), § 13; the legal nature of the *Busse* used to be and perhaps still is strongly disputed. There are three theories: (a) the theory of punishment, (b) the theory of damages, and (c) the combined theory, representing the intermediate position, which holds that the *Busse* is the material and idealistic indemnification of the victim, interwoven with the idea of private vengeance.

of these civil and penal functions is a serious defect in the modern system of fines, which go only to the state, while the injured victim suffers all the hardships of the civil process. However, there is still a tendency to remove the question of restitution or compensation more and more from criminal procedure, palpably in the desire to avoid representation of the victim along with the public prosecution.[20] The victim, so the argument runs, should not be interested financially in the outcome of the prosecution, and concern for the victim should not disturb the criminal-political purposes.[21] History suggests that growing interest in the reformation of the criminal is matched by decreasing care for the victim.

[20] Hentig, *op. cit.*, pp. 216–217.
[21] Carlo Waeckerling, *Die Sorge für den Verletzten im Strafrecht* (Zürich, 1946), p. 15.

PART TWO

LEGISLATION OUTSIDE THE UNITED KINGDOM
TO 1960

3

AIMS AND METHODS OF THE SURVEY

*A copy of the Questionnaire used in the inquiry
is printed in the Appendix*

FIRST of all the inquiry examines two preliminary questions, whether the victim or his dependants have any legal right at all to claim restitution or damages from the offender, and, if so, to what offences this right applies. The question then raised is whether damages are restricted to compensation for financial loss only, or whether they also include compensation for moral damage or any other non-material injury.

The inquiry then asks what type of court it is which has jurisdiction to entertain claims for restitution or damages in different legal systems, and what are the essential points of that court's procedure. The main interest lies in ascertaining whether the court is a criminal court, and whether the question of restitution or damages is entertained within the scope of the criminal procedure, or whether it is an independent procedure. This involves the examination of the practice of the courts concerning the substantive issues involved in the decision, and of the basis on which the amount of restitution (damages) is determined. The inquiry considers whether the concept of restitution or damages has been involved with a penal element in any legal system; and whether the award or non-award of restitution or damages has any effect on the punitive element in the court's sentence.

Next, the inquiry asks, " Against what assets can the victim or his dependants enforce their claim?" and goes on to examine the financial position of prisoners in different countries (on the hypothesis that recourse may eventually be had to the earnings of offenders in prison). Are the offenders allowed or compelled to work in prison? Are they paid for such work? Are their wages (if any) different from those earned by free workers, and, if so, what is the difference, and are the prisoners permitted to keep their earnings at their discretion?

Finally, the investigation was extended to include some general impressions as to how restitution works in practice, and whether any

15

trend to improve or to modify the present provisions can be seen in any legal system.

The investigation was based on information given by the Ministries of Justice, university faculties, and the institutes of criminology or comparative criminal law of the countries concerned, or by individual qualified experts. The information on foreign legislation was collected between September 7, 1958, and December 31, 1959.

The survey was world-wide, but is not intended to, and does not, cover all the countries in the world. It was clearly advisable to concentrate on the countries whose legal systems were the most immediately relevant.

Twenty-nine countries were surveyed as follows:

(A) Western Europe:
         (a) Belgium
         (b) France
         (c) Holland

(B) Central Europe:
         (a) Austria
         (b) German Federal Republic
         (c) Switzerland

(C) Northern Europe:
         (a) Denmark
         (b) Finland
         (c) Norway
         (d) Sweden

(D) Southern Europe:
         Italy

(E) Eastern Europe:
         (a) Greece
         (b) Turkey

(F) North America:
         (a) Canada
         (b) United States of America

(G) Central America:
         (a) Cuba
         (b) Dominica
         (c) Mexico

(H) South America:
         Argentina

(I) Middle East:
           (a) Egypt
           (b) Israel
           (c) Persia

(J) Far East:
           (a) India
           (b) Pakistan

(K) Pacific:
           (a) Australia
           (b) New Zealand

(L) Africa:
           Union of South Africa

(M) Communist territories:
           (a) Hungary
           (b) Soviet Union

4

WESTERN EUROPE

BELGIUM

IN Belgian legislation restitution to victims of crime belongs to the sphere of civil law. The victim has a legal right to claim restitution, or, according to the Belgian terminology, damages for or reparation of the injury; and this right attaches to all offences against the civil law, damages compensating for moral as well as material injury. As in other legislations, the words " restitution," " compensation " and " damages " cover different concepts, and it is necessary to distinguish between restitution and damages.

Restitution, with which the law is concerned, and which the law contrasts with damages, is exclusively applied to the recognised right of ownership or possession by the injured party of the articles which have been removed from him, wherever these articles are recovered in kind and placed in the hands of the law. Damages are the indirect reparation for the offence, and are equivalent to what we call restitution, paid by the offender to the victim of his crime.

Concerning damages in this sense, the operative provisions are civil. According to these, any action whatsoever committed by a person which causes damage to another, obliges the one through whose fault the damage was done, to repair it. It is a general rule in Belgian legislation, that everyone is responsible for the damage he has caused not only by his own positive actions, but also by his negligence or imprudence.[1]

It should be noted, however, that in certain cases the person responsible for the damage may not be the perpetrator of the criminal offence. However, damages can be awarded against him as well as against the perpetrator of the offence in the judgment by which the latter is condemned. A man can be responsible, for example, not only for the damage which he causes by his own actions, but also for that caused by the action of some person for whom he is answerable. Similarly, a man can be responsible for damage caused by another to property entrusted

---

[1] *Code Civil* of 1803, Arts. 1382–1383 (the Belgian Civil Code is the French Code Civil of 1803, which has been altered in many respects, but not in the articles referred to here).

18

to his care. Thus, the father, and the mother after the death of her husband, are responsible for the damage caused by their children living with them who are minors; landlords and employers are responsible for the damage caused by their servants and overseers in carrying out the duties for which they are employed; and teachers and workmen are responsible for the damage caused by their pupils and apprentices during the time when they are under their supervision. These responsibilities apply, unless the people concerned (parents, teachers, workmen, etc.) prove that they were unable to prevent the action which gave rise to the liability.[2]

Damages bear almost entirely civil characteristics. The exception to this appears in the possibility of a victim claiming damages (in the Belgian sense) within the scope of criminal proceedings. Due to the civil character of damages, the victim's action can be first of all the object of a separate hearing before the civil court. In this procedure the application for damages is made by means of a summons either before a Justice of the Peace or a Tribunal of First Instance, depending upon the size of the sum applied for by the injured party.

In addition to this, however, Belgian law offers to the victim the chance of criminal procedure, and victims frequently avail themselves of this chance. The action for damages is generally brought before the criminal court (*juridiction répressive*) by the injured person, who becomes here the plaintiff. The court can award damages only in cases where the action ascribed to the accused constitutes an offence against the penal law. Legal action taken by the victim can either be by means of a charge (or plaint), or by application to an examining magistrate; and in neither of the cases is any special form of procedure insisted upon, provided that the wish to intervene is made known.

In order to establish the amount of material damage, the court may consult experts, whose conclusions, however, are not binding. The award of damages in any case takes the form of the payment of a sum of money. It is a matter of indemnifying the injured party for the damage he has suffered; however this is only concerned with immediate and direct damage.

The possibility of the victim choosing the criminal procedure for his claim raises the question of the effect of an award of damages on the sentences of the court. The court estimates the severity of sentence

[2] *Ibid*. Art. 1384.

required by considering all the factors in the case and, in particular, the indemnification or non-indemnification of the victim.

In cases where damages are awarded to the injured party within the scope of the criminal procedure, the victim can enforce his claim by means of civil proceedings only. He has no recourse to the earnings of the offender while a prisoner.

In principle, any prisoner who asks to do so, may work during his term of imprisonment. He may be deprived of work as a disciplinary measure, or because of a shortage of work, or on medical grounds. Generally, with the exception of prisoners sentenced to detention (*peine de la détention*, a sentence reserved for offences of a political nature), or of police punishment (*peine de police*), all prisoners are required to work, and every prisoner must do the work allotted to him.

Whereas workers who are free receive a wage, prisoners who work receive a gratuity only, the amount of which varies according to the amount of work done; and it is estimated that the gratuities granted correspond to about a third of wages paid in ordinary life. Those who are sentenced to the detention reserved for political offences, or to police punishment, can enjoy the whole of this gratuity; other prisoners, however, receive only a proportion of it. This proportion may not exceed three-tenths for those sentenced to hard labour, four-tenths for those sentenced to solitary confinement, and five-tenths for prisoners undergoing correctional detention; in cases where it is deserved this latter may be used partly to obtain certain " treats." The rest of their earnings belongs to the state. Moreover, the Government may dispose of half of the prisoner's portion as a reserve fund for the benefit of the prisoner, while he is serving his sentence, or for the benefit of the prisoner's family, if they are found to be in need. The other half of the prisoner's portion is given to him on his release or at stated times after his release.[3] This sum cannot in any way be touched, and, therefore, the victim cannot enforce his claims for damages from any money earned by the offender during his imprisonment.[4]

As mentioned before, the term " restitution " here covers a different concept, and is concerned with the right of ownership or possession by the injured party of certain articles, mainly in cases of theft. This feature belongs entirely to civil disputes, and restitution may be ordered even in the case of acquittal.[5]

---

[3] *Code Pénal* (Penal Code) of 1867, Arts. 15, 27.
[4] *Règlement Général des Prisons* (General Prison Regulations) of 1905, Art. 346.
[5] *Code Civil*, Arts. 2279–2280.

The impression gained is that in Belgium, generally speaking, no fundamental criticisms have been levelled against this system of damages (in the Belgian sense) to the victims of crime, and there seems to be no expectation that it will be modified.[6]

FRANCE

French legislation offers a model example of a system whereby the victim's claim for restitution may be entertained together with the criminal offence within the scope of criminal proceedings, despite the exclusively civil character of the restitution.

It is a general provision in penal law as well as in civil law[7] that a person who causes damage to another person is obliged to repair it. More especially, the victim of crime receives reparation for the damage he has suffered: " *l'action civile* in reparation for damage resulting from crime, misdemeanour, or offence, is the right of those who have suffered injury as a direct result of an offence." [8]

This wording of the law provides for the indemnification of all those who have suffered directly in consequence of a criminal offence, that is to say not only the victim himself, but also his rightful claimants (for example, his dependants in cases where the crime caused the victim's death). At the same time the law attempts to lay stress on the purely civil character of such claims, expressly providing not a criminal claim but an *action civile*, that is to say a civil procedural action. This civil action, as a claim for compensation in return for individual damage, can be exercised in criminal procedure in all cases of penal offences which have caused any direct injury: the law provides no restriction in this respect. The indemnity granted by the courts means reparation for all the damage caused, irrespective of whether the injury was a material one or caused non-material or moral damage.

It should be noted, that this is a form of restitution (or as it is mostly called in France " reparation ") to be paid by the offender, since compensation is not guaranteed by the state. Only in the case of motor-car accidents,[9] does the state take part in a certain sense, in compensating the victim. For that purpose the so-called *Fonds de garantie automobile* was set up. This undertakes the responsibility of paying damages to those victims of motor-car accidents who are bodily injured. However, this

---

[6] Derived from information supplied by P. Cornil, Secretary General of the Ministère de la Justice (Ministry of Justice), Bruxelles, 1959.
[7] *Code Civil* (Civil Code), Art. 1382; *Code Pénal* (Penal Code), Art 51.
[8] *Code de Procédure Pénale* (Code of Criminal Procedure) of December 31, 1957, Art. 2.
[9] Act of December 31, 1951.

state agency is only obliged to pay this compensation in cases where the offender or other liable person is not known, or if he is partly or totally insolvent.

The victim has the right to choose the kind of procedure by which his claim for restitution should be decided. In either case his claim keeps its character of *action civile*, but it may, in reparation for either material or non-material (moral) damage, be brought before the civil courts, or before the criminal courts. In spite of the expressly civil character of restitution French law in the order of Articles seems to show a preference for entertaining the claim to criminal proceedings: " the civil action may be pursued at the same time as the prosecution and before the same jurisdiction " [10] but is followed by: " can also be pursued independently of the prosecution." [11]

If the victim claims the reparation of his injury in civil proceedings, the ordinary rules of civil procedure are applied; provided, however, that the decision of the civil court does not contradict any decisions of the court which heard the criminal case.

On the other hand, if the victim claims in the criminal court, his action is an accessory to the criminal case, somewhat similar to the German adhesive procedure. But his claim is an *action civile*, although it is heard in a criminal court, and he makes his appearance in court as a civil party (*partie civil*). If the victim chooses to bring his action before the civil court, he may not change his mind and return to the *juridictions répressives*.[12]

The conditions and time limits for *l'action civile* demonstrate the penal nature of the action, since the periods of limitation are generally the same as those for prosecutions: ten years for crime, three years for misdemeanours, and one year for minor offences. However, in all other respects this civil action conforms to the rules of civil law and civil procedure.[13]

It should be noted that joint responsibility is established between co-authors or accomplices of the same crime or misdemeanour: the whole of the civil conviction may thus be recovered from the estate of one of the authors of the offence.[14] Generally, it is for the court alone to prove both the existence and the gravity of the injury. The evaluation of the injury is particularly difficult in the case of moral damage, but it is a

[10] *Code de Procédure Pénale*, Art. 3.
[11] *Ibid*. Art 4.
[12] *Ibid*. Art. 5.
[13] *Ibid*. Art. 10.   [14] *Code Pénal*, Art. 55.

tenet of French law, that reparation must be in full.[15] However, damages can only be granted to the victim of an offence if he has sought them. It throws some light on previous French practice, that the legislature formally forbids [16] the payment of damages, even with the victim's consent, to charitable objects. It is the victim to whom the damages must be paid.

In contrast to most countries' legislation, in France the victim has a fair chance of enforcing his claim for restitution against the prisoner's earnings, and through the working of the prisoners' earnings system, the execution of a sentence for damages has a definite effect on the offender's income from his work in the prison.

Those condemned to a *peine définitive* (imprisonment for a definite period) are compelled to work in prison. Those who are held in custody pending trial of their case, may request work, but for them this is purely optional and not an obligation.

Prisoners, who are required to work, are paid for the work they do at, as far as possible, similar rates of pay as free workers carrying out similar work. Their remuneration is calculated on the basis of the *Code du travail pour les travailleurs à domicile* (code of work for the home-workers): in practice they are hardly more than half or two-fifths of free workers' earnings.

These earnings are not given to the prisoner in cash, but are paid into his savings account. Further, the prisoner's income from this source is divided up in varying proportions, dependent on the nature and length of the sentence being served, and according to different purposes:

So-called liquid assets may be used at once by the prisoner (in particular for purchases in the canteen of the prison and certain payments to his family).

Finally, the so-called guaranteed earnings (*le pécule de garantie*) are applied in the first instance to the payment of fines and legal costs due to the state. If and when, however, the sums due to the Treasury have been paid, they are devoted to the payment of damages awarded by law to the plaintiff (victim), who has made known to the Public Prosecutor attached to the jurisdiction which pronounced sentence, his intention of taking proceedings to establish his claim to this fraction of the prisoner's earnings.

As a rule, the proceeds of the prisoner's work are divided in this way:

[15] *Code de Procédure Pénale,* Art. 3, para. 2.
[16] *Code Pénal,* Art. 51.

One-half is used for liquid assets, one-quarter is used for the formation of the savings account, and one-quarter is used for the formation of the guaranteed fund. (Once the damages have been paid, the guaranteed fund has no further point, and for this reason disappears. Then the prisoner may use three-quarters of the whole of his earnings.) Generally, taking into account that only one-quarter is destined for those purposes which include, among others, the satisfaction of the claim for restitution, the victim's chances may be slim; but, compared with many other countries, this chance is better, and is expressly provided by law.

It should be noted that, until very recently a plaintiff who had not received indemnification could obtain, in a purely civil procedure, *la contrainte par corps* (imprisonment for debts) against an offender who had not indemnified his offence. The new Code of Penal Procedure, however, has allowed the continuation of this provision only in favour of the Treasury.

The French solution to the question of restitution to victims of crime has raised a great many problems and prompted some criticism, particularly with regard to the link between the prosecution and the *action civile*, but by and large one gains the impression that the system operates in a relatively satisfactory manner.[17]

HOLLAND

In the Netherlands the problem of restitution belongs to the civil law. Anybody who, through another person's wrongful conduct, suffers a material damage or non-material loss (that is to say moral damage), has a right to claim restoration of the previous position (*restitutio in integrum*), compensation or damages from the offender, but from the offender or his property alone. The injured party has no right to claim any compensation from the state, unless the Government itself infringes the law. The whole question is in principle ruled by civil law, is entertained within the scope of the civil procedure inside the jurisdiction of the civil court, and only in cases of small awards of damages has the victim a right of compensation in a criminal court.

In general, the victim or his heirs, as the case may be, has a right to claim damages from anyone whose action causes loss or damage.[18]

---

[17] Based on information supplied by the French Ministry of Justice, and G. Stefani, Professor of Criminal Law, Université de Paris, Faculté de Droit, Institut de Criminologie (University of Paris, Faculty of Law, Institute of Criminology), Paris, 1959.

[18] *Burgerlijk Wetboek* (Code of Civil Law), Royal Decree of April 10, 1838 (Staatsblad No. 12), Sect. 1401.

Such an action is a tort. But an action lies for three specific criminal offences:

(a) In the case of manslaughter or culpable homicide, the surviving spouse, the children, or the parents of the victim can bring an action for damages (but only in cases where they used to be maintained by the work of the victim, and they can succeed in their action only in so far as they need the sum of damages for their subsistence). In fixing the amount of the indemnification, the position and the financial situation of the parties involved, as well as the attendant circumstances are to be taken into account.[19]

(b) Wilful or negligent injuring or maiming of any part of the body gives the injured party, but the injured person only, a right to claim indemnification for the damage resulting from the injuring or maiming, in addition to indemnification for the costs of his recovery; these indemnifications shall again be fixed by taking into account the position and financial situation of the parties involved and the circumstances attending the case; and this provision is generally applicable in all cases where a valuation has to be made of the damage caused by an offence against the person, *e.g.*, rape, abduction, unlawful detention, etc.[20]

(c) An action lies for criminal insult, which tries to indemnify both for the material loss and damage and also to mitigate the damage sustained to honour and reputation; and again, in their valuation the court shall take into account the degree of the insult, as well as the standing and the financial situation of the parties involved, and any other circumstances attending the case. At the same time, the insulted party has a right to demand that it be pronounced in the judgment that the act done was slanderous or insulting, and that the judgment be publicly placarded at the expense of the party against whom the judgment is given.[21]

All actions for damages arising from criminal offences are brought before the civil courts. In these cases the normal rules of civil procedure [22] are applicable. *By way of exception, however, and exclusively*

---

[19] *Ibid*. Sect. 1406.
[20] *Ibid*. Sect. 1407.
[21] *Ibid*. Sects. 1408 and 1409, amended by Act of April 26, 1884 (Staatsblad No. 93).
[22] *Wetboek van Burgerlijke Regtsvordering* (Code of Civil Procedure), Royal Decree of September 16, 1896 (Staatsblad No. 156), based on a great number of laws of 1828.

in cases of small damages, not exceeding fl.300.—. (about £30),[23] the victim may join his civil action to criminal procedure.[24] The victim is not obliged to do so, but this method has certain advantages:

(a) the rules of criminal procedure are far simpler than those of civil procedure. The victim has a right but is not obliged to be legally represented; the victim or his representative is entitled to introduce and to conduct the claim in court personally and verbally without any previous formality, and for evidence of the kind and extent of damages, documentary evidence will suffice.

(b) The costs of a suit are considerably less.

(c) Criminal procedure is quicker.

There are, however, a number of drawbacks. For instance:

(a) If the compensation claimed is more than the stated limit of fl.300.—, the surplus over that sum cannot be recovered. According to established jurisprudence of the Supreme Court, the victim who claims compensation in a criminal court, thereby abandons his claim for the amount above the maximum fl.300.—. This limit can only be exceeded by an aggregate of the claims of several injured parties. Further, it is unlawful to make use of the criminal procedure for the maximum amount allowed, and to reserve a civil action for the balance of the damages. For this reason the criminal court is frequently used in cases of small material damages in connection with motoring accidents, petty offences against property and offences against the person. For these offences recourse to the criminal courts is quite satisfactory.

(b) The injured party is only allowed to influence the issue of indemnification for the damage; not the major issue of whether the accused is guilty or not. Conviction is, however, an essential condition of the success of the victim's claim.[25] The victim or his counsel has the right to put questions to witnesses and experts, but only concerning the extent and nature of the damages. Moreover the examination is conducted through the president of the court.[26]

---

23 *De Wet op de Zamenstelling der Regterlijke Magt en het Beleid der Justitie* (Act of Judicial Organisation) of April 18, 1827 (Staatsblad No. 20), Art. 44, para. 3 and Art. 56, para. 3, altered by Act of May 4, 1954 (Staatsblad No. 169).

24 *Wetboek van Strafvordering* (Code of Criminal Procedure) of January 15, 1921, Royal Decree of December 4, 1925 (Staatsblad No. 465), Sect. 332.

25 *Ibid.* Sect. 337.   26 *Ibid.* Sect. 335.

(c) The injured party is not allowed to widen the scope of the inquiry, neither as regards the points at issue, nor as regards the evidence to be led. In proof of the nature and extent of the damages sustained, the plaintiff victim has a right to submit documents, but is not allowed to have witnesses or experts summoned.[27] Consequently his evidence in this joint procedure is often sketchy. On the other hand, whatever is lawful evidence in the criminal procedure may somehow contribute to the substantiation of the claim, including as appears from the case law, a statement by the injured party. That the scope of inquiry is limited by the criminal procedure, follows not only from the implication of the law that, in general, no right of action for damages is available if facts are ascertained which form a tort but not a criminal offence, but also from certain other restrictions, which have become accepted in case law and legal literature. For example, that the damages claimed may only have regard to the damage or loss directly resulting from the offence with which the accused is charged; that in a joint procedure the damages can only be claimed by the person who is directly affected by the offence; that the action can only be brought against the accused, and that a counterclaim by the accused is out of the question, etc.

As a rule, it is obligatory for the offender to indemnify the victim in full, in accordance with the principle that the victim is to be restored as far as possible to the situation that would have existed if the offence had not been committed. With the three exceptions of damages arising from offences of manslaughter or culpable homicide, wilful or negligent injuring or maiming of any part of the body, and insult, the court has no right of mitigation. In these specified cases, however, the law allows a reduction of liability according to the standing and financial situation of each of the parties involved, and according to other circumstances, *e.g.*, whether either party is insured, partial fault of the victim, etc.

Material damage consists in loss sustained and/or profit lost. In principle, the perpetrator of a tort is required to make good, in addition to material damages, the non-material damage, *e.g.*, on account of pain, mental suffering, fright, lessening of joy in life, except in the cases of manslaughter or culpable homicide. This non-material damage is usually fixed *ex aequo et bono*.

---

[27] *Ibid*. Sect. 334.

Generally, in assessing damages, the court fixes the amount *ex aequo et bono* where the offence has been proved, but where the extent of the damage has not been established by strict rules of evidence. Under certain circumstances, a claim for a future obvious damage may be sustained.

It is usual for the amount of the damage to be expressed in terms of money, but sometimes it is expressed in goods (for instance if the thief is still in possession of the object stolen).

It is possible for the victim to have recourse to all available items of property or income of the offender. Civil imprisonment may be applied to enforce the payment of damages, costs and interests where judgment has been given against the defendant for a sum exceeding 150 guilders (about £15).[28]

Though persons serving sentences, prisoners in the State Labour Colonies and in the State Asylums for Psychopaths, as well as persons sentenced to a certain term of detention, are required to work and earn wages, these earnings are not available for restitution or compensation to victims of their crime. Not only because wages for prison work are a mere fraction of wages in a free society, but because part of prison wages are intended for pocket-money, and the balance is to be paid on release. The victim thus has no recourse to the prisoner's earnings.

In the largely civil atmosphere of the Dutch system of restitution, there is only one indication of the effect of performance or non-performance of restitution on sentence. The fulfilment of his obligation to pay damages may be of importance to the offender, as regards both prosecution and punishment. Whether this obligation has been fulfilled or not is taken into account when the decision to prosecute is made. Further, prosecution may be withheld on condition that the offender pays damages to the injured party within a certain time. If the matter of indemnification has not been settled, it is in general not possible to make an arrangement with the Public Prosecutor to settle the criminal case out of court. The fact that the damage has been made good, may also be taken into account if a petition for mercy is considered.

Generally speaking, Dutch opinion concerning indemnification for damages seems to be satisfied with this present system. Joinder with criminal procedure, however, meets with some criticism. Clearly, in some cases it offers a good chance of obtaining quick and cheap justice :

---

[28] *Op. cit., Wetboek van Burgerlijke Regisvordering,* Sect. 585.

the summary rules of evidence cause few difficulties in practice. Criticism is directed on the one hand at the very principle of joinder, but on the other hand at the smallness of the amount for which such joinder is possible, the strict limitations on evidence, and dependence of the award on a finding of guilt.[29]

[29] Based on information supplied by J. C. Tenkink, Secretary-General of Ministerie van Justitie (Ministry of Justice), 'S-Gravenhage, 1959; and A. L. Melai, Tutor of the Strafrechtelijk en Criminologisch Instituut aan de Rijksuniversiteit te Leiden (Institute of Criminal Law and Criminology at the University of Leiden), Leiden, 1959.

5

CENTRAL EUROPE

AUSTRIA

As a general rule, in Austrian legislation, a person who wilfully or by gross negligence causes criminal injury, is bound to make compensation. Though the victim's claim for restitution may be entertained within the scope of criminal procedure, it bears a civil character.[1] The victim has a legal right to claim restitution in the criminal court, and has the status of *Privatbeteiligter* (civil party). This right descends to his heirs. If the victim joins the criminal procedure, his claim will be regarded as an *Adhäsionsprozess* (adhesive procedure). The court is required to warn victims of criminal injury of their right, which includes a claim for non-material damage.[2]

The court must make some award, unless the claim is not established on the evidence, or unless the extent of the injury is not certain. In these cases, the court turns the claim over to civil procedure, and it is the victim's business to claim compensation in the civil court.[3]

Generally, in the criminal courts, only those claims are awarded which can be decided without too much difficulty, without, in particular, protracting or hindering the course of the criminal proceedings. For example, in a case of bodily injury the expenses for medical treatment of the victim are usually awarded if proved by bills: but a claim for moral damage is generally referred to the civil court.

The only other connection which restitution has with criminal law is its effect on sentencing policy. The performance of restitution before sentence may be considered as a mitigating factor.

The victim has little hope of enforcing his claim against the offender's prison earnings, and recourse is practically limited to the ordinary procedure of civil execution. Prisoners are certainly required to work in the prison, but their *peculium* is insignificant in comparison with the

---

[1] *Allgemeine Bürgerliche Gesetzbuch* (Civil Code) of June 11, 1811 (in some parts amended in 1914–16, text in force published in 1955), Arts, 1295–1341.
[2] *Ibid*. Art. 1325.
[3] *Osterreichische Strafprozessordnung* (Code of Criminal Procedure) of May 23, 1873 (amended text published in 1945 and 1959), Arts. 36–50, 265–379.

normal wages of free workers. Half of the prisoner's earnings are kept for his release, the other half is at his disposal and with special permission can be spent voluntarily for the maintenance of his family or for restitution.

This system of restitution is familiar to the Austrian people. It affords a good example of a claim for civil restitution being successfully made in criminal courts. In Austria the system has the advantage that victims claiming restitution in criminal proceedings are not required to pay any procedural costs or expenses.[4]

SWITZERLAND

In investigating Swiss penal practice, one has to face the difficulty that Swiss criminal procedure may involve the provisions of twenty-six legislations in addition to that of the legislation of the Swiss Federation itself.[5] They have at the best similar but not identical provisions. Even the claimant is called by different names: *private complainant, civil plaintiff, interested party, informer, injured party* are only a few of the various cantonal terms. However, this recital by itself suggests that though restitution has some relation to both criminal law and to what may be called " neutral " procedure, generally it is an institution of a civil character.

The victim has first of all to choose between joining the criminal procedure or claiming independently in a civil court. If he claims restitution in the criminal court, this is dealt with by the so-called adhesive procedure (*Adhäsionsprozess*), similar to the provisions of German law with a similar limited chance of success, that is to say the claim will succeed only if it does not hold up the exclusively criminal proceedings.

If, however, the victim forgoes his claim for restitution, with the result that the trial proceeds smoothly, he may obtain damages as follows:

1. The victim of a criminal injury, for which the offender will not make compensation, may be awarded the proceeds (*den Erlös*) (to the extent of his claim established by court decision or by agreement) from the sale of confiscated objects, gifts or similar things which go to the state, and may further be awarded a sum which the state has demanded

---

4 Based essentially on information supplied by Professor Roland Grassberger, Director of Universitätsinstituts für Kriminologie (University Institute of Criminology), Wien, 1959.

5 Claude Baumann, *Die Stellung des Geschädigten im schweizerischen Strafprozess* (Aarau, 1958), p. 5.

from the offender as a guarantee that he will keep the peace (*den Betrag der Friedensbürgschaft*).[6]

2. In the case of a person who has suffered severe hardship through a criminal injury, for which compensation is not forthcoming, an award may be made even from the *Busse* paid by the convicted person.[7]

This seems to involve a procedure independent of either the civil courts or the criminal court which heard the case. However, the state is under no obligation to make this kind of award, and in practice the procedure is seldom used.

The victim has little chance of enforcing his claim against the prisoner's earnings, and usually can turn to civil execution only. Prisoners are allowed to offer a part of their prison earnings towards compensating the victim (some Cantons seem to envisage this in their legislation), but their earnings, the so-called *peculium*, are far less than those of free workers and have no real significance as far as restitution is concerned.[8]

Revision of Switzerland's penal provisions is in hand, but there are no signs that those rules which deal with restitution are likely to be altered.[9]

GERMAN FEDERAL REPUBLIC

In German law the term " damages " includes " restitution," as defined in this survey. Moreover, in German legal terminology the term " damages " comprises both " restitution in kind " (*Naturalrestitution*) and " monetary compensation."

The distinction between the two kinds of damages is clearly shown, however, in the provisions by which a person who is bound to make compensation must restore the injured party to the position in which he would have been if the circumstances from which the liability to compensate had not occurred. If compensation has to be made for injury to a person or damage to a thing, the injured party may demand, instead of restitution in kind, a lump sum or an annuity sufficient to effect such restitution. Furthermore, in so far as restitution in kind is impossible or is insufficient to compensate the injured, the person liable shall compensate the victim in money; so, too, he may pay monetary compensation if restitution in kind would be unreasonably expensive.[10]

---

[6] *Schweiz, Strafgesetzbuch* (StGB) (Swiss Penal Code) of December 21, 1937, Art. 60 (1).
[7] *Ibid.* Art. 60 (2).
[8] *Ibid.* Arts. 376–378.
[9] Based essentially on information supplied by Erwin R. Frey, Professor of the University of Zürich, Uitikon, 1959.
[10] *Bürgerliches Gesetzbuch* (" BGB ") (German Civil Code) of August 18, 1896, Arts. 249, 251, 842–847.

These provisions indicate that the victim has the legal right to claim restitution, or, according to German terminology, damages, from the offender. He enjoys this right in respect of all kinds of injury caused to him by a criminal offence. He can claim damages for material and moral injury. In addition to his claim for restitutive damages, the victim has other remedies available to him, such as a claim for restoration of a position, the return of an article, an interdict restraining the wrongdoer from future illegal actions, the retraction of a statement, etc. The ambit of his possible claims is, however, circumscribed by the provisions of civil law.

As a general rule, a person who, wilfully or negligently, unlawfully injures the life,[11] body, health, freedom or property of another, or infringes any right to which another is entitled, is bound to compensate his victim for any damage arising therefrom. A person who infringes a statutory provision intended for the protection of others, incurs the same obligation. If, however, infringement is possible without any fault on the part of the wrongdoer, the duty to compensate arises only if some fault can be imputed to him.[12]

Where the wrongdoing consists of a defamatory statement, the injured party can recover damages for any material loss he may have suffered therefrom, and in addition he can recover a solatium for his injured feelings. Such damages may be awarded against a transgressor even if he were ignorant of the untruth of his statement, if he ought so to have known. Similarly, liability to make compensation arises for any wilful damage caused to another *contra bonos mores*.[13]

Compensation can also be awarded to a woman against whom a crime of an immoral nature has been committed, or who has been induced by fraud or threats, or by an abuse of a relation of dependence, to permit illicit intercourse, even though she has suffered no material loss.[14] Similarly in the case of injury to the body or health of another, or in the case of deprivation of liberty, the injured party may demand equitable monetary compensation for the transgression, though this has occasioned no pecuniary loss.[15] According to a decision of the Federal Supreme Court (*Bundesgerichtshof*),[16] this latter provision is by analogy to be

---

[11] Injury to life means in German law killing. Other injuries, although endangering the life of the injured victim, are deemed to be injuries to " body " or " health."

[12] BGB. Art. 823.

[13] *Ibid*. Arts. 824, 826.

[14] *Ibid*. Art, 825.   [15] *Ibid*. Art. 847.

[16] *Entscheidungen des Bundesgerichtshofs in Zivilsachen* (Decisions of the Federal Supreme Court in civil matters), Vol. 26, p. 349.

applied also to those interferences which violate the right to free exercise of the will, the "inherent right to self-determination in the personal sphere of life." [17]

All these kinds of damages concern the victim (in other words: the injured party) personally, and only this person, the immediately injured, is, in principle, entitled to compensation.

Mediately injured persons, particularly dependants, may claim their own damages only in exceptional circumstances.

Where death has been caused, the person bound to make compensation must make good the deceased's funeral expenses to the person on whom the obligation to pay such expenses lies (the person bound to furnish maintenance to the deceased, or the deceased's heir). If the deceased at the time of the injury stood in a relationship to a third party by virtue of which he was or might be bound by law to furnish maintenance to such a third party, and if in consequence of the death such third party is deprived of the right to claim maintenance, the person bound to make compensation must compensate the third party by the payment of an annuity, to the extent that the deceased would have been bound to furnish maintenance during the presumable duration of his life. (The obligation to make compensation arises even if at the time of the injury the third party was only *en ventre sa mère*.) [18]

Similarly, in the case of causing death, or of causing injury to the body or health of another, or in the case of deprivation of liberty, if the injured party was by law bound to perform services for a third party (*e.g.*, a husband or parent; not the employer of a domestic servant, this relationship arising not by the operation of law, but by virtue of a contract of service), the person bound to make compensation, must compensate the third party for the loss of service by the payment of a money annuity.[19]

Further similar cases have been acknowledged by the jurisdiction under the name of *Drittschadensersatz* (which means compensation for damage caused to a third party). For example, an agent may claim for damage suffered by his principal when goods, bought on his behalf by the agent, are destroyed by a third party before delivery; so too an

---

[17] By this reasoning, the Federal Supreme Court awarded to the injured person a compensation for the moral damage suffered in a case, in which a photograph was published for purposes of advertisement by a third party without the knowledge and consent of the person reproduced and without having obtained the latter's authority.

[18] BGB. Art. 844.

[19] *Ibid*. Art. 845.

employer can claim compensation for damage suffered through continuing to pay salary to an injured employee.[20]

State compensation can be awarded if the person convicted was a public official,[21] but only in that case. If, in the exercise of the public office entrusted to him, he caused damage to a third party through wilful or negligent violation of an official duty to that third party, the victim may, instead of the official, hold liable the state or the public authority in whose service the official was employed.

In such cases, the following special provisions apply:

If an official wilfully or negligently commits a breach of duty incumbent upon him in his official capacity towards a third party, he must compensate such third party for any damage arising therefrom. If negligence only is imputable to the official, he may be held liable, only if the injured party is unable to obtain compensation elsewhere, the *onus probandi* resting upon the injured party.[22] If, however, an official commits a breach of his official duty in giving judgment in an action, he is not liable for any damage arising therefrom, unless the breach of duty is punishable with a public penalty, enforceable by criminal proceedings.[23] It is otherwise, however, with a breach of duty consisting of refusal or delay in the exercise of the office. The duty to make compensation does not arise if the injured party has wilfully or negligently omitted to mitigate the injury by making use of a legal remedy.

Further, if any person, in exercising the duties of a public office entrusted to him, violates his official obligations towards a third party, liability, in principle, rests with the state or his employing authority. In the case of wilful intent or gross negligence, the state or employing authority is entitled to be indemnified by the transgressing official. An appeal lies to the ordinary courts in respect of both the claim for damages and the right to an indemnity.[24]

The victim may claim damages for any criminal offences. Moreover, he may claim even if the injury does not at the same time amount to a contravention of the criminal law.

The victim of a criminal offence can bring his claim for damages against the offender first of all before the ordinary civil courts. As the punishable act is usually at the same time an unlawful act within the

---

[20] *Op. cit., Entscheidungen*, Vol. 10, p. 107.
[21] *Amtsträger*—holder of a public office.   [22] BGB. Art. 839.
[23] *Strafgesetzbuch* ("StGB") (German Criminal Code) of May 15, 1871, as published amended on August 25, 1953, Arts. 334, 336.
[24] *Grundgesetz für die Bundesrepublik Deutschland* (Basic Law for the Federal Republic of Germany) of May 23, 1949, Art. 34.

meaning of civil law, that court within whose district the unlawful act was committed has jurisdiction.[25]   In addition, the action may also be brought to the court having general jurisdiction over the defendant.

Besides this civil procedure, however, the victim can, as part of the criminal procedure, bring a claim for material damage suffered as a result of the criminal offence.   This is called " adhesion," or " the adhesive procedure." [26]

According to the provisions concerning the adhesion procedure, the injured person or his heir may during the criminal proceedings assert a claim against the accused for material damage arising out of the criminal offence, if the claim is within the jurisdiction of the ordinary courts, that is to say, is for not more than DM.1,000, and is not yet pending before another court.   In the District Court, however, this can only occur if the claim is within its jurisdiction.   The injured person (the victim of the criminal offence) or his heir should be notified of the criminal proceedings as early as possible; at the same time he should be informed of the possibility of asserting his claim in the criminal proceedings.   He can submit his claim verbally, and in spite of the fact that he is a " party " he can be questioned as a witness as well.

In two cases the court will not decide the claim in its judgment.   First, if the accused is not found guilty of a criminal offence, and no giving of security or reformatory order is made against him, or if the claim appears unfounded; and secondly, if it is inappropriate to settle the motion in a criminal procedure, in particular if its examination would protract the proceedings or if the claim is inadmissible; such action may be taken at any stage of the proceedings.

On the other hand, if the result of the trial shows that the claim is well founded, the court will grant it in the judgment; but the decision need not be limited to the grounds of the asserted claim.   In a decision of this kind, the court may declare it provisionally executable, subject to the furnishing of security.   The decision on the claim, however, is equivalent to a final judgment passed in civil litigation.   If the claim is not accepted, it may be brought elsewhere.

Disputes between the victim and the offender concerning the amount of damages may be decided by the court in its discretion considering all

---

[25] *Zivilprozessordnung* (" ZPO ") (German Code of Civil Procedure) of January 30, 1877, as published amended on September 12, 1950, Art. 32.
[26] *Adhäsionsverfahren*; *Strafprozessordnung* (StPO) (German Code of Criminal Procedure) of February 1, 1877, as published amended on September 12, 1950, Arts. 403–406.

the circumstances. Whether and to what extent requested evidence or expert opinion shall be ordered, is left to the discretion of the court. It is also for the court to decide whether the act complained of was the true cause of the damage suffered.[27] The court has complete discretion to decide, in the light of the evidence given, and of the rest of the proceedings, the truth or otherwise of any facts alleged. It must, however, give reasons for its decision.

The victim or his dependants may not attach the prisoner's earnings, but he may voluntarily pay his earnings in prison towards compensation for damage caused by the criminal offence.

Generally speaking, all prisoners are allowed to work in prison. Those prisoners, moreover, are compelled to work, who are undergoing a sentence of penal servitude, imprisonment, rigorous detention, youth imprisonment, penal arrest, or a measure of security and correction involving deprivation of liberty, except those who are in an asylum.[28] Prisoners of full age awaiting trial are not compelled to work, nor are prisoners in detention and confinement.[29]

Prisoners, generally, receive remuneration for their work (except where an authority of the Federal Armed Forces executes a punishment). The remuneration for prisoners' work differs from the wages of non-criminal free workers, in so far as there exists no legal right to them, and that they are governed, with regard to their amount, by considerations of the education and readaptation of the prisoners to the community; collective agreements regarding free workers are not applicable to prisoners.

The prisoner is not permitted to dispose of his earnings at his discretion. He is, however, allowed to dispose of half of his remuneration (prisoners under preventive detention are permitted to dispose of two-thirds) for the maintenance of his dependants, for his personal needs, and for compensation for the damage caused by his criminal offence. In addition, his remuneration should, at the same time, serve the purpose of providing him with a little sum in hand at the time of his release.[30] This is the sole way, in which the victim's claim can be met from the prisoner's earnings, otherwise the victim may not have recourse to

---

[27] ZPO, Arts. 287, 452.
[28] StGB, Arts. 15, 16, 42, 362: *Jugendgerichtsgesetz* (Juvenile Court Act) of August 4, 1953, as published amended on March 30, 1957, Art. 91; *Rechtsverordnung über den Vollzug des Strafarrestes* (Regulation on the Execution of Penal Arrest) of August 25, 1958, Arts. 5, 12.
[29] StPO, Art. 116; StGB, Arts. 17–18.
[30] Wolfgang Mittermaier, *Gefängniskunde* (Berlin, 1954), Chap. 13.

earnings of this kind, nor can he enforce his claim against them.[31]   It is for the prisoner voluntarily to decide if he wishes to pay compensation out of his earnings.

Certainly the civil character of the victim's damages is not affected by the fact that the punishment awarded may be affected by the payment or non-payment of damages.   When awarding punishment, the court will generally take into account whether or not the accused has voluntarily made compensation for the damage caused by his crime, or at least shown a sincere willingness to do so.

Similarly, the question of damages is taken into account when the court considers the possibility of suspension of the sentence or of probation.   When the court suspends a sentence and places the accused on probation, the provision of the Criminal Code concerned stipulates, *inter alia*, that the court shall impose certain obligations upon the person convicted for the duration of the probation, and in particular it may require him to make compensation for the damage caused by his offence. However, the court may refrain from imposing certain obligations, if it is to be expected that the person convicted will even without them lead an orderly and law-abiding life, and especially will make compensation, as far as possible, for the damage caused by the offence.[32]

In the Swiss legal system there is another remedy besides damages. The person injured by a punishable act may, in certain cases, request a so-called *Busse*, which is roughly a " compensatory fine," and though its legal character is strongly disputed in scientific literature, according to the official German views it seems to be considered not as a penalty, but as a civil remedy.   In its imposition it is concerned primarily with the circumstances of the victim, and compensation by means of it has the flexible limit of DM.3–10,000.

The right to claim this *Busse* arises in case of insult and personal injury, and is also to be found in other penal secondary Acts (secondary Acts are any Acts besides the original Criminal Code) which deal with unfair business competition, trade marks, models and designs, patents, copyright in works of art and photography, etc., but all the relative provisions are, in substance, the same.   Generally, if the wrong injures the economic position, livelihood or the future prospects of the person insulted, *Busse* compensation payable to him may, at his request, be

---

[31] This is the practice, but the only express provision can be found in the *Dienst und Vollzugsordnung für die Gefangenenanstalten der Justizverwaltung in Preussen* (Service and Execution Rules for Prisons) of August 1, 1923, Art. 109; applicable in Berlin.   [32] StGB, Arts. 23–24.

imposed in addition to the penalty, and this award of compensation debars any further claim to damages. Similarly, *Busse* is payable in all cases of bodily injury,[33] without, however, any precondition. In other words, in cases of insult *Busse*-compensation may be imposed only if certain consequences (such as prejudice to the economic position, the livelihood, or the future prospects of the victim) flow from the misdeed; moreover, in the case of prejudice to the future prospects, non-material damages may also be awarded. In cases of bodily injury, however, liability to pay *Busse*-compensation arises from the bodily injury itself. In this latter case, the compensation is not only an indemnification for pecuniary loss suffered by the victim but also a reparation for the physical or psychical damage suffered by him, and unconnected with any material loss, *e.g.*, reparation for the disturbance of his wellbeing or for pain suffered. It is for the court to assess in money terms the gravity of the personal injury to the victim both with regard to his pecuniary situation and in other respects, and award accordingly an appropriate compensation.

Claims for *Busse* can only be asserted through criminal procedure. In this connection, the provisions for " adhesive procedure " apply.[34]

The practice in the German Federal Republic is that claims for damages almost always make use of the civil procedure, and the " adhesive procedure " as well as the special institution of *Busse* plays a role of secondary and mainly theoretical importance. In general, the victim will wait for the result of the criminal procedure in order to obtain certain evidence for the enforcement of his civil claim. In many cases the victim will, however, not bring an action for damages, if he realises that the offender is a man of straw.

The possibility of putting forward a civil claim for damages in connection with criminal procedure by means of the adhesive procedure has not reached any importance in practice, though many theorists have held high hopes of its efficiency. Similarly to the French system, the German law also provides the *droit d'option de la personne lésée*,[35] but this right is not, in practice, utilised. The adhesive procedure was originally planned in order to avoid the double work of both civil and criminal work for the courts.[36] The criminal courts, and the State

---

[33] *Op. cit.*, StGB, Arts. 188, 231.

[34] *sinngemäss.*

[35] However, the French principles " *le criminel tient le civil en état* " and the " *autorité de la chose jugée au pénal sur le civil* " are not effective ones in German law : Nicholas Valticos, *L'autorité de la chose jugée au criminel sur le civil* (Paris, 1953).

[36] Schönke, *op. cit.*, pp. 8, 28.

Prosecution authorities, however, seem to feel that civil claims are inappropriate to criminal procedure. This is probably why the courts frequently make use of the aforementioned provisions of the Code, which enable them to decline to give judgment in criminal proceedings on a civil claim.

Claims for the compensatory fine, *Busse*, are filed relatively seldom in practice. This is presumably due, above all, to the fact that, according to the previously mentioned provisions, the award of this *Busse* compensation, be it even a very small one, excludes any possibility of claiming any further restitution or indemnification in another, civil, procedure.[37]

---

[37] Based essentially on information supplied by H. Gossrau, Bundesministerium der Justiz (Ministry of Justice), Bonn, 1959; Hans-Heinrich Jescheck, Professor of Criminal Law, Director of the Institut für ausländisches und internationales Strafrecht an der Universität (Institute of foreign and international Criminal Law at the University), Freiburg, 1959; Hans Heinz Heldmann, Institut für ausländisches und internationales Strafrecht an der Universität (Institute of foreign and international Criminal Law at the University), Freiburg, 1959; Th. Würtenberger, Professor of Criminology, Director of the Institut für Kriminologie und Strafvollzugskunde an der Universität (Institute of Criminology and Penology at the University), Freiburg. 1959; Wolfgang Starke, Institute für Kriminologie und Strafvollzugskunde an der Universität (Institute of Criminology and Penology at the University), Freiburg, 1959.

6

NORTHERN EUROPE

DENMARK

RESTITUTION by the offender is an accepted institution in Danish law.

Any person who is responsible for violation of the body or freedom of another person, and any person who is found guilty of any other punishable violation of the person of another, his peace or honour, may be ordered to pay damages to compensate the victim for his financial prejudice or loss. He may, in addition, be ordered to pay damages for any non-material injury suffered, such as pain and suffering, disfigurement, loss of marriage or business or career prospects, and generally for disturbing the other's peace.

Furthermore, any person, who is responsible for the death of another person, may be ordered to pay damages to the dependants of the latter, in respect of the loss they have suffered therefrom. Damages can be fixed either as a lump sum or as a regular subsistence allowance, in which latter case they may be either subject to or without security.[1]

The law recognises that the making of restitution or payment of damages may be taken into consideration in deciding what punishment should be imposed. Thus, the punishment prescribed may be mitigated if, after the commission of the crime, the perpetrator has made full recompense for the damage caused by his act. This is also true if the offender has somehow tried to prevent the completion of the act and has tried to make good the damage he has caused.[2]

So much importance is attached to the victim's right to restitution, that even claims in respect of non-material loss pass on his death to his successors. But in order for such a claim to be hereditable, it must have been admitted, or civil proceedings to enforce it must have been taken, or a claim for damages put forward during a criminal trial by the

---

[1] Act No. 127 of April 15, 1930, on the Coming into Force of the Criminal Code, Art. 15 (1) and (2).
[2] Criminal Code of April 15, 1930, s. 84 (1), para. (VII) and (VIII).

adhesive process, or at any rate a summons have been filed with the court. Until this has been done, the claim is not transferable.[3]

The victim of a crime, or his dependants, can choose where to claim restitution. His claim may be put forward and decided either during the criminal proceedings, or during the trial of a case brought separately under the rules governing the public administration of justice.[4]

Though criminal justice is, to this extent, involved with the question of restitution to the victim, the victim's recourse to the offender's earnings seems to lie through the ordinary civil channels, and the possibility of enforcing his claim against the offender while the latter is a prisoner is rather slight. Prisoners are required to carry out the work which, due regard being had to their abilities, skills and opportunities of employment after discharge, they are ordered to do; and for the execution of this work a remuneration is credited to the prisoner. This remuneration is determined either at a fixed daily amount, a rather small sum, or according to the piece-rate system, in which case the daily earnings will be somewhat higher though still fairly small. The amount cannot be attached by creditors until it is paid, nor can the prisoner dispose of it before that time. In any case, however, one half of what the prisoner earns in this way is saved for his discharge, while he may spend the remaining half on the purchase of personal requirements, books, etc. No claim for damages can therefore be enforced against the prisoner's earnings in prison until they have actually been paid over to him, and the amount he is required to have at his discharge has been set aside. Claims can, however, be satisfied out of the other assets of the prisoner, if any.[5]

It should be noted that this system of restitution seems to work satisfactorily and competent authorities have at present no intention of amending the rules in force in that field. It is, however, noteworthy that at the Fourth Congress of Nordic Criminologists the Finns raised the question of modernising the rules relating to restitution to victims of crime.[6]

---

[3] Act No. 127 of April 15, 1930, on the Coming into Force of the Criminal Code, Art. 15 (3).

[4] Notification No. 265 of September 15, 1953, of the Administration of Justice Act, Chap. 89.

[5] Order No. 364 of May 10, 1947, on the Execution of Sentences of Imprisonment in State Prisons; Order No. 389 of September 3, 1948, on the Execution of Sentences of Imprisonment in Local Jail.

[6] *Nordisk Kriminalistisk A'rsbok 1957* (Stockholm, 1959) pp. 201–203. Based essentially on information supplied by Niels Madsen, Justitsministeriet (Ministry of Justice), Copenhagen, 1959.

FINLAND

Finnish legislation allows restitution for victims of crime to be claimed in criminal proceedings. In all other respects, however, the claim remains a civil one.

The victim of a criminal offence can make a claim for restitution during the course of the trial of the alleged offender. In his capacity of claimant he is then described as being the " plaintiff " in the suit. It is immaterial whether the crime was committed intentionally or negligently and only in the case of contributory liability for the damage by the victim himself or by a third party can the claim for restitution be reduced.[7]

Restitution can be claimed for any diminution in the value of goods or property, for loss of income or support, for pain, suffering or disability, for any expenses incurred as a result of the crime, including medical expenses, and for moral damage such as is caused by rape or the deprivation of liberty.[8] The last cannot be claimed by the dependants or successors of the victim after his death,[9] but apart from this restriction, compensation can be awarded both for actual financial loss and for non-material moral damages.

Where the crime results in the death of the victim and he leaves dependants who are thus deprived of their essential means of support, they are entitled to restitution. Such restitution may be awarded in the form either of a lump sum or periodic payments until they are able to provide for themselves. When awarding such compensation, due regard must be had to the financial position of the offender and to any other relevant circumstances.[10]

Where a criminal offence is committed by two or more offenders, each of them is liable for the whole restitution claim, having however a right of recourse against the others.[11] If the damage is caused by a child under fifteen or by a mentally ill or otherwise irresponsible person, and the person responsible has been negligent, he will be liable for the damage. If, however, he cannot pay the damages awarded they will be paid out of the offender's property.[12]

A legal right to claim compensation is attached to every crime, but the state is liable to pay compensation only in respect of offences committed by officials in the course of their duty. This cannot be considered

---

[7] Criminal Code of December 19, 1889, Chap. IX, para. 1.
[8] *Ibid.* Chap. IX, para. 2.
[9] *Ibid.* Chap. IX, para. 8; Act of May 18, 1927, para. 6.
[10] *Ibid.* Chap. IX, para. 3.
[11] *Ibid.* Chap. IX, para. 4.   [12] *Ibid.* Chap. IX, para. 5.

as a state compensation system in its criminological term, and is merely a civil obligation of the state. The state is liable directly for damage and suffering, if an imprisonment has been enforced without the person concerned being found guilty of any crime, or if property in the custody of an official has been lost; and it is secondarily liable for all damage and suffering, caused by an official through breach of his official duty, which has not been made good by the official himself.[13]

Claims for restitution can be dealt with either in criminal or in civil proceedings, independently of the criminal case, according to the choice of the victim who suffered the damage. Compensation for damage caused by an official can also be claimed directly from the common courts.[14] To claim restitution within the scope of criminal proceedings is only a possible way of proceeding. The victim's claim for restitution is not in any way connected with the criminal proceedings; the victim can claim restitution even where such proceedings have already begun or a penalty prescribed, or where the proceedings have not yet commenced.[15]

The performance or non-performance of compensation has, as a rule, no effect on the decision or execution of the punishment. It may, however, affect the " qualified " (suspended) sentence. The court may impose as one of the conditions for giving a qualified sentence the offender's readiness to pay compensation to the victim of his crime. A qualified sentence may also be given on the condition that compensation is paid within a certain time, and a failure to pay may cause the sentence to be carried out in full.[16]

Generally, the victim can enforce his claim for compensation against all the property of the offender, with the exception of some personal assets, which are not subject to the right of enforcement, such as indispensable household goods, clothes, tools, etc.[17] In addition, there exists, in certain exceptional cases, a right for the victim to enforce his claim against the offender's earnings in prison.

The victim cannot, as a general rule, have recourse to the prisoner's prison earnings[18]; but if a person, to whom the prisoner has been ordered to pay restitution by a court, is in need of maintenance and requires money for his support, the Prison Board can, even against the prisoner's will and without his consent, use up to half the prisoner's

---

[13] Act of May 18, 1927, paras. 1–5.
[14] *Ibid.* paras. 8–9.
[15] *Op. cit.*, Code, Chap. IX, para. 6.
[16] Act of June 20, 1918, on Conditional Sentence, paras. 3–5.
[17] Act of December 3, 1895, on Civil Execution, Chap. 4, para. 5.
[18] Decree of December 19, 1889, on Execution of Punishments, Chap. 3, para. 10.

savings and wages to pay an award of restitution or damages.[19] In addition, by permission of the director of the prison and with his assistance, the prisoner can voluntarily use his savings and wages to indemnify those who have suffered by his crime.[20]

These possibilities have a realistic basis, as certain prisoners earn quite a considerable amount in prison, depending upon the sort of penal institution in which their punishment is carried out:

(a) A prisoner held for trial cannot be compelled to work. If he still wants to work, a suitable opportunity must be, so far as possible, arranged for him; and the whole income of his work is at his disposal.

(b) A prisoner serving hard labour (penal servitude) must work entirely for the benefit of the state.[21]

(c) A prisoner serving simple imprisonment is required to work, but, in so far as is possible in his prison, he is allowed to choose suitable work, and can even perform such work with his own tools. He is given some wages.[22]

(d) Prisoners serving their sentence in State Labour Colonies or in State Prison Colonies [23] are required to work; the emphasis in these institutions being on work, rather than on education. Their wages are similar to those of free workers, corresponding to current wages in the free market, though reductions are made to cover taxes, food, clothes, family care, and obligatory savings.

This Finnish system of restitution seems in practice to work, though certain claims have been put forward for its modernisation. It often happens that the offender lacks pecuniary resources, and the victim cannot, therefore, in spite of the amount awarded him, get any compensation. This question was raised at the Fourth Nordic Congress of Criminologists,[24] which called attention to this unsatisfactory state of things.[25]

19 *Ibid*. Chap. 3, para. 10; Chap. 5, para. 4.
20 *Ibid*. Chap. 3, para. 10; Chap. 5, para. 4; Regulations of Ministry of Justice of May 30, 1958, on Savings and Wages of Prisoners, Art. 12.
21 *Ibid*. Chap. 3, para. 2.
22 *Ibid*. Chap. 4, paras. 2–10: *op. cit.*, Regulations of May 30, 1958.
23 Act of April 26, 1946, on State Labour Colonies; Act of 1954 on Prisoners' Colonies.
24 *Nordisk Kriminalistisk A'rsbok 1957* (Stockholm, 1959), pp. 201–203.
25 Based essentially on information supplied by Kai Korte, Secretary of Government, Valtioneuvosto Oikensministeriö (Ministry of Justice), Helsinki, 1959; Bruno A. Salmiala, Professor of Criminal Law, Institute of Criminal Law, University of Helsinki, Porthania, Helsinki, 1959; and Viljo O. Eloranta, Master of Laws, Assistant at the Institute of Criminal Law of the University of Helsinki, Porthania, Helsinki, 1959.

NORWAY

Apart from some features of secondary importance, restitution to victims of crime belongs in the Norwegian legal system to the field of civil law. According to Norwegian restitution principles, the offending party is generally liable to pay compensation (the term used there instead of restitution) if he has caused unlawful injury deliberately or through carelessness. If the injury is caused " by an act that is punishable " (*i.e.*, by a criminal offence), this general provision will normally apply.[26] Where the cause of action is a criminal act, third parties (*i.e.*, neither malefactor nor victim) will not normally be able to be parties to the action.

Where, however, death has been caused, the deceased's relatives may have a claim for compensation, in accordance with the provision[27] by which the dependants of a person wrongfully killed are entitled to compensation for loss of support.

Although it is nowhere expressly stated in Norwegian law, an obligation to pay compensation arises whenever anyone has suffered damage through the criminal act of another.

The normal rule is that only the victim's economic loss is compensated. In certain cases, however, moral or non-material damages may be awarded,[28] mainly in cases of injury to the body or health, infringement of freedom,[29] false accusation,[30] gross sexual crimes, rape, sexual intercourse with persons under sixteen years of age,[31] and certain serious criminal offences in family relationships.[32] In certain other cases, too, damages may be awarded for non-material injury suffered, but these causes of action are not necessarily crimes. Where a wrongdoer is liable to pay compensation for his crime, he must give the injured party (that is to say the victim of the crime), besides compensation for the damage suffered, such compensation for loss of his future livelihood, as the court finds equitable. If the criminal act was carried out intentionally

---

[26] There may be an exception, if it is a safety regulation which has been broken to a punishable extent. It should be considered that the safety regulations involve stricter demands for care than what follows from the demand that an action is to be careful and that breach of the regulations, in spite of being punishable, will not entail liability for compensation for injury in Norwegian law.

[27] Law on coming into force of the General Penal Code of May 22, 1902, para. 21. (This Penal Code has been amended several times, but not in respect of compensation. A permanent committee has been set up, the so-called *Straffelovsradet*, that is to say the Advisory Committee on Criminal Law, whose task is to prepare amendments and improvements.)

[28] *Op. cit.* Penal Code, paras. 19, 19a.

[29] *Ibid.* para. 19.

[30] *Ibid.* paras. 168–169.

[31] *Ibid.* paras. 191–196, 201.

[32] *Ibid.* paras. 217–221.

or with gross negligence, the court may in addition order the guilty party (that is to say the offender) to pay the victim an equitable sum as reparation for pain and suffering and for the disturbance of the victim's rights caused by the act, or for other damage not of an economic kind.

Similarly,[33] if anyone has defamed or insulted another, he must, provided the act be punishable or he has acted negligently, pay such compensation for future loss of earnings as the court, considering *inter alia* the culpability of the criminal act, finds equitable. Where a libel has been printed and the author of the libel wrote it while acting in the service of the owner or publisher of the printed material, the latter, as well as the original author of the libel, is liable to pay compensation. The same provision applies to compensation awarded for insult or infringement of privacy, unless the court considers that for special reasons the owner or publisher should be relieved. Owner or publisher may also be required to pay such further compensation as the court finds equitable. In a judgment involving punishment or an order for retraction the court may order the convicted party to pay a sum to the victim for publication of the judgment.

Although a person may be injured as a result of a breach of the criminal law, he is not necessarily, strictly speaking, considered the " injured party " in Norwegian law. The injured party in cases involving the criminal law is *stricto sensu* he for the protection of whose rights the law was passed. In cases of punishable damage to another person's property, the owner is the injured party; if embezzlement has been committed, he on whom the loss falls is the injured party; if murder has been committed, the wife and children are counted as injured persons as well; if a damaged object was insured, the insurance company is regarded as injured as well as the owner.[34] Under penal provisions for the protection of public interests, such as public peace and order, the regulation of traffic, etc., no private individual can be an injured party. If, however, he is injured as the result of the breach of such a law, his claim for compensation or restitution can be combined with the actual criminal procedure.[35]

Some criminal characteristics attach to the institution of compensation, since, for example, the injured party (the victim) must be informed that he may have his claim for compensation adjudicated at the same

---

[33] *Ibid.* para. 19a.
[34] *Ibid.* para. 78.
[35] Penal Procedure Law of July 1, 1887, Chap. 32, para. 3. (This law is, at present, under review.)

time as the criminal charge, within the scope of the criminal procedure.[36] If he wishes to join the criminal procedure with his claim for compensation, he must inform the accused of his intention to join, and of the evidence he intends to lead, and he must do so within a certain time.

At the request of the injured party, the prosecuting authority may undertake to present his (the victim's) case if he (the prosecutor) can do so without much inconvenience; he will do so even without any request being made, unless it is assumed that the reason for the victim's failure to make such a request is that the injured party does not wish to present his claim during the criminal case.

The court may refuse to adjudge the claim of the victim within the scope of the criminal trial if the inclusion of it is considered likely to lead to considerable inconvenience; and judgment must not be given if the court does not find the victim's claim sufficiently established.[37]

If the accused is sentenced to punishment, the claim of the injured party is adjudged simultaneously, if the necessary preconditions have been fulfilled. If that is not the case, *e.g.*, because the court is of the opinion that the injured party has not suffered any loss, the court cannot decide on his claim and this will be left for civil action. If the accused is not sentenced to punishment, he must also be dismissed from the claim of the injured party, if it is clear that the injured party's claim has no basis. If, however, in spite of an acquittal of the accused it seems possible or probable that the injured party's claim is well founded, it cannot be decided within the scope of the criminal proceedings but is transferred to the civil proceedings. The victim may, however, receive judgment in his favour even though the accused is acquitted, *e.g.*, where the accused is acquitted because his crime has been time barred, while the civil claim has not. Where the court has ordered the retraction of a defamatory statement the claim for compensation must also be decided.

The Norwegian legal system provides that if the victim's claim is decided in the course of the criminal procedure without his requesting it, he may, if not satisfied with the decision, withdraw his claim for compensation and bring it in a separate civil action.[38] If, however, the injured party's claim is adjudged at his request, he can, if dissatisfied with the result, only submit an appeal, which appeal will be entertained as a civil case.

It is a claim against the accused alone that the injured party can

[36] *Ibid.* paras. 438–440.
[37] *Ibid.* paras. 441–442.   [38] *Ibid.* para. 446

submit in the criminal procedure, and claims against others cannot be included.[39]

Besides being able to bring his claim through the criminal procedure, it is open to the injured party to choose instead to institute a civil action.

Similar provisions apply where the victim claims the restitution of money or goods. In such cases, however, a decision of the court, as a judgment on the civil claim, is not necessary, and if objects are confiscated from the wrongdoer, they will be returned to the victim.

There is little chance for the victim to enforce his claim against the prisoner's prison earnings. Convicted prisoners are required to work, and prisoners awaiting trial may work if this does not conflict with the order and safety of the prison.[40] For their work prisoners *may* be awarded " work-money," but they have no legal right to claim remuneration; their income is at present about 5 to 10 per cent. of that of ordinary free workers. If the prisoner agrees, up to half of any " work-money " saved may be paid out for compensation purposes to the injured party. In exceptional cases the governor of the prison may order this even without the prisoner's consent.

And as with most legal systems, the question of compensation is relevant to the suspension of sentences and to probation.[41] The law allows a sentence to be suspended when it is not necessary for the sentence to be enforced either as a deterrent to the accused himself and to others, or to prevent the wrongdoer from committing new crimes. As a condition for suspending the sentence, the court may order the offender while on probation, which is usually for a period of two years, to pay the injured party such compensation as he is entitled to and has claimed and the offender has the means to pay. If a large sum is involved, it is usually ordered that the offender should pay it in monthly instalments. The amount of compensation is adjusted according to the financial position of the offender, so that it sometimes happens that the amount of compensation ordered to be paid by the offender on probation is less than that claimed by the victim.

Apparently very little criticism has been raised against the principles governing restitution (compensation) in the Norwegian legal system.

[39] *Ibid.* para. 3 (there is, however, an exception, where the injured party has been exposed to libel in print, in which case the claim for compensation may be extended to the owner or publisher).

[40] It should be noted, on the coming into force of a new Norwegian prison law of April 1, 1959, the custody prisoners' duty to work will drop out, but their right to work will continue.

[41] *Op. cit.*, Penal Code, para. 52.

One of the most important principles is that in cases where the victim's claim for compensation is joined to the criminal proceedings, the criminal case is to be regarded as the main item; another that the victim (injured party) cannot be allowed to join the case with his claim, if this may disrupt and protract the main proceedings. These two principles illustrate the dominantly civil character of the institution of restitution.[42]

SWEDEN

Though Swedish law allows claims for restitution to the victim to be brought within the scope of the criminal trial, restitution remains in Swedish law an entirely civil matter.

The victim, or his dependants, has a legal right to claim restitution and damages from the offender, and damages includes compensation for moral injury. This right applies to practically all offences, for, according to Swedish law, compensation for damage, which one person's criminal action has caused another person to sustain, must be paid by the offender, whether the crime was committed intentionally or unintentionally.[43] If the person who has suffered the damage has unintentionally contributed towards bringing it about, compensation for the damage should be reasonably adjusted.[44]

Otherwise damages must fully compensate for the loss sustained, except where damages must be paid for the loss of a provider; the amount of such damages is limited to a reasonable sum.

In a case where bodily injuries have been sustained damages shall include not only doctor's fees and other expenses, but also compensation for loss of earnings or prospects, and loss of amenities.[45]

Restitution must also be made for the humiliation inflicted by the wrongful detention of a person or by defamation. A person who is guilty of libel may, if the injured party requires, be ordered to pay for printing in the national or local press the verdict of the court by which he was convicted.[46]

In cases where a crime has caused death, if the deceased had dependants whom he was legally bound to support, and who now, as a result of his death, lack the means of support, they are entitled to receive such damages by way of restitution for their deprivation of support as the

---

[42] Based essentially on information supplied by Andreas Endresen, Director of the Legal Section, Norwegian Ministry of Justice, Oslo, 1959.
[43] Strafflag (Criminal Law) of February 16, 1864, No. 11, s. 1, Chap. 6, para. 1.
[44] *Ibid*. Chap. 6, para. 1.
[45] *Ibid*. Chap. 6, para. 2.
[46] *Ibid*. Chap. 6, para. 3, amended by Act of June 30, 1948, No. 448.

court may consider just, having regard to the criminal's assets and means. Such compensation may be ordered to be paid either in a lump sum or in the form of periodic payments.[47]

Claims for restitution and damages can be entertained within the scope of criminal proceedings, and this is the usual procedure. If this procedure is adopted, it is incumbent upon the prosecutor, at the request of the plaintiff, to prefer his claim at the trial, provided that this can be done without causing inconvenience, and provided the claim is not considered to be unjustified. The court may, however, order that the claim for restitution or damages be heard as a civil action at separate proceedings. Such an order would be made, for example, if the claim for restitution called for extensive examination.

If punishment cannot be imposed or the time for the resumption of criminal proceedings which were interrupted, has elapsed, the plaintiff is not on this account precluded from claiming such compensation as he is otherwise entitled to receive.[48]

The victim is, however, not bound to avail himself of his remedies through the criminal procedure. He can also institute special proceedings for restitution or damages, which are then regarded as being a civil action. Such a course may be particularly appropriate, when the case is a long one. Sometimes this is necessary, since criminal proceedings are not instituted. If, however, criminal proceedings are taken at the same time, the court may order that the claim for restitution or damages shall be entertained within the scope of the criminal procedure.

Cases in which claims for restitution or damages are entertained within the scope of the criminal procedure, differ from those in which such claims are heard as a civil action, primarily in respect of the preliminary trial of the case, but there is little difference in the composition of the court.

The victim has a better chance of enforcing his claim in cases where the offender is free, or when he proceeds against his property; he has but a very slight chance of having recourse to the offender's earnings as a prisoner, though an offender, who is sentenced to simple imprisonment, can, to a considerable extent, use his earnings at his own discretion. Depending upon the nature of the prisoner's earnings, however, the victim has a limited chance of enforcing his claim.

The offender may use a small sum of money per week for buying

---

[47] *Ibid.* Chap. 6, para. 4, amended by Act of March 19, 1926, No. 48.
[48] *Ibid.* Chap. 6, para. 7, amended by Act of March 31, 1926, No. 70; and Chap. 5, paras. 13, 14, 15, 17, 18, 19.

tobacco, coffee, fruit, etc. Part of his earnings are set aside to cover expenses connected with his release. The rest of his earnings may be used for the support of his dependants, payment of restitution and damages, dental hygiene, books and newspapers, study-material, expenses in connection with his leave, etc. He may either be paid a fixed sum per day as a gratuity, or payment may be made according to piecework rates. In either case remuneration is considerably lower than that in the open market (about one-seventh). If the offender's earnings are by way of the gratuity, the victim cannot enforce his claim through the usual legal channels; *inter alia*, a distress cannot be levied upon the offender. On the other hand, the prison authorities endeavour to persuade the offender to pay restitution and damages voluntarily.

In exceptional cases, an offender is allowed to work on the premises of his employer outside the institution. As a rule, under such conditions he receives standard wages. If remuneration is received by the offender as ordinary wages, the victim may have recourse to the usual legal means for obtaining payment, in competition, however, with other creditors, since he has no right of priority.

The entirely civil character of restitution is finally shown by its lack of influence on the award of punishment. It should be pointed out, however, that when considering what is known as " facultative conditional release," the offender's readiness to pay compensation for the damage caused by his crime must *inter alia* be taken into account.

The unsatisfactory state of the law on restitution to victims of crime was, as mentioned earlier, brought up by the Finns at the Fourth Nordic Congress of Criminologists.[49]

---

[49] *Nordisk Kriminalistisk A'rsbok 1957* (Stockholm, 1959), pp. 201–203. Based essentially on information supplied by Carl Holmberg, Justitie-departementet (Ministry of Justice), Stockholm, 1959.

7

SOUTHERN EUROPE

ITALY

THE Italian legal system seems to deal with restitution as a civil institution, since " any crime compels restitution under civil laws." [1] Thus,
if the criminal offence has caused an injury, the offender and all other
persons who are liable under the civil law for what was done, must pay
damages.

The victim may claim in either the civil courts or the criminal
courts. Civil actions for damages for a crime may be brought by " the
person to whom the crime has brought injury " (that is to say by the
victim), or by his heirs.[2] An action for damages may thus be brought
by those having *locus standi in judicio* either before the appropriate
civil court having jurisdiction, or at criminal sessions when the trial of
the malefactor takes place. The criminal court may, however, decide
the civil action only if it convicts the accused.[3]

The civil character of the institution of restitution to the victim of
crime (which is called just " damages " in the Italian legal system) is
stressed by the provision by which those having the right to bring a civil
action are joined in criminal proceedings as " civil parties." [4]

Where a civil action is so brought during criminal proceedings, the
two cases, civil and criminal, are heard jointly, and the criminal court
deals with the question of damages to the victim during the criminal proceedings, and the victim, as a civil party, may suggest to the court how
facts should be decided and damages awarded.[5] In this procedure the
victim is a civil party only, but such a party enjoys great rights in the
proceedings: he may, *inter alia*, present petitions, be present at investigations, and when the court receives evidence where the value of something is in dispute, he may appoint his own technical consultant, who
participates in the final discussions at the end of the hearing and gives

---

[1] Codice Penale (Penal Code), Art. 185.
[2] Codice Procedura Penale (Penal Procedure Code), Art. 22.
[3] *Ibid.* Art. 23.
[4] *Ibid.* Arts. 91–106.
[5] *Ibid.* Art. 104.

his conclusions, including his evaluation of the appropriate quantum of damages (here called "compensation") if he is asked to do so.[6]

This right to bring a civil action in a criminal court provides the victim of crime with a right "to restitution or to compensation" for injury. Damages for injuries deriving from crimes can thus be claimed for physical as well as moral injuries.

The court may, when attempting to assess damages, hear any expert witness to whom the parties may have agreed. When passing sentence, the criminal court will also award damages, unless it is not possible to assess damages accurately, on account of the nature of the injury suffered, when it will pass the matter to a civil court for a settlement of the question of the quantum of damages. In such a case, the criminal court may require the criminal to give a certain sum to the injured party in the nature of a down-payment to be set against the damages when these are definitely fixed.[7]

The victim, or his dependants, can, to a certain extent, enforce an award of damages against the prisoner's prison earnings. As part of his penalty, the convicted person is obliged to work in the penal institution. For this work he is paid a certain remuneration from which must be deducted: first, the amount due as damages, then, the cost of his maintenance in prison, and lastly the cost of his trial. One-third, however, of the money he earns by his prison labour must be left him, to be saved against the day when he emerges from prison.[8]

The amount of the remuneration is fixed by the Ministry of Justice for the various categories of workers, regard being had to the nature of the work and to the capacity and efficiency of the prisoner. Payment may also be made on a piecework basis. A certain proportion of the amount earned may also be taken by the state by way of a penalty from the earnings of the prisoner.[9]

The victim and his heirs may enforce their claim against the prisoner's earnings in prison, as well as against his movable and immovable property. To ensure the sum owing to the "claimant for compensation for injury" (*i.e.*, the victim), legal hypothec over and, if necessary, sequestration of the offender's goods is provided for; such hypothec or sequestration is cancelled by a decree of irrevocable acquittal being pronounced

---

[6] *Ibid.* Arts. 304–305, 468.
[7] *Ibid.* Art. 489.
[8] Codice Penale, Art. 145.
[9] Penitentiary Regulations of June 18, 1931, Art. 125.

(penal sanctions are also provided for the recovery of financial penalties imposed for breaches of the law).[10]

The only respect in which restitution for damages can truly be said to be part of the criminal law is that it may have an effect upon sentence. If the prisoner has entirely redressed the damage before judgment, or has at least endeavoured spontaneously and efficaciously to mitigate the consequences of his crime, this will constitute extenuating or mitigating circumstances. In such a case, the penalty can be reduced by not more than one-third. It can have an effect on capital punishment as well, where imprisonment for twenty to twenty-four years can be substituted for the death penalty.[11]

If compensation for the injury of the victim has already been made, the prisoner's earnings in prison are applied to his other liabilities in their aforementioned order and to his savings against his release.

It appears that in Italy this system works satisfactorily. Even though the penal code and the penal procedure code have been subjected to not a few modifications, and others are in the process of being made, the provisions relating to the payment of restitution to victims of crime have not formed the subject of significant proposals for modification.[12]

[10] Codice Penale, Arts. 189–198.
[11] *Ibid*. Arts. 62–65.
[12] Based essentially on information supplied by the Italian Ministry of Justice, Rome, 1959.

8

EASTERN EUROPE

Turkey

RESTITUTION is in Turkey an accepted institution; generally speaking, it is embodied in the civil law. Any person who, intentionally or by negligence, causes unlawful damage to another person, must pay restitution.[1] Consequently any person who has suffered damage as a result of a criminal offence has a right to claim restitution from the offender. All offences, committed intentionally or by negligence and against property or against the person, give this right.

The victim's claim for restitution and damages is generally tried by a civil court. He has, however, the right to apply to a criminal court if his injuries were caused by a criminal offence. In this case the question of restitution is entertained within the scope of the criminal trial, provided such action is accepted by the criminal court as necessary.[2] Where the victim is alive, the right to claim restitution belongs exclusively to him; in the case of the victim's death, however, the legal right to claim restitution passes, with other legal rights, to his dependants. In the case of the death of such a dependent person, the right to claim damages still survives.[3]

In Turkish law these damages are not restricted to material loss, and include compensation for moral damage also. The ascertainment and estimation of moral damage is at the court's discretion.[4]

Where the case involves some matter requiring technical knowledge, the court's decision is based upon the opinion of an expert.[5]

Persons who are convicted of crimes involving imprisonment are compelled to work if they are put in prison for a second or third term. Prisoners who are serving their second term, work in the workshops of the central prisons; those who are serving their third term, in the workshops of the new prisons.[6]

---

[1] Act No. 818 of May 8, 1926, on Law of Obligations, Art. 41.
[2] Act No. 1412 of April 20, 1929, on Law of Criminal Procedure, Art. 365.
[3] Act No. 818 of May 8, 1926, on Law of Obligations, Art. 45, ult. para.
[4] Act No. 818 of May 8, 1926, on Law of Obligations, Art. 49.
[5] Act No. 1086 of July 4, 1927, on Law of Civil Procedure, Art. 275.
[6] Act No. 4358 of January 13, 1943, on Law of Prison System.

When the offender is compelled to work in prison, he is paid for such work, and there are some circumstances in which the victim can have recourse to such earnings. In the Turkish prison system work is of primary importance in the physical and moral reform of the prisoners.[7]

After the deduction of necessary expenses, such as for food, etc., the remaining money is in a sense his own. This money is banked and is given to the prisoner when he is released from the prison. The victim (or in case of his death, his dependants) can, however, enforce his claim for restitution against this asset. This is quite a valuable right of the victim, for although the basic wages of prisoners are different from those of free workers, nevertheless, if they do extra or very arduous work, they receive cash premiums which may make up the prison wages to something like the wages of free workers.

The law of restitution to victims of crime seems to work satisfactorily in Turkey.[8]

GREECE

Restitution to victims of crime is mainly of a civil character in Greek law. Both the civil action, and the alternative of pursuing one's claim at the criminal trial are similar to the provisions of French law.

In general, anyone who through his own fault causes unlawful damage to another is bound to make reparation therefor. In addition to an indemnity for material loss the court may grant damages for moral injury. This applies particularly when the victim has been insulted or has suffered injury to his or her health, reputation or chastity, or has been unlawfully deprived of his or her freedom. Where the victim has died as a result of the crime, moral damages may be granted to the victim's family in the guise of a *pretium doloris*.[9]

The victim or anyone else who has suffered injury, including moral injury, as the result of a criminal offence, is entitled to sue the offender or offenders for restitution. He may bring this action either before a competent civil court according to the general provisions of the Code of Civil Procedure, or before the criminal court. In either case it is called an *action civile*.

Where it is intended to bring an *action civile* before a criminal court for the recovery of material damages, the accused must be given due

---

[7] Act No. 6988 of June 7, 1957, on Amendments of the Turkish Criminal Law, Art. 13.
[8] Based essentially on information supplied by Esat Budakoglu, Minister of Justice, Ankara, 1959.
[9] Law No. 2250/1940 (Civil Code) of February 23, 1946, Arts. 914–932.

warning thereof, within the time limit fixed for civil cases. Where only damages for moral injury or a *pretium doloris* is sought there is no need to give previous notice to the accused, and the victim's claim may be submitted to the criminal court at any time up to the commencement of the hearing of the criminal trial, without even preliminary written application to the criminal court.

Should the victim not be present when the trial commences, the court may not on that account adjourn. The absent plaintiff is not prevented by his absence from presenting his case before the civil court, nor, even if the trial should be adjourned for any reason whatever, from bringing it on before the penal court. If the plaintiff was originally present at the trial, but has absented himself during its course, he may be barred from the trial if the court thinks fit. Any person barred in this way may bring his case before the civil court.

An *action civile* originally brought before the civil court may be recommenced before the penal court if a final judgment has not yet been pronounced in the civil court. A penal court before whom an *action civile* is brought under these circumstances may either give judgment on the case or refer the case back to the civil court.[10]

The victim's injury is of some importance in deciding the gravity of the offence, since the court takes into account the actual or potential damage caused by the offence. In addition, it is considered an extenuating circumstance if the offender has manifested sincere regret and has sought to annul or to mitigate the consequences of his actions. Thus, the reparation made by the accused himself for loss caused to his victim may influence the court's sentence, but this is entirely within the court's discretion.[11]

The victim has in theory the right, but in practice little chance, of enforcing his award of restitution against the prisoner's prison earnings.

Work is permitted but is not compulsory. The prisoner who works is paid. During his term of imprisonment, he can dispose of half the amount he receives, but not more, unless in a case of exceptional need the governor of the prison rules otherwise. At the time of his release, the prisoner has the right to withdraw the remainder of his earnings. The prisoner's rate of pay in prison is equal to nearly half the normal amount received by a free worker for the same work.

No legal provision exists to forbid the injured victim from seizing

10 Law No. 1493/1950 (Code of Penal Procedure) of January 1, 1951, Art. 63.
11 Law No. 1492/1950 (Penal Code) of January 1, 1951, Arts. 79–84.

the offender's prison earnings; normally, however, these are very small and not worth the trouble. The prisoner's personal property, however, if any, is available to meet the victim's claim

The Greek law regarding restitution to victims of crime appears to work satisfactorily except that the courts generally seem to award low damages to the victim, especially when he asks for damages for non-material injury (*i.e.*, for damages in respect of moral injury or a *pretium doloris*).[12]

YUGOSLAVIA

Under Yugoslav law the victim of an offence has the right to claim indemnity from the offender. This right falls entirely within the ambit of the civil law.

The victim may bring his claim either through civil action or before a criminal court, by asking that criminal proceedings already under way against the offender should decide his claim at the same time. Where the claim for this " restitution " is submitted to the criminal court, this court will decide it according to the civil law.

If the criminal court is of the opinion that a decision on the civil claim will not be dealt with, the victim will be directed to bring his claim in a civil action. The criminal court will also direct the victim to bring a civil action if the criminal procedure does not prove the victim's right to recompense from the criminal; or where the criminal court only partly accepts his claim for recompense, and in such a case the victim will have to bring that part of his claim which has not been decided upon, by means of a civil action.[13]

12 Based essentially on information supplied by Professor P. G. Vallindas and B. Lambadarios (Hellenic Institute of International and Foreign Law), Athens, 1959.
13 The Criminal Law Procedure of September 10, 1953 (official *Gazette* of the FPRY, No. 40). Based essentially on information supplied by the Secretariat of State for Foreign Affairs of Yugoslavia (Belgrade, 1959).

9

NORTH AMERICA

CANADA

RESTITUTION in Canada is of a civil nature, though a claim for restitution can be brought during criminal proceedings.

A court that convicts an accused of an indictable offence may, upon the application of his victim, concurrently with passing sentence, order the criminal to compensate his victim for any material loss he has caused him by his crime.[1]

Where such compensation is not paid forthwith, the applicant may file the order in the superior court of the province in which the trial was held. This will give the order the effect of a judgment rendered against the accused in that court in civil proceedings. Such an order may be enforced against any money found in the possession of the accused at the time of his arrest, except where there is a dispute as to the ownership or the right of possession of such money by claimants other than the accused.[2]

There seems to be no reason why the victim or his dependants should not pursue any civil remedy that might be available to them against the offender during his imprisonment, and, if successful, have recourse to the prisoner's earnings in prison. The practical value of such a procedure, however, is rather low, and there seems to be no case in which such proceedings have been instituted in Canada.

An offender, who is sentenced to imprisonment in the penitentiary, is required to work at whatever labour he is assigned to by the prison authorities. He is paid at the rate of twelve, eighteen or twenty-four cents a day, depending upon his length of service and the conduct, industry and attitude that he has shown during that period. A proportion of his earnings is set aside as compulsory savings to be handed to him on the day of his release. The balance may be spent by him at the inmates' canteen. It is obvious that the amount that is available to a prisoner, by way of earnings in the prison, is relatively small, and that is

[1] Criminal Code of Canada of April 1, 1955 (Chap. 51 of the Statutes of Canada, 1953–54), s. 628 (1).
[2] *Ibid.* s. 628 (2) and (3).

the main reason why these earnings are of little importance in connection with the victim's claim for restitution.

In Canada there exists one factor which does in effect connect restitution with the criminal jurisprudence, and that is its relation with the probation system. Where it is expedient that the accused be released on probation, and the court, instead of sentencing him to punishment, suspends the passing of sentence, the court may prescribe as a condition of such suspension that the accused shall make restitution and reparation to any person aggrieved or injured, for the actual loss or damage caused by the commission of the offence.[3]

There are also in Canada some legal provisions providing remedies closely akin to restitution, but concerning rather the reparation of the injury or the restoration of the *status quo ante*. Thus, where an accused is convicted of an indictable offence and any property obtained as a result of the commission of the offence has been sold to an innocent purchaser, the court may, upon the application of the purchaser, after the restitution of the property to its owner, order the accused to pay to the purchaser an amount not exceeding the amount paid by the purchaser for the property.[4] Similarly, where an accused is convicted of an indictable offence, or is tried for an indictable offence but is not convicted, the court must order that any property obtained by the commission of the offence shall be restored to the person entitled to it, if at the time of the trial the property is before the court or has been detained so that it can be restored to the person entitled to it. Exceptions are made in respect of property to which an innocent purchaser has acquired a lawful title; in respect of a valuable security that has been paid or discharged in good faith by a person who was liable to pay or discharge it; in respect of a negotiable instrument that has, in good faith, been taken or received by transfer or delivery for valuable consideration by a person who had no notice and no reasonable cause to suspect that an indictable offence had been committed in connection with it; or in respect of property over which there is a dispute as to ownership or the right of possession by claimants other than the accused.[5]

UNITED STATES OF AMERICA

Restitution to victims of crime is treated separately by Federal law and the various state laws. Since the Federal legislature and the respective

---

[3] *Ibid.* s. 638 (2).   [4] *Ibid.* s. 629.
[5] Based essentially on information supplied by A. J. Macleod, Director of Criminal Law Section in the Department of Justice, Ottawa, 1958–59.

state legislatures are sovereign within their respective sphere of legislation (assigned to them by the Constitution), it will be found that the approaches of the fifty-one legislatures concerned are not by any means identical. This is very readily understandable if it be remembered that some of the states have common law, some civil law. Federal law does not to any great extent concern itself with the problem of restitution to victims of crime. In so far as it does so, it seems to regard it as within the province of the civil law, although it is occasionally treated as being part of the punishment for the crime.

Federal law does not provide for civil parties in criminal proceedings. The injured party is left to his civil action before a civil court.

The only relevant Federal statutory provision relates to probation. A criminal court, when suspending sentence, may require the defendant to make restitution or reparation to the aggrieved party or parties for actual damages or loss caused by the offence for which he was convicted.[6] It is common, as a condition for the suspension of a sentence, to require him to make restitution or reparation in an amount which he is able to pay, and such payment is commonly made on the instalment plan from his earnings. The word " restitution " is normally used in the United States only when an offender has been given an opportunity to repay money stolen, with the understanding that he be placed on probation instead of being sent to prison. The probation department of New York State collects about $200,000 a year from probationers as restitution. In Massachusetts, a man who had discharged a rifle within the city limits, resulting in the loss of an eye to a boy, was placed on probation for five years and ordered to make weekly payments of damages to the boy during that period and, if at the end of the five years the damages had not been adequately satisfied, to be continued on probation for a longer period with a continuation of payments.[7]

State laws have not all adopted the same system, and various rules apply to one who is the victim of a criminal wrong.[8]

The outstanding and most universal system of restitution permits the compromise of misdemeanours, for which an offender is brought before a magistrate, and for which the injured victim has a remedy by means of a civil action. Three kinds of misdemeanours are excluded: those committed by or upon a police officer while executing his official

---

[6] United States Code, Title 18, s. 3651.
[7] Sutherland, *op. cit.* p. 577.
[8] " Restitution and Criminal Law, Notes and Legislation," *Columbia Law Review*, Vol. XXXIX, No. 7 (New York, November 1939), p. 1186.

duties, misdemeanours committed riotously, or with the intent to commit a felony.[9] Apart from these exceptions, however, the aggrieved party may appear in court and acknowledge the satisfaction of his injury, whereupon the court may, in its discretion, discharge the offender. When, in these cases, leave is granted to withdraw the complaint (which is somewhat reminiscent of the medieval system of composition), the complainant victim must submit a sworn statement [10] to the effect " that there was no intent on the part of the defendant to commit the within mentioned crime " and " that he has not been unduly influenced or threatened in any way in making this request." These kinds of provision seem to represent a system by which restitution may apply in lieu of criminal procedure, or at least in lieu of punitive sentence.

A less uniform or common, but perhaps more striking development of this conception in other states' laws is the provision for restitution or reparation in lieu of or in addition to fines or imprisonment. In these cases criminal procedure is followed and sentence is actually passed, and restitution takes its place roughly among the penalties, or at any rate bearing a punitive character. Or, upon application during the same term to the court in which the offender was convicted, an order for restitution or reparation in damages may be obtained.[11]

In other jurisdictions either the property must be returned or its value must be paid to the owner.[12] In other states again the punitive character of restitution is more marked, requiring the payment of double the value of the property, in addition to a fine or imprisonment. And in cases such as embezzlement of public funds, a fine of twice the value of the property may be imposed in addition to imprisonment, which operates as a judgment in favour of the injured parties, and only the latter may absolve the wrongdoer from the fine or give a quittance for it.[13] A similar formula, providing for double or treble damages in

---

9 New York Code of Criminal Procedure, ss. 663–666. Similarly Arizona Rev. Code Ann. (Struckmeyer, 1928), paras. 5202–5203; California Penal Code (Deering, 1937), paras. 1377–1379; Iowa Code (1935), paras. 14019–14022; Ne. Rev. Stat. (1930), Chap. 145, para. 20; Miss. Code Ann. (1930), paras. 1317–1318; Mont. Rev. Code Ann. (Anderson and MacFarland, 1935), paras. 12220–12222; Nev. Comp. Laws (Hillyer, 1929), paras. 11209–11211; N.D. Comp. Laws Ann. (1913), paras. 11074–11077; Oklahoma Stat. (Harlow, 1931), paras. 2703–2706; Ore. Code Ann. (1930), paras. 13.1501–13.1504; S.D. Comp. Laws (1929), paras. 4803–4806; Utah Rev. Stat. Ann. (1933), paras. 105–50–1, 2, 3; Va. Code (Michie, 1936), para. 4849; Wash. Rev. Stat. Ann. (Remington, 1932), paras. 2126–2127; Wis. Stat. (1937), para. 361.28.

10 In the magistrates' courts in New York City, where this practice is frequently employed.   11 Kentucky Stat. (Carroll, 1936), paras. 1132, 1134, 1135.

12 Alabama Code Ann. (Michie, 1928), para. 4910; (Michie Supp. 1936), para. 4159.

13 Nebraska Comp. Stat. Ann. (1929), para. 28-550; Arkansas Dig. Stat. (Pope, 1937), paras. 3167, 3077–3079; Delaware Rev. Code (1935), paras. 5192, 5196–5198, 5200, 5201, 5210.

addition to a fine or imprisonment in the criminal proceedings, is frequently found in the criminal codes. There is, however, some difficulty in ascertaining the intended character of restitution, whether it is merely a civil restoration, or whether, as seems more probable, it is in the nature of an atonement for transgression. Perhaps the most interesting mixture can be seen in a prohibition against making fraudulent conveyances, contracts and agreements; such instruments are void; the parties to them must forfeit the property affected, " and such forfeiture shall be recovered in an action of tort, on this statute, half to go to the party aggrieved, and half to the county in which the offence is committed." [14]

As to whether the performance or non-performance of restitution or damages has any effect on the decision of the court, generally speaking, there has been no statutory modification of the established rule that neither restitution nor the tender of restitution, either at the time of the trial or previously, serves as a defence in a criminal prosecution for larceny, embezzlement or other criminal offences against property.[15] Nevertheless, a distinction has been drawn in some states between restitution before and restitution after the initiation of criminal proceedings. Virtually identical, or at any rate similar, statutes provide that whenever, prior to an information being laid before a magistrate or a true bill being found by a grand jury charging a person with embezzlement, he voluntarily restores or tenders restoration of the property alleged to have been embezzled, or any part thereof, such fact, while not a defence, will authorise the court in its discretion to mitigate the punishment.[16] Of course, the absence of statutory provision does not mean that voluntary restitution may not influence the court in its attitude to a case.[17] On May 29, 1939, for example, in the New York Court of General Sessions, a one-time millionaire manufacturer and speculator was granted a suspended sentence after being convicted on a charge of

[14] Vermont Pub. Laws (1933), paras. 8474–8475.
[15] *Op. cit.* article in *Columbia Law Review*, p. 1190.
[16] California Penal Code (Deering, 1937), para. 513; Arizona Rev. Code Ann. (Struckmeyer, 1928), para. 4768; Idaho Code Ann. (1932), para. 17-3611–17-3612; N.D. Comp. Laws Ann. (1913), paras. 9939–9940; Okla. Stat. (Harlow, 1931), para. 2040; S.D. Comp. Laws (1929), para. 4236; Florida Comp. Gen. Law. Ann. (Skillman, 1927), para. 7240; Maine Rev. Stat. (1930), Chap. 131, para. 12; Massachusetts Gen. Laws (1932), Chap. 266, para. 61; Texas Ann. Pen. Code (Vernon, 1925), art. 1424; Tennessee Code Ann. (Michie, 1938), para. 10972; Kan. Rev. Stat. Ann. (Corrick, 1935), paras. 21-556; S.C. Code (1932), paras. 1222–1225; New York Penal Law, para. 1307; Minn. Stat. (Mason, 1927), para. 10373.
[17] *Op. cit.* article in *Columbia Law Review*, p. 1192.

grand larceny, this being his first criminal offence; one of the conditions of his being put on probation was that he should pay restitution.[18]

The victim, however, can enforce his claim by ordinary civil methods of execution only, and here again the practice in the Federal and state jurisdictions varies in details. The offender, if sent to prison, has to work there, but his earnings as a prisoner are too small to make them worth attaching.

Work is compulsory in both Federal and state prisons, but the respective laws restrict the labour of prisoners, which cannot be used for private purposes. In other words, prisoners can be required for work for the Federal Government so far as Federal institutions are concerned, and for the state Government so far as state institutions are concerned. Prisoners are paid wages both by the Federal Government and the state Governments, but the amount varies. In New York State, for example, prisoners are paid from a minimum of about 5 cents to a maximum of 50 cents per day, depending upon the character of the work. Money earned by prisoners can be used for the benefit of their families, or can be held until their release, or, in some states, can be used to purchase additional food or to satisfy the prisoner's personal needs, all, of course, in accordance with the state's specific regulations. Prison earnings, however, in no case represent a sizeable sum.

The making of restitution probably hinders somewhat the success of criminal prosecutions. The victim, after having received private satisfaction, frequently exhibits such apathy that he becomes a weak witness. It seems that extra-official negotiations with thieves are commonplace.[19] The police are frequently the agents of the criminals in persuading victims to accept restitution. They inform the victim that a criminal trial will cause him great inconvenience and expense, and may be continued for many months. Sometimes the criminals themselves make contact with the victim and make the same arrangement together with an offer of restitution, thereby inducing the victim not to testify and not to press the prosecution.[20] On the other hand, there seems to exist a sentiment among United States citizens to the effect that committal to prison for a criminal act is not always adequate, and that there should be some way of making the offender pay the victim for his violence.[21]

18 *Ibid.* p. 1193; *New York Post*, May 29, 1939.
19 Proceedings of Governors' Conference on Crime and Criminal (1935), p. 356.
20 Sutherland, *op. cit.* pp. 208–209.
21 Based essentially on information supplied by Paul A. Sweeney, Asst. Attorney-General in Department of Justice, Washington, 1958; E. R. Cass, General Secretary of the American Correctional Association, New York, 1958; and Herbert Wechsler, Professor of School of Law, Columbia University, New York, 1959.

10

CENTRAL AMERICA

CUBA

RESTITUTION to victims of crime covers a broad field in Cuba. Restitution by the offender is combined with compensation by the state, and is available to victims of all criminal offences.

Every offence entails consequent civil responsibility. The criminal court must decide to whom this is owed and its extent. Convicted persons must also satisfy their civil responsibility. This civil responsibility comprises:

1. *restitutio in integrum*;
2. reparation of the material damage;
3. reparation of the moral damage; and
4. indemnification for all expenses and losses.[1]

1. Restitutio in integrum

The object itself must, if possible, be restored, with compensation for any deterioration or impairment, such compensation to be assessed by the court. The object must be restored to its owner even if in the possession of a third party, who acquired it by legal means. The third party can then claim against the person responsible. This provision, however, shall not apply to a third party who has acquired the object in such manner and under such conditions as to acquire an indefeasible title.[2]

2. Reparation of the material damage

This must be ordered by the court, taking into account the extent of the damage, including, according to the case:

    (a) compensation for the loss of the head of the family, being the amount necessary to maintain the home;

    (b) the loss of earning power of the head of the family;

---

[1] Código de Defensa Social (Code of Social Defence) of 1938, Arts. 110–111. (This Code has substituted, as the criminal legislation, the ancient Spanish Code in force there since 1879.)

[2] *Ibid*. Art. 112.

(c) damage or impairment of the object;

(d) loss of income suffered by the injured party, which has been directly caused by the criminal offence.[3]

3. **Moral reparation includes, where appropriate:**

(a) a public correction or apology to which the victim may be entitled;

(b) marriage of the offender with the injured party where appropriate and provided in every case that the injured party consents;

(c) monetary compensation instead of marriage, the amount whereof to be assessed by the court

(i) when there is an absolute impediment to marriage with the offender,

(ii) when the injured party's objection to contracting marriage is based on the offender being repugnant to her, or an habitual criminal, or if there is any permanent circumstance of danger;

(d) recognition of the children, if not rendered impossible because of relationship with the father;

(e) compensation, in the form of a dowry, for the reduced marital prospects of the woman;

(f) compensation, in the form of a pension, for diminution of the public standing of the victim;

(g) monetary compensation for the moral damage suffered by the victim of defamation or slander, and for damage caused thereby (in these cases the offender must always pay compensation of not less than five times the fine prescribed for the offence by the law; and this compensation is to be paid by the tribunal directly to the victim, and if not paid the injured party may claim it by the procedure laid down by the law).[4] The foregoing provisions do not apply to offences causing little damage or annoyance.[5]

4. **The indemnification of damage shall include, where appropriate:**

(a) working days lost by the victim, both as a direct result of the offence and through presenting his case;

(b) payments to doctors or nurses, and for medicines, special foods, medical examinations, operations and hospital expenses;

(c) payment for work and material required to repair the damage;

(d) payment of any other expenses occasioned by the offence;

[3] *Ibid.* Art. 113.
[4] Order No. 124 of 1902.
[5] *Op. cit.* Código, Art. 114, Part B of Art. 509.

(e) payment of the fees and expenses of advocates, experts and witnesses, if claimed;

(f) payment for damage caused by the offence to relatives of the victim or to third parties.

In each of these cases the court shall assess the amount of compensation when passing sentence.[6]

In determining the amount the court shall take into account the age, status, social and economic position, occupation and working and productive capacity of both the victim and the offender. Where there is more than one offender the court must allocate responsibility according to the degree of participation in the crime and the circumstances of each, stating expressly on what basis the allocation is made. Where the victim caused or provoked the offence, he is not entitled to compensation.[7]

An offender must not leave the country without having satisfied his civil liabilities, except by leave of the court or with the agreement of the victim or his heirs or legal assigns. Nor may he, without leave of the court or the agreement of the parties, dispose of or pledge his property until he has satisfied his civil liabilities for his crime or guaranteed them in one of the forms legally recognised.[8]

In certain cases third parties are civilly liable. These cases are:

1. The state, the province or the municipality are liable for offences committed against individuals by them or their agents or public officials while in the execution of their duties.

2. Those having the charge or legal guardianship of an insane person, a person under twelve years of age, or a deaf-mute, are normally liable for their charge's offences, but if it be shown that the offence was committed despite all reasonable training and precautions by the said guardians, the latter are exempted from liability.[9] In such a case, or if the guardian be insolvent, the property of the insane person, minor or deaf-mute shall be used for the purpose of indemnification in so far as it exceeds what is necessary for his maintenance.

3. Where the offence was committed as a result of irresistible coercion by a third party.[10]

4. Where the offence was committed because the offender was put in fear by a third party.[11]

---

[6] *Ibid.* Art. 115.
[7] *Ibid.* Art. 116.
[8] *Ibid.* Art. 117.
[9] *Ibid.* Art. 55.
[10] *Ibid.* Part F of Art. 35.
[11] *Ibid.* Part G of Art. 35.

5. Where a third party has benefited from the act he may be civilly liable.[12]

In default of those criminally responsible, the following are civilly responsible :

1. Persons or corporations for offences, in establishments belonging to them, committed by their servants or agents (who have infringed the regulations or the rules of the authority).

2. Communities, fraternities and associations for offences committed by their representatives or officials or members while carrying on the functions entrusted to them by the bodies of which they were members.

3. Persons or corporations owning hotels, inns, guest-houses or boarding-houses for thefts from their guests, provided these abided by the rules of the establishment; thefts not committed by employees of the establishment or by persons in connivance with them are excepted.

4. Persons or corporations owning newspapers, magazines, printing works, radio stations, or any other means of publishing news or information, for offences committed by using the means of publicity at their disposal.

5. Persons or corporations owning vehicles of any kind, used for business, the transport of persons or goods or for public service, for offences committed by their drivers or employees in using such vehicles.

6. The owners of or concerns engaged in any kind of industry for offences committed by their employees, officials or apprentices in the course of their employment

7. Professional persons for offences committed by their employees, attornies, agents, or other persons responsible directly to and appointed by them, if committed in fulfilling their engagements or performing their services.[13]

Accomplices are jointly liable to satisfy the civil liability arising from their crime,[14] but if one pays more than his share he can recover his overpayment from the others or from any of them. The obligation to satisfy the civil liability is a firm one, and in the case of the death of the person liable, liability passes to his heirs in favour of the victim or the victim's heirs.[15]

In order to make civil responsibility effective there is a system of state compensation with an Indemnity Fund [16] in the custody of the Financial Secretary of Cuba.[17] Into this Fund are paid:

---

12 *Ibid*. Parts B, C, D and E of Art. 35.
14 " Solidaria entre los correos."
16 Secretario de Hacienda de la Republica.

13 *Ibid*. Arts. 118–119.
15 *Op. cit*. Código, Art. 120.
17 Caja de Resarcimientos.

1. Sums paid in satisfaction of civil responsibility.

2. A proportion, defined by law, of the earnings of prisoners.[18] Work is obligatory for all persons sentenced to imprisonment,[19] and the regulations determine the conditions, wages and other matters regarding their compulsory labour.[20] The earnings of a prisoner are to be applied, first, to satisfying the civil responsibility to which he was condemned, then to paying the cost of his maintenance, *i.e.*, food, clothing and bedding issued to him, and then to creating a reserve fund to be available to him on his release, or to his heirs should he die before then.[21]

3. Fines imposed and recovered, after covering the requirements of certain funds established by law.[22]

4. Donations to the Indemnity Fund.

5. The unclaimed estates of the victims of a criminal offence.

6. Property confiscated in connection with an offence.

7. Any compensation not claimed within two years of confirmation of the sentence.

8. Money defined as *corpus delicti* and not claimed within one year of confirmation of the sentence.

9. Interest earned by money belonging to the Fund.

10. Sums allocated in the general estimates of the nation for the maintenance of the Fund.[23]

The Indemnity Fund is charged with the execution of verdicts referring to civil responsibility. The Fund is concerned with the rights of the victim and it can therefore pay his legal expenses if necessarily incurred in obtaining payment of the compensation due to him as the result of a criminal offence.[24]

There is also a somewhat similar fund to meet cases where a prisoner, in the course of doing work imposed on him, has been the victim of an accident which he has not negligently, carelessly or deliberately caused and which has resulted in permanent incapacity for work or in his death.

---

[18] *Op. cit.* Código, Arts. 90–91.
[19] Ley de Ejecución de Sanciones (Law of Execution of Sanctions), Del Regimen del Trabajo (Regulations concerning labour), Arts. 67–68; *op. cit.* Código, Arts. 88–89. (Prisoners over the age of sixty years, those suffering from any malady rendering them unable to work, and pregnant women after the third month of pregnancy only, shall be exempted from the obligation to work, except if they want to work voluntarily.)
[20] *Op. cit.* Ley de Ejecución de Sanciones, Art. 78.
[21] *Ibid.* Art. 75.
[22] Law of March 18, 1927, amended by Decree Law No. 139 of 1935 and in accordance with Decree Law No. 751 of 1934.
[23] *Op. cit.* Código, Art. 121.
[24] *Ibid.* Arts. 122–123.

He is entitled to compensation from this fund, or his heirs will be so entitled. This compensation must be paid by the Administrative Section of the Chief Council of Social Defence [25] from the Special Fund. The Special Fund is provided from profits earned by the work of the prisoners, and is applied to different purposes, *inter alia*, the compensation of victims.[26]

To revert to the position of victims of crime, however, once sentence is confirmed the Indemnity Fund guarantees the court's award, whether this be in the form of a lump sum compensation or periodic payments. The Fund pays the court's award, and reimburses itself from the prisoner in the following ways:

1. The convicted person must pay to the Indemnity Fund the monetary obligations imposed on him.

2. If he fails to do so, because of insolvency, his property shall be judicially seized and sufficient of it to meet his obligations to the Fund sold by public auction.

3. If there should still be insufficient to meet his obligations to the Fund, he must pay to the Indemnity Fund one-quarter of his monthly income until his obligation is discharged; if he does not do so voluntarily, he will also have to pay the costs of any judicial procedure necessary to compel him to pay.

4. If the penalty includes periodic payments the offender must pay these in the form decreed in the sentence.

5. If the offender is not working, or is insolvent, or refuses to pay the civil liability to which he has been condemned, he shall be confined to a penal establishment, workshop or place of detention until such time as the product of his labour is sufficient to satisfy his obligations; and if this is not possible, the court must indicate in sentencing him to what subsidiary prison he is to be committed—in no case for more than six months. Whenever imprisonment becomes necessary on account of a failure to discharge the civil liabilities arising from a crime or crimes, the period of imprisonment shall be one day for every three pesos unpaid.

6. Sums which artificial persons (corporations) are sentenced to pay must be satisfied in a single payment. If this is not possible the court, on the application of the Fund, must order the corporation to be put under judicial management, and the entire profits, if any after

[25] Sección Administrativa del Consejo Superior de Defensa Social.
[26] *Op. cit.* Ley de Ejecución de Sanciones, Arts. 69–71.

payment of the expenses of the judicial management, to go to pay off the corporation's indebtedness to the Indemnity Fund.[27]

Restitution is thus considered, in Cuba, to be part of the penalty for the crime. That this is so is shown by the fact that non-compliance with an order for restitution, or non-payment of damages, incurs a penalty additional to any already prescribed by the court, the extent of the extra penalty being proportional to the amount of damages unpaid. Cuba also has the institution of "rehabilitation," which cannot be obtained unless the offender submits proof that he has fully paid the compensation awarded by the court to the victim.[28] By contrast, perhaps the only civil characteristic is the provision that civil liability arising from offences is extinguished in the same manner as obligations arising under the Civil Code.[29]

The Cubans seem to believe that their legislation is as perfect as possible, though in practice the Indemnity Fund does not sometimes have sufficient funds to meet all its obligations. When this happens, claims are paid *pro rata*. If the Fund were furnished with sufficient funds the Cuban system would probably work well.[30]

DOMINICA

The Code Napoleon has been received in Dominica, and the Dominican law of restitution to victims of crime is similar to that of France. Those who have suffered damage through a contravention of the criminal law are entitled to bring an action against the wrongdoer to have the damage made good.[31] Although in principle damages can be awarded only to those who have suffered directly through the criminal act, a succession of cases have allowed the action to be brought by all who have been prejudiced by the criminal act, including the assigns or descendants of the victim, and even those who were bound to him by ties of deep affection, such as a concubine or lover if they were living together as man and wife.

The action brought by the victim himself must not, however, be confused with that of an assign or dependant, a successor or heir. The latter's claim need not arise at the time that the wrongful act takes

---

[27] *Op. cit.* Código, Arts. 124–126.
[28] *Ibid.* Art. 128.
[29] *Ibid.* Art. 127.
[30] Based essentially on information supplied by Jose Agustin Martinez, President of the Instituto Nacional de Criminologia (National Institute of Criminology), La Havana, 1958 (J. A. Martinez has drafted the Cuban legislation concerned).
[31] Código de Procedimiento Criminal (Code of Criminal Procedure), Art. 10.

place. Where compensation is claimed for the victim's death the right of action arises only at the moment of his decease, while the victim's right of action accrues at the moment of the criminal act which caused his subsequent death. This can be important from the point of view of the limitation of actions. If the two rights of action accrue at different times, they will become time-barred at different times. The right of action of the victim himself derives from a different provision of the law from that of those who claim through him. It seems, further, that the burden of proof is higher for the victim himself,[32] than for his heirs, creditors, assigns, descendants, etc.[33]

The liability of the wrongdoer comprehends any loss or prejudice suffered by the victim as a result of the crime. A man may also be liable for damage suffered as a result of the criminal act of somebody for whom he is civilly liable. The courts need not and do not make a distinction between material and moral damage.

The claim for restitution can be brought at the same time and before the same criminal court as the criminal prosecution.[34] The victim may, however, if he prefers, bring his claim for restitution by way of civil proceedings before a civil court, and even if he in fact brings his claim before a criminal court, that court can refer the proceedings to a civil court for decision. The law allows the court, when assessing damages, to take into consideration the victim's situation and circumstances and the courts have taken full advantage of this provision.

Fines, restitutory damages, and costs may be recovered by proceeding against the person of the debtor.[35] A convicted offender can thus be ordered to undergo additional imprisonment of up to ten years should he fail to meet a compensatory order which has been made against him. Prison earnings are not available to satisfy claims for restitution, but if the property of the offender is not sufficient to cover the obligations simultaneously laid on him in respect of restitution, damages and fines, the former shall always take priority over the latter.[36]

In practice, Dominican institutions do not seem to be sufficiently efficacious to achieve the object of restitution to victims of crime. Nor is the inefficient and anachronistic prison system, which many feel is ripe for reform, of any use in achieving this object.[37]

[32] Canon (Precept) 1382. [33] Canon 1384.
[34] Código Criminal (Criminal Code), Art. 30. [35] *Ibid*. Art. 52. [36] *Ibid*. Art. 54.
[37] Based essentially on information supplied by Gustavo Adolfo Mejia Ricart, Professor of Criminology, President of the Instituto Nacional de Criminologia (National Institute of Criminology), Ciudad Trujillo, 1958.

MEXICO .

Between the two World Wars Mexican legislation restored restitution to its historical position. The Mexican Penal Code of 1931 regarded the victim's claim as being closely tied up with the concept of punishment and invested it with strong criminal characteristics. For this reason the victim has less and the public prosecutor more to do with claim restitution in the criminal trial.

The *sanción pecuniaria* (pecuniary sanction) comprises both fine and damages.[38] The restitution which must be made by the offender is in the nature of public punishment. When, however, the restitution is to be exacted from a third party, it becomes a civil liability and is dealt with separately, in accordance with the Code of Penal Procedure.

Should the convicted person be unable to pay the fine imposed, or be able to pay part only, the court will sentence him to a corresponding term of imprisonment instead. In doing so it will take his economic circumstances into account. Such a term of imprisonment must not exceed four months.

Restitution comprehends the restitution of the thing obtained through the offence, or if this be impossible, payment of its value, and indemnification for material or moral damage caused to the victim or to his family. The court, in fixing the amount to be paid by the wrongdoer, will take into consideration not only the amount of damage he has caused but also his ability to pay.[39]

Where possible, the sum which the wrongdoer has been ordered to pay is recovered by the public service. The amount to be recovered includes both any compensation which the wrongdoer may have been ordered to pay, and any fine to which he may have been sentenced. If the amount recovered be insufficient to cover both the compensation and the fine the compensation must be paid in full from the amount recovered before any of the money goes towards payment of the fine. If insufficient be recovered to pay all the compensation awarded to different claimants the money will be distributed *pro rata*. If an accused person on bail endeavours to escape justice his bail bond can be estreated and used for the payment of compensation and fine.[40]

An award of compensation must be satisfied in cash in the same manner as a fine. If a prisoner's assets, including any earnings he may

---

[38] Codigo Penal para el Distrito y Territorios Federales (Penal Code) of August 13, 1931, Art. 29; Schönke, *op. cit.*, pp. 144–145.
[39] Codigo Penal, Chap. V, Arts. 30–31.
[40] *Ibid.* Chap. V, Arts. 34–35.

have made in prison, be insufficient to satisfy in full any award of compensation made against him, he will, on the expiration of his sentence, continue to be liable for the remainder, and he may be ordered by the authority charged with the collection of fines and compulsory awards to make fixed payments at fixed intervals.[41]

Mexican criminal legislation is based on the principle of social defence, and this affects the concept of restitution.[42]

[41] *Ibid.* Chap. V, Arts. 37–39.
[42] Based essentially on information supplied by Oscar Trevino Rios, Direccion Juridica y Consultiva (Juridical and Consultative Dept.), Mexico, 1959.

11

SOUTH AMERICA

ARGENTINA

IN the Argentine restitution (called there " indemnification of damage ") to victims of crime is dealt with by both the criminal law and the civil law. Basically it is of a civil nature, but it displays certain penal characteristics too.

Since about half a century ago, Argentine jurisprudence has recognised the existence of a social need to facilitate or simplify or even to guarantee indemnification. Nevertheless, " the fact that both public and private interests are involved does not transform reparation into a penalty, but modifies the strictly private nature of the action, and introduces into it the element of public protection." The projected Penal Codes of 1891 and 1906 required the court to decide the question of indemnification to the victim when pronouncing sentence in a criminal trial. The Penal Code of 1917 was similarly drafted. The Argentine Senate Committee, however, amended the phrase " shall order " in the present Penal Code to " may order," on the grounds that " in this form judges can still determine the indemnification of the damage without being obliged to do so on the application of the injured party."

As a result of this change, the present Argentine Penal Code does not conform with the theory of the identification of the penalty and the indemnification or reparation as had the earlier Codes. Nevertheless, Argentine legislation does not regard the civil action as being independent of the criminal one, for the court may pronounce judgment on the civil matter in the course of sentencing in the criminal action.

According to the Criminal Code,[1] civil reparation has the following objects: restitution, indemnification, costs. The court may order:

(1) restitution of the thing obtained by the criminal offence, and if this is not possible, payment by the offender of the current price of the thing and in addition the cost of valuation if any;

(2) indemnification of the material and moral damage caused to the

---

[1] Código Penal (Penal Code of Argentine Republic), Law No. 1179 of September 30, 1921, Art. 29.

76

victim, to his family, or to third parties, the amount of which to be assessed by the court when it cannot be accurately proved;

(3) payment of costs.

The problem of indemnification is, however, dealt with by the civil law, too. The concept of damage, referred to in the penal provisions, is defined by the Civil Code. " Damage arises whenever any prejudice capable of pecuniary assessment is caused to another person, or where harm is done to things he owns or to things in his possession; or indirectly when any harm is done to his person or to his rights or amenities." [2] Moreover, the civil law, rather than the criminal law, lays down the detailed rules relating to the law of restitution for injuries suffered as a result of a criminal act.

As a general rule, every delict gives rise to an obligation to make good any prejudice (damage) caused to another person thereby; and " if the act was a criminal offence, the obligation arising therefrom comprises not only indemnification for losses, with interest, but also reparation for any moral damage inflicted on the person for endangering his personal safety, or interfering with his enjoyment of his property, or wounding his legitimate affections." [3]   In addition to this general provision, there are also provisions for particular offences.

If the " crime " was homicide, " the guilty party " has to pay all the expenses in connection with the death, including the funeral, as well as having to pay for the support of the widow and children of the deceased. The assessment of the amount to be paid is in the discretion of the court, as is the method of payment. If the offence was one of wounding or assault, the indemnification is to consist in the payment of all the costs of the treatment and convalescence of the victim and of any loss of earnings up to the day of his full restoration to health. If the liberty of an individual was infringed, the indemnification shall consist only of an amount corresponding to the loss of earnings suffered by the victim. If the crime was rape, indemnification shall consist of payment of a sum of money to the victim, if she has not married the offender; this provision also applies if the offence was carnal copulation with any honest woman by violence or threats, or seduction of an honest female under the age of eighteen. If the crime was calumny or slander, the victim is entitled to claim pecuniary indemnification, if it be proved that the calumny or slander caused any harm or loss of earnings assessable in

---

[2] Código Civil (Code of Civil Laws of Argentine Republic), Law No. 340 of September 29, 1869, Art. 1068.   [3] *Ibid*. Arts. 1077–1078.

money, provided the offender does not prove the truth of what he alleged.[4]

If the crime was theft, the stolen article must be returned to the owner with all its accessories and with indemnification for any damage done to it even if caused accidentally or by *force majeure*; if, however, restitution of the stolen article should not be possible, indemnification must be paid as for the total destruction of the property of another. If the offence was the misappropriation of money, the guilty party must pay interest from the date of the crime.[5]

The obligation to make good damage caused by criminal offence lies not only towards the person directly harmed by the crime, but also towards any person who has suffered even indirectly from it,[6] that is to say towards third parties who suffer any consequences of the offence: first to the wife and children of the victim[7]; and to the parents, where children are killed or injured, whether or not they be of full age.[8] Regarding concubines, the question is complex since it involves not only a legal but a moral problem, and the cases do not seem finally to have resolved the point. In a case recorded in the city of Rosario, a widow was denied the right to indemnification as heir of her husband because he died within thirty days of the marriage, and the court did not take into consideration her rights as his concubine up to the time of the the marriage.[9] The right to claim restitution for damage caused by offences against property lies with the owner of the property, or with the person who had possession or detention of it, such as the lessee, tenant, or depositee. A mortgagee has this right even against the owner of the thing mortgaged if he was responsible for the damage.[10]

Execution for any compensation awarded can be levied not only against the guilty party but also against the property he leaves on his death.[11] If his civil liability has not been discharged during the serving of his sentence, or if a " penalty of indemnification " was pronounced in favour of the victim (or his family), and the wrongdoer becomes bankrupt, the court may determine what proportion of the wages of the

[4] *Ibid.* Arts. 1084–1090.
[5] *Ibid.* Arts. 1091–1094.
[6] *Ibid.* Art. 1079.
[7] *Ibid.* Art. 1084.
[8] Practice of courts.
[9] Cited by Raimundo Salvat, *Derecho Civil Argentino.* Vol. III, Chap. IV.
[10] *Op. cit.* Código Civil, Art. 1095.
[11] *Op. cit.* Código Penal, Art. 70.

offender are " to be applied to the discharge of his liability for restitution before granting him conditional release." [12]

The victim also has some chance of enforcing his claim against the prisoner's earnings in prison. Prisoners work in prison, and the product of a prisoner's labour shall be applied:

(a) to make restitution for any harm or prejudice caused by the offence, which has not been satisfied by any other means,

(b) to the support of his dependants in accordance with the civil law,

(c) to the cost of his maintenance in prison, and

(d) to form a fund to be given to the prisoner on his discharge. [13]

These claims on the prisoner's earnings rank concurrently.

Generally speaking, the partly civil, partly criminal character of restitution, and the diversity of legal bodies dealing with this problem, has inspired in the Argentine numerous explanations and controversies regarding the applicability of the civil law or the penal law. It has also led to various legal interpretations regarding the validity, priority or effect of actions in civil or penal courts. [14]

[12] *Ibid.* Art. 11 (2).
[13] *Ibid.* Art. 11.
[14] Based essentially on information supplied by Juan Carlos Pizarro, Director of the Nacional Institutos Penale, Ministerio de Educacion y Justicia (National Penal Institution, Ministry of Education and Justice) and Jose Salez Zamora, technical assistant, Buenos Aires, 1959.

12

MIDDLE EAST

ISRAEL

IN the State of Israel a clear distinction is drawn between damages under the rules of tort and compensation obtainable as an adjunct to criminal proceedings. On the one hand, it shall not be a bar to action in respect of a civil wrong, that the facts upon which such action is based constitute a criminal offence [1]; on the other hand it is provided, that neither an acquittal in criminal proceedings, nor the imposition of a penalty, nor an adjudication to pay compensation under the penal law, shall detract from liability for damages under any other law. [2]

The victim of crime can claim restitution in the following ways:

1. In the case of a person who has been convicted of an offence, the court may order him to pay to a person who sustained damage through the offence and who has not constituted himself a civil party, an amount not exceeding £I.500 as compensation for the damage or suffering caused to him. [3]

2. In the case of a person who has constituted himself a civil party and the court has not decided on his claim, the judgment shall be deemed to contain a decision not to adjudicate on the civil claim. [4]

3. In Ottoman law a civil suit arising out of and based on a criminal offence can be attached to the criminal proceedings by the injured party. [5]

4. Between persons of the Moslem faith, but only when the case is heard by a Moslem religious court or a tribal court, there is the possibility of what is called *diyet*, that is to say a compensation by the offender, either, in the case of death, to the heirs of the dead person, or, in the case of injury resulting in the loss of a part of the body, to the victim.

This right to claim restitution applies to all of the offences, and,

---

[1] Civil Wrongs Ordinance of 1944, s. 67.
[2] Penal Law Revision (Modes of Punishment) Law of 5714–1954, s. 34.
[3] *Ibid*. s. 31. (This replaced s. 43 of the Criminal Code Ordinance of 1936, which provided for an award not exceeding £I.100 " by way of satisfaction or compensation for any loss caused by the offence.")
[4] *Ibid*. s. 33.   [5] Ottoman Code of Criminal Procedure, Arts. 1–4, 58–63.

except in the case of *diyet*, an award of compensation is not limited to specific crimes. Damages used to be restricted to compensation for financial loss only, but the court may now also award compensation for " damage or suffering," [6] which suggests that damages include compensation for moral damage also.

Where a victim of crime claims compensation, there need not be a formal application by the complainant,[7] and the court hearing the criminal case may also deal with the compensation question.

A person bringing a claim for damages for a civil wrong, can ask for it to be heard by the court hearing the parallel criminal prosecution; the plaintiff. however, has to claim a specified sum and pay the usual court fees.[8]

Preliminary inquiries are held only for the most serious offences, and on the application of either side. Where they do take place, however, the civil claimant can join, but he has no standing at this stage, and his joinder becomes effective only when the case is sent for trial.[9]

The rules of procedure, where a civil claim is brought informally without joinder as a civil party in a criminal trial, provide that the plaintiff can examine all witnesses brought by the prosecution or the defence in connection with his claim. He may also bring evidence at the close of the prosecution's case or at a later stage, or even after conviction.

This is a matter for the court's discretion. He may not, however, examine witnesses or offer argument in connection with the charge against the defendant, unless the court allows him so to do.[10] If the civil claim is formally joined to the criminal case, the procedure is just as in any ordinary civil action in tort.[11]

In addition, there is the ordinary civil action in tort, unconnected with the criminal proceedings. This is unconditionally open to the victim. Even when the Attorney-General has, in pursuance of his powers, ordered a stay of criminal proceedings, this will have no effect on any civil claim brought in a civil court, even though the evidence in the civil case may reveal that the defendant is guilty of an offence.[12]

---

6 Penal Law Revision Law, s. 31.
7 Civil Appeal Tel-Aviv 90/50, District Court Decisions, Vol. 7, Summary 11.
8 Ottoman Code of Criminal Procedure, Art. 3.
9 High Court of Justice 90/50, Supreme Court Decisions, Vol. 6, p. 169.
10 Criminal Procedure (Trial on Information) Ordinance, s. 43 (Laws of Palestine, Drayton. Chap. 36).
11 In this respect. the law in Israel is similar to that in England.
12 Civil Wrongs Ordinance, p. 67; Penal Law Revision Law, p. 34; Trial on Information Ordinance, p. 60; Magistrates' Courts Ordinance of 1947, s. 20. (Ordinary civil claims may be brought in the magistrates' court, where the claim does not exceed £I.1,500, or in the district court, if the claim exceeds this amount.)

If the victim has a judgment in a civil claim, he can have recourse to the offender's earnings as a prisoner. Prisoners are required to work during their period of imprisonment, unless a special dispensation is given them.[13] The so-called Releases Committee is empowered to exempt a prisoner from his obligation to work, or to limit this obligation, but on one of the three following grounds only:

  (a) for health reasons,
  (b) if the limitation may help the prisoner to repent of his ways and make good,
  (c) on any other reasonable ground.

They receive wages for their work, at least 40 per cent. of which is paid to them immediately upon their release from prison; they are entitled to use the other 60 per cent. of their wages for the purchase of items in the prison canteen.[14] If, however, the victim has a civil judgment, he may apply to the Execution Office to have the prisoner's earnings attached to the extent of 75 per cent. The victim, however, has little hope of gaining much from the prisoner's earnings, as they amount to a relatively small sum. Prisoners' wages differ considerably from those of free workers, as the prisoner is not called upon to contribute towards the cost of his detention, nor towards his upkeep in prison. The present relationship between the two rates of pay seems to be:

  Prisoners: from 120 prutot to £I.1 per day;
  Free workers: from £I.4 to £I.12 per day.[15]

The civil character of restitution is also shown by the lack of any legal provision, whereby the performance or non-performance of restitution or damages will affect the punishment. The judge, however, when passing sentence, will take into account the fact that the offender has made restitution of, say, stolen property or embezzled funds, but this matter is entirely in the judge's discretion.

Regarding matters closely akin to restitution, there are provisions for the " restitution," for example, of stolen property which has come into the possession of the police in connection with any criminal charge, to the owner thereof. This may take place by order of the court, on application by a police officer, or by a claimant to the property. It does not affect the right of any person to take legal proceedings for recovery

---

13 Prisons Ordinance of 1946.
14 Prison Regulations (Ministry of Police).
15 There are 1,000 prutot to the Israeli pound, and the official rate of exchange is £I.5·040 to the pound sterling. On this basis the prisoner receives between 6d. and 4s. per day: as against between 16s. and £2 8s. per day for similar work by non-prisoners.

against the person in possession of the property by virtue of the order. These proceedings, however, must be instituted within six months from the date of the order. In the case of immovable property of which a person has been dispossessed by the offence of forcible entry [16] or of criminal trespass,[17] there is provision for the granting of ejection or possession orders.[18]

It is apparent that the institution of restitution works similarly in Israel and in England, where kindred provisions exist. The question of restitution to victims of crime seems to be under consideration, and the State of Israel is interested in this problem.[19]

<h2 style="text-align:center">PERSIA</h2>

In Persian law the victim of a criminal act has the legal right to claim damages from the offender. Although the remedy is apparently civil in character, it can be sought even in criminal proceedings.

As a general rule, a person who has suffered loss is entitled to demand damages from the person who inflicted the loss. This right of the victim exists in every kind of material loss. In addition, in certain circumstances and in certain cases, the victim may also claim damages for a moral injury resulting from a " guilty act." This right obviously applies to all offences causing injury.

Both civil and criminal courts have jurisdiction to entertain claims for restitution, called " damages " in Persia. Civil courts are normally used to pursue such claims, but restitution can also be sought during the course of a trial, where the source of the damage or loss is the criminal act being tried. In this latter case the criminal court entertains the question of damages also, and will give judgment on the victim's claim.

Where a technical matter is involved, the court will normally seek the advice of an expert before arriving at a decision on the scale and nature of the damages. It is, however, not bound to do so, and need not accept all or any of his opinions.

Performance or non-performance of restitution, that is to say, the payment of damages, has no legal effect on the sentence; but can, in the court's discretion, count as a mitigating circumstance.

There is no legal impediment to the victim's attempting to have

[16] Criminal Code Ordinance, s. 96.
[17] *Ibid.* s. 286.
[18] *Ibid.* s. 388.
[19] Based essentially on information supplied by Moshe Rimel, Assistant State Attorney in the Ministry of Justice, Jerusalem, 1959.

recourse to the offender's earnings in prison. Prisoners are obliged to do a specified amount of work if sentenced to imprisonment with hard labour, and may do so if sentenced to correctional imprisonment. A portion of their earnings is spent on the maintenance of their families, and another part is set aside and given to them when they are released. Since such income derives from his own labour, it is regarded as the prisoner's own property. Consequently, as the victim has the right to enforce his claim against the wrongdoer's income, of whatever nature, he may also do so against his prison income.[20]

EGYPT

In accordance with general principles, the victim who is awarded restitution or damages against the offender may enforce this judgment against the latter's property, by means of the seizure and sale of this property, according to the provisions of civil law. In addition to these ordinary civil methods of enforcing a judgment to make restitution to a victim of crime, the criminal law also proves special methods for such enforcement.

If the wrongdoer does not comply with an order to pay damages for his crime, the court can condemn him to up to three months' imprisonment for debt. Before the court issues a warrant for his imprisonment, however, a wrongdoer who is capable of working may choose to do manual or industrial work instead of being imprisoned.[21]

He is then employed in such work without remuneration. He remains in the service of a government or municipal department for a number of days equal to the duration of the imprisonment he would otherwise have had to undergo. The accused is not sent away from the town or district in which he lives in order to do this work. His daily work is fixed with regard to his physical strength and is limited to a working day of six hours. If he does not carry out the work, he is sent to prison to serve the sentence for which he was otherwise liable.

Should it happen, however, that there is no work in which the accused may usefully be employed, he must be imprisoned in spite of his offer to work instead.[22]

---

[20] Based essentially on information supplied by Bagir Ali, Ministry of Justice, Legal Department, Teheran, 1328 (1959).

[21] Code of Criminal Instruction, Arts. 519–520.

[22] *Op. cit.* Arts. 521–522. Based essentially on information supplied by the Minister of Foreign Affairs of Egypt, by courtesy of the Swiss Embassy, Cairo, 1959.

13

FAR EAST

INDIA

IN India, as in Pakistan, the criminal law hardly deals with the problem of restitution to victims of crime, and restitution finds its place, if any, in the sphere of civil law. Thus the victim and his dependants have a legal right to claim damages from the offender, but only if the crime is at the same time a tort.

Apart from this, and certain provisions of the law of criminal procedure,[1] the system of restitution or compensation to victims of crime is unknown in India. Under the law regulating criminal procedure[2] it is open to the criminal courts to order payment of costs or compensation to the complainant out of the fine imposed on the offender. There is thus restitution of a kind. The victim, however, is not entitled to such restitution as of right, and its award is entirely within the court's discretion. In addition to these somewhat limited forms of restitution, the owner has a right to claim back his property either from the wrongdoer who has unlawfully deprived him of it, or from the person into whose hands the chattel or property has come.

In the crime and tort of defamation, moral injury is a relevant factor in considering the amount of damages, but only if the complainant's character has been traduced. So too with regard to the crimes of malicious prosecution, wrongful confinement, cheating, forgery, theft, robbery, rioting, criminal trespass, adultery, bigamy. Generally speaking, where a tort is at the same time a criminal offence, the court, when assessing damages, will consider the moral injury too.

The civil nature of the victim's remedies in India is shown by the provision that only civil courts can entertain suits for damages, where a criminal offence is both a crime and a tort. The claim can be brought only by way of a civil action in tort, and not for the crime as such. Apart from the exceptions already noted, criminal courts have no jurisdiction to award restitution to victims of crime. The plaintiff victim

---

[1] Code of Criminal Procedure of 1898, amended by the Criminal Procedure Amending Act, No. XXVI of 1955.   [2] *Ibid.* ss. 545–546.

must sue in a civil court on the basis of the *damnum* suffered by him as a result of the criminal act.

In keeping with the civil character of restitution in India, the question of whether or not the wrongdoer has attempted to make restitution to his victim has no legal effect upon the sentence imposed upon him. The punishment imposed will depend upon the nature of the crime and the character or personality of the offender; the only relevance of restitution to the sentence imposed is that if the criminal has made reparation it may lead to a lighter sentence, or even to the release of the offender on probation if the court accepts it as evidence of the offender's remorse and repentance.[3]

Though a prisoner has a small income in prison, the victim cannot enforce his claim against the prisoner's earnings. In " simple " imprisonment, the prisoner is not compelled to work at all. If he wants to work, however, he may be allowed to do so, and such work counts towards remission of his term of imprisonment. In " rigorous " imprisonment, the prisoner has to work for about six hours a day. Although he is paid for such work, the payment is far less than he would earn outside the prison as a free man.[4] Every prisoner gets the same wages for his work. A prisoner is allowed to spend or save these earnings entirely at his discretion. He is not required to pay a portion thereof towards his upkeep in prison, nor is he obliged to remit any part of it for the maintenance of his wife or children or other dependants. Furthermore, no part of his prison wages can be used for compensation to the aggrieved party. The victim can thus have no recourse to the prisoner's earnings, and can enforce his claim only against the other assets of the offender, provided, of course, he has obtained a judgment from a civil court for the damage suffered by him.

There seem to be certain shortcomings in the Indian prison system, as well as in the system of restitution to victims of crime. The system has excited a certain amount of complaint, and compulsory compensation has been strongly advocated.[5]

---

[3] Probation of Offenders Act, 1959.

[4] The prisoners' wages are about one-third of that which a free man would get outside prison for the same work.

[5] M. J. Sethna, *Society and the Criminal* (Bombay, 1952); M. J. Sethna, *Jurisprudence* (Bombay, 1959). Based essentially on information supplied by M. P. Amin, Dean of the Faculty of Law, University of Bombay, and M. J. Sethna, Professor of Criminal Law, Government Law College in Bombay, Bombay, 1959.

PAKISTAN

In Pakistani law, restitution to victims of crime is considered as a question for the civil law, and the criminal law has little to do with it.

Generally the victim or his dependants have no legal right to claim restitution or damages from the offender at the criminal proceedings. However, a criminal court which imposes a fine, or confirms in an appeal, revision or otherwise a sentence of a fine or of which a fine forms part, may order the whole or any part of the fine to be applied in defraying expenses properly incurred in the prosecution, or to be applied to the payment of compensation for any loss or injury caused by the offence, when substantial compensation is, in the opinion of the court, recoverable by the injured person in a civil court. In addition, any fine imposed for any of the following offences, that is theft, criminal misappropriation, criminal breach of trust, cheating, dishonestly receiving or retaining, or voluntarily assisting in the disposal of, stolen property, knowing or having reason to believe the same to be stolen, may be in part applied in compensating any bona fide purchaser of such property, if the property is restored to the possession of the person entitled thereto.[6]

The payment of compensation out of the fine is not restricted to particular offences. Compensation is to be awarded when loss or injury has been caused by the offence, if, in the opinion of the court, such compensation would be recoverable in a civil court by the person to whom the criminal court seeks to award compensation. It is entirely within the discretion of the court whether or not to award compensation to the party injured by an offence. All criminal courts have jurisdiction to award this sort of compensation.

The amount of the damages is arrived at after a consideration of the evidence led to prove the criminal offence. The damages awarded are usually approximate. Damages for moral injury are seldom awarded, compensation usually being awarded for financial loss only.

The victim can under no circumstances enforce his claim for restitution or compensation against the earnings of the offender in prison. Offenders, if undergoing " rigorous " imprisonment, can be compelled to work in prison. For such work, however, they are not paid. There are therefore no prisoners' wages to form a basis for restitution.

As a general rule, restitution is not regarded as of much importance in Pakistan, and even in passing sentence no account is taken of whether restitution is to be made or not, or of the payment of compensation or

6 Act No. V of 1898, Code of Criminal Procedure, s. 545.

damages to the victim by the offender. If there is no fine, there can be no order for compensation. And no order for compensation can be passed unless the court is first satisfied that substantial compensation is recoverable in a civil court. Compensation is seldom awarded out of the fine imposed, and it is consequently difficult to evaluate the success or otherwise of so little used an institution. There is little public interest in Pakistan in the question of restitution to victims of crime.[7]

[7] Based essentially on information supplied by A. R. Kazi, and Edward Snelson, Ministry of Law, Karachi, 1959.

14

AUSTRALASIA

AUSTRALIA

AUSTRALIA has a Federal Constitution. Each state, and those territories controlled by the Commonwealth Government, therefore has its own laws on restitution to victims of crime. The only Commonwealth legislation of relevance to the question of restitution is the criminal law.[1]

This Commonwealth legislation, however, states only that when any person is convicted of an offence against any law of the Commonwealth, the court may, in addition to any penalty imposed upon him, order the offender to make reparation to the Commonwealth, whether by way of money payment or otherwise, in respect of any loss suffered by the Commonwealth by virtue of the offence.[2] That is to say, restitution can be ordered to be made to the state for a criminal offence, but not to an individual victim. In addition, though such a claim for restitution (by the state) can be entertained within the scope of criminal proceedings, the award seems to bear a civil character. Restitution to an individual victim bears an entirely civil character.[3]

As for the individual states, in *Queensland* restitution bears strong civil characteristics. The general principle applicable there is that the criminal jurisdiction of the courts of Queensland is not to be used for the purpose of securing recompense to a person who regards himself as injured by an offence against the criminal law. If he wishes, the victim can bring a civil suit for damages, when he must rely on his civil rights alone.

The courts in Queensland have both criminal and civil jurisdiction, but claims for damages or restitution must be brought before the court sitting as a civil court, unless the claim is for the return of the actual article misappropriated by the criminal.

---

1 Act No. 12 of 1914, Crimes Act, amended several times, now the principal Act and the amending Acts cited as the Crimes Act, 1914–55.
2 *Op. cit.* Crimes Act, s. 21B; inserted by Act No. 9 of 1926, amending Crimes Act, s. 15.
3 Based essentially on the information supplied by the Attorney-General's Department, Canberra, 1959.

To this general principle there are a few exceptions, arising from *e.g.,*

(a) the Auctioneers and Commission Agents Acts, where some of the offences are designated as crimes and the court may award compensation for persons who suffered loss or damage;

(b) the Traffic Acts, according to which if a person uses any vehicle without the consent of the owner and does damage to the vehicle, he may be required to pay compensation;

(c) the Cattle Stealing Prevention Act, under which compensation for damage may be awarded;

(d) the Criminal Code, which provides that the court may order property to be restored to its owner, or the person lawfully entitled to its possession, and may make the suspension of punishment dependent on the payment of compensation for the injury done to the victim.

Any restitution awarded by a civil court to the victim can be enforced by civil execution. Although prisoners are required to work in Queensland and certain pay is credited to them this is insignificant compared with the wages of free workers, and any damages which the victim might obtain against an offender would, for all practical purposes, have to be recovered from the offender otherwise than from his prison earnings.

Restitution has no legal effect on punishment, but, if a convicted offender makes restitution in some way to the victim of his offence, the judge may be influenced in the punishment he awards.

In practice, restitution is so seldom awarded to victims of crime in Queensland that it is difficult to gain an impression of how the system works in practice.[4]

In another Australian state, *Tasmania*, though " the criminal courts do not regard themselves as in any way debt collecting courts and the question of restitution has little effect on the punishment to be decided upon," restitution appears to a certain extent to be connected with the criminal law.

During the course of a criminal trial, upon the application of any person aggrieved, and immediately after the conviction of any person for any crime, there may be awarded a sum of money not exceeding £100, by way of satisfaction or compensation for any loss of property suffered by the applicant (*i.e.*, the victim) through or by means of the

---

4 Based essentially on information supplied by L. J. Murray, Assistant Crown Prosecutor, Queensland, 1959.

crime.[5] This remedy, however, in no way derogates from the civil remedies.

Another connection between restitution and the criminal law can be found in the Infants Welfare Act, 1935, which provides that when a child is dealt with under the provisions of this Act the court may make his discharge subject to the condition that he shall pay damages; and, if the court has reason to believe that his parent has contributed to the commission of the offence, the parent may be required to pay such restitution.

Finally, when placing anyone on probation the court may order him to pay damages for injury or compensation for loss.

In general, however, restitution to victims of crime is still regarded in Tasmania as being primarily a civil matter.

In the State of *Western Australia*, the law gives victims of crime the right to claim restitution in wide terms, although in fact it applies only in offences involving property, while special damages can be claimed for assault. The restitution, however, which a criminal court can award, is only to reimburse the victim for his costs, expenses and time lost through the act of the offender, and is limited to £25 in summary courts and £100 in superior courts.[6] Apart from this, damages can be awarded only in civil actions.

Damages for non-material injury can be awarded only in civil actions sounding in tort.

Except where the law prescribes a maximum or a minimum penalty the question of punishment is wholly in the discretion of the court. In practice the performance or non-performance of restitution is one of the factors considered by the court in deciding on the appropriate penalty.

Prisoners are generally compelled to work, except those undergoing imprisonment without hard labour who pay sufficient for their maintenance during their imprisonment.[7] Prisoners are paid for this work, but the payment of these wages is described as a gratuity, and execution cannot be levied against it.[8]

In the State of *Victoria* the victim's right to claim restitution applies to any offence which consists in whole or in part in a wilful or negligent act of omission constituting a breach of duty by the accused to the

---

[5] Criminal Code Act, 1924 (amended in 1924, 1934, 1943, 1946, 1954, and by the Criminal Code Act, 1957), Chap. XLVIII, s. 425 (2).

[6] The Criminal Code, 1913–56, No. 28 of 1913, s. 719.

[7] The Prisons Act, 1903–18, No. 14 of 1903, s. 29.

[8] Based essentially on information supplied by E. J. Hork, Secretary to the Attorney-General's Department, Canberra, 1959.

victim and whereby the victim suffers personal injury or loss of or damage to his property. The civil courts have jurisdiction to entertain the claims and the procedure is the same as in English civil courts. In practice damages are generally restricted to compensation for financial loss.

Each prisoner who is able to work can be employed for work and may earn credits of money. These earnings, however, are applied towards the maintenance of the prisoner's wife and family, satisfaction of costs, education and training, and the personal needs of the prisoner. Neither the victim nor his dependants have recourse to the prisoner's earnings.[9]

A criminal court entertains only the restitution of stolen property. In addition, in certain cases the justice may, if he thinks fit, discharge the offender from his conviction upon his making such satisfaction to the party aggrieved for damages and costs or either of them as is decided by the justice.[10]

NEW ZEALAND

In New Zealand restitution to victims of crime is not treated as a separate compartment of the law. Restitution to victims of crime is left to be dealt with by the civil law, which, as in all civil suits for damages, is substantially the same as the law of England. The victim of crime has available to him the ordinary civil remedies, and, in addition, in certain circumstances a court which has convicted an offender may as part of its sentence order him to make restitution to the victim of his crime.

The general rule is, that whenever an offence is also a civil wrong, and most serious crimes are, the victim (and in some cases his dependants) may bring an ordinary civil action in the courts. No civil remedy, moreover, whether for an act or an omission shall be suspended because such act or omission is also a criminal offence.[11]

In addition to the ordinary civil remedies there are in New Zealand certain provisions which enable a court, which convicts a person of a criminal offence, to make, in certain cases, an order restoring stolen property or ordering the payment of its value. It may also require the offender to compensate his victim for injury or loss suffered.[12] Apart from this, in only one case does restitution fail to be considered within the scope of the criminal procedure. Where an offender is admitted to

9 Gaols Regulations, 1931, paras. 56, 60, 62, 65.
10 The Crimes Act of September 30, 1958, No. 6231, ss. 440–443, 480.
11 Crimes, Act, 1908, s. 355.
12 Crimes Act, 1908, ss. 449 and 451 ; Summary Proceedings Act, 1957, ss. 70 and 79.

probation, the court may, as one of the conditions of probation, require him to pay such sum as it may direct by way of damages for injury or compensation for loss suffered.[13]

Apart from these special provisions, the only remedies available to the victim are the ordinary civil actions, brought in any civil court possessing jurisdiction, and in accordance with the ordinary civil procedure.

Even if there were any provisions requiring prisoners to pay restitution from their earnings in prison, these provisions, owing to the small and uncertain nature of such earnings, would be nugatory. Though persons convicted of offences are compelled to work in prison, they are not paid wages in the ordinary sense. Prisoners may earn a small allowance for good conduct, but this is not comparable in amount to outside wages, which are about twenty times such an allowance. A prisoner is permitted to spend a certain proportion of this allowance on goods such as tobacco, sweets or books, and the balance of his earnings are paid to him on his discharge to assist his rehabilitation. His earnings, however, including his past earnings, may be forfeited for misconduct and legally are paid at the discretion of the authorities.

For that reason, a person, who has obtained judgment in a civil action against a prisoner, has no right of recourse to his prison earnings, because a prisoner has, as has been said, no legal right to such earnings. Whether a victim or his dependants, could in law have recourse to the prisoner's earnings, has in New Zealand never been tested. Generally speaking, however, a civil judgment can be enforced against any of the defendant's assets, except personal and family clothing, personal and household effects, and tools or implements of trade not exceeding £100 in value all told.

Restitution to victims of crime is regarded in New Zealand as a civil matter to the extent that the performance or non-performance of restitution or the payment or non-payment of damages has no legal effect on the award of punishment.[14]

---

[13] Criminal Justice Act, 1954, s. 8 (1) (*b*) and (2).
[14] Based essentially on information supplied by S. T. Barnett, Secretary for Justice, Department of Justice, Wellington, 1958.

15

AFRICA

Union of South Africa

In South Africa there is a general rule for restitution, when any person is convicted of an offence which has caused damage to or loss of property belonging to some other person. The court trying the case may, after recording the conviction and upon the application of the injured party, or of the person conducting the prosecution, acting on the instructions of such party, forthwith award the injured party compensation for such loss or damage, provided that the compensation claimed does not exceed five hundred pounds.[1]

Similarly, the court may order a person convicted upon a private prosecution to pay, besides the costs and expenses, compensation for loss or damage caused by the criminal offence. Private prosecutions can only be instituted after the Attorney-General has declined to prosecute, except for bodies such as the railways or municipalities statutorily authorised to prosecute.

It has been held that compensation can be awarded only on the application of the injured party; nevertheless, when the court has convicted a person under the provisions of the Children's Act, it may order the convicted person to pay compensation to the injured party, even though such party has not applied for it.[2]

The practice of the courts in dealing with the substantive issues involved in the decision is, that every case is dealt with on its own merits, and for the purposes of determining the amount of compensation or the liability of the accused for this, the court may refer to the proceedings and evidence at the trial or hear further evidence either upon affidavit or verbally. When any person is convicted of an offence under the Act for the Prevention of Cruelty to Animals, and it appears that this offence has caused damage to any person, the court may, on the oral or written request of the aggrieved person, and in the presence of the convicted person, inquire summarily and without pleadings into the extent of the damage. Then, upon proof of this damage the court shall give judgment

[1] Act No. 56 of 1955, Criminal Procedure Act, s. 357.
[2] Act No. 31 of 1937, Children's Act, s. 23.

94

in favour of the aggrieved person against the convicted one, provided that the sum awarded does not exceed one hundred pounds.[3]

When a court has made any award of compensation, the award has the effect of a civil judgment, and is executable in the same manner as if it had been given in a civil action.[4] These provisions demonstrate the civil character of restitution in South Africa, even when entertained within the scope of the criminal trial. Indeed, perhaps the only criminal aspect of restitution to victims of crime in South Africa is that if restitution has been made it may be taken into consideration in mitigation of sentence. This part of the criminal procedure provides an alternative to the ordinary civil procedure. Therefore, no person against whom such an award has been made can be sued in any civil proceedings by the person in whose favour the award was made, in respect of the injury for which compensation was awarded.

The injured victim can recover any damages awarded him only through the ordinary civil procedure unless any money has been taken from the accused on his arrest. In this case the court may order payment to be made to the victim from such money, in satisfaction or on account, as the case may be, of any damages awarded him. The victim has, however, no recourse to the prisoner's earnings, partly on principle, and partly because they are so insignificant. Offenders are either allowed and compelled to work in prison (prisoners awaiting trial are offered opportunities to work, but are not required to do so), and may be paid a gratuity, not exceeding 2s. 6d. per week.[5] Money so earned, however, is paid out to the prisoner only on his discharge, except that he may, during the term of his imprisonment, utilise one-half of the monthly amount to purchase groceries and toilet requisites for his own use. The Government makes provision for the payment of grants to destitute dependants of prisoners, sentenced to at least six months' imprisonment,[6] but there are no similar provisions in favour of the victim.

In addition, there are special restitutive provisions concerning stolen property, and the usual provision with respect to the restoration of

3 Act No. 8 of 1914, Prevention of Cruelty to Animals Act, s. 6.
4 Criminal Procedure Act, s. 357 (5); Prevention of Cruelty to Animals Act, s. 6 (2).
5 This amount is under reconsideration, in connection with the new Prisons Act.
6 This grant depends upon the locality and the size of the family. For instance, if there is only one child, the grants payable are £13 10s. per month in respect of a city area, and if the family consists of, say, six children, the respective amount is £24 10s. Where the father has been sentenced to a term of imprisonment of less than six months, the family may be assisted in terms of the Poor Relief Memorandum; this assistance includes the issue of food rations, clothes, the payment of rent, etc.

unlawfully obtained property is effective.[7] Furthermore, when any person is convicted of theft or of any other offence, whereby he has unlawfully obtained any property which he has then sold to a purchaser, who has no knowledge that it was stolen, the court may order that a sum not exceeding the amount of the proceeds of the sale be given to such purchaser out of the money taken from the convicted person at his arrest. The property must first have been restored by the purchaser to its original owner.[8]

Although restitution to victims of crime in South Africa is, in general, of an entirely civil character, there is a special system of restitution, somewhat similar to the German-Swiss *Busse*, which has criminal characteristics and applies to thefts of stock or produce. It is a mixture of fine and compensation, applied when a person, who is charged with the theft of stock or produce, is found guilty of:

(a) the theft of, or an attempt to commit the theft of, such stock or produce; or

(b) receiving such stock or produce knowing the same to have been stolen; or

(c) inciting, instigating, commanding or procuring another person—
  (i) to steal such stock or produce, or
  (ii) to receive such stock or produce; or

(d) knowingly disposing of, or knowingly assisting in the disposal of, stock or produce which has been stolen or which has been received with knowledge of its having been stolen.[9]

In all cases of a conviction for the said offences, in which:

(a) the court is satisfied that the stock or produce which forms the subject-matter of the charge is the property of some particular person;

(b) such stock or produce has not been recovered or, if recovered, is worth less than its market value at the time of the theft; and

(c) the owner of such stock or produce does not apply under the provisions of the Criminal Procedure Act for compensation,

the court shall, in addition to any sentence which it may have imposed upon a person convicted of any such offence, who is twenty-one years of age or older—

(a) if the stock or produce has not been recovered: sentence this

---

[7] *Op. cit.* Criminal Procedure Act, s. 359.
[8] *Ibid.* s. 358.
[9] Act No. 26 of 1923, Stock Theft Act, s. 4 (1).

person to a fine, not exceeding the market value of the stock or produce at the time when it was stolen, or

(b) if the stock or produce has been recovered and is worth less than its market value at the time when it was stolen: sentence the said person to a fine, not exceeding the difference between the said market value and the value of the stock or produce when it was recovered.

In either case the court shall sentence the offender to a term of imprisonment not exceeding twelve months, if the fine is not paid or is not recovered according to the provisions of the criminal procedure. If the court has imposed that sentence in addition to any other sentence of imprisonment, which is imposed for any such aforementioned offence, the offender serves the additional sentence after the expiration of the other sentence. If, however, the convicted person or any other person acting on his behalf, has compensated the owner of the stolen stock or produce in any way for its loss or depreciation, the fine must not exceed the amount by which the compensation fell short of the market value, and, in the other case, the fine imposed shall not exceed the amount by which the compensation fell short of the difference.

Such fine may be recovered in the manner provided by the rules of criminal procedure,[10] and any amount so recovered is paid to the owner of the stolen stock or produce, subject to the said owner giving security *de restituendo* in case the judgment of the court be reversed on appeal or review.[11]

[10] Criminal Procedure Act, s. 337.
[11] Stock Theft Act. s. 10; this provision is not applied to the care of any person sentenced to whipping without imprisonment, unless it be proved that such offender has the means of satisfying any fine imposed thereunder. Based essentially on information supplied by the Department of Justice (G. J. Goosen, Secretary for Justice), Pretoria, 1959.

16

COMMUNIST TERRITORIES

HUNGARY

HUNGARIAN law, both pre-war and Communist, treats the question of restitution to victims of crime as belonging to the sphere of civil law. The victim has a legal right to claim restitution; because of the civil nature of his claim, which is similar to the French civil action, his claim is called *magánjogi igény* or *polgári jogi igény* (civil claim). In spite of its civil nature, however, the victim can submit his claim during the criminal trial, if he wishes.[1]

Hungarian law offers to the victim the choice between claiming through civil or criminal procedure. If he turns to the criminal court he joins the case as a civil party. This right applies to all offences, and both the victim's economic loss and his moral damage are to be compensated.

Prosecution for the criminal offence naturally takes precedence over the victim's civil claim and is dealt with first irrespective of whether the victim intends to bring his claim during the criminal procedure or not. Criminal courts are generally reluctant to consider the victim's claim and usually make use of their right to abstain from a decision on the question of restitution, on the grounds that the examination of the claim would protract the criminal proceedings. In such a case, the criminal court transfers the victim's restitutive claim to the civil court, or it may even, without transferring the case, merely warn the victim of his right to submit his claim through a separate civil action. Only in exceptional circumstances has a criminal court entertained the victim's claim *in merito*; and this applies even more so to the post-war practice of the courts, as, according to the Communist concept of crime, most offences are committed not against individual interests but against the state.

If restitution has been made or damages paid before sentence, they are taken into consideration in mitigation of the punishment.

The victim can enforce his claim through the ordinary civil channels; and though it is not forbidden to have recourse to the prisoner's earnings, these are insignificant and never worth attaching.

---

[1] *Büntetöperrendtartás* (Law of Penal Procedure).

While pre-war Hungarian criminal law safeguarded primarily individual interests,[2] post-war Hungarian criminal law's aim is to safeguard the interests of the community.[3]

In general it should be noted that in accordance with Communist legal thinking, which regards crimes against individual interests as being of secondary importance, the problem of restitution to victims of crime is not regarded in Hungary as being of great significance.

SOVIET UNION

In the Soviet Union there are no special rules concerning restitution to victims of crime. If damage is caused by a criminal offence, it is considered merely as a civil case. The plaintiff, however, or his dependants, has a civil right to full restitution for his losses, that is to say for injury suffered as well as for loss of profits.[4]

This right exists because his rights at civil law have been infringed. There is no special provision for the hearing of claims for restitution by victims of crime. Matters of this nature are dealt with by the ordinary courts, but actions between the so-called socialist organisations must be settled by arbitration. Soviet courts, incidentally, do not recognise "moral harm," and damages for moral injury are never awarded, damages being awarded only for material injury suffered.

Though restitution can be sought, as any other civil claim can be pursued, in the civil courts, such claims can also be entertained during criminal proceedings. Such a court can decide on the appropriate form of restitution, such as restitution in kind, in addition to deciding on the appropriate punishment and sentencing the criminal; the court has a wide discretion in this field, and is not tramelled by detailed legislation on this count.

Since offenders are compelled to work in prison and they are paid for their work, the prisoner's earnings can be an asset against which the victim can enforce his claim. In accordance with the Soviet corrective labour policy and law, labour is considered as one of the most important methods of correction and re-education of prisoners. The administration of corrective labour establishments and their officers accordingly insist that prisoners undertake non-specialised productive work. Both readiness to undertake such work and exemplary conduct are of primary

---

2 P. Angyal, *A Magyar Büntetöjog Tankönyve* (Budapest, 1920), p. 12.
3 S. Schafer, "Some Basic Principles of Hungarian Criminal Law," *The Modern Law Review*, Vol. 22, No. 2, London, March, 1959.
4 Soviet Civil Code, Arts. 117 and 410.

importance when applying for the remission of a sentence of detention. All work done is paid for. In every corrective labour establishment compulsory trade training is organised for the prisoners, so that they may strive to improve standards of work while in the detention centre. For those prisoners, however, who refuse to apply themselves to their tasks (although it is in their own interests to do so) the usual methods of coercion are employed—disciplinary action and restricted diet. This is an administrative decision at the detention centre, and is not a decision of the court.

Prisoners receive wages for their work. The amount of the remuneration depends on the quality and the amount of work done, and is calculated in relation to the earnings of free workers and other wage-earners doing similar jobs. Prisoners' earnings are, however, approximately one-third lower than those of free workers. These wages help to defray the expense of the maintenance of living quarters and community centres in the corrective labour establishments. In addition, prisoners must contribute towards their food and clothing out of their earnings. Against what remains an award of restitution can be enforced.

If damage to property is caused by a crime, then, in accordance with the ordinary civil rules, execution can be enforced against possessions held by the prisoner prior to his arrest (*e.g.*, musical instruments, etc.). Certain articles are protected, however, and execution cannot be levied against them. With certain limitations, execution can be levied against the prisoner's earnings in prison. These earnings must not be cancelled completely. At present the law provides that a prisoner doing his work satisfactorily must receive at least 10 per cent. of his earnings for his own personal account.[5]

[5] Based essentially on information supplied by B. S. Nikiforov, Doctor of Legal Sciences, Criminal Law; B. S. Antimonov, Professor of Civil Law and Lawsuits, and A. I. Pergament, Candidate in Legal Sciences, Scientific Secretary of the National Institute of Legal Sciences, Moscow, 1959.

17

COMPARATIVE SUMMARY

In glancing through the legal systems of these different countries, one notices firstly that the subject of this survey is not universally called "restitution." In fact, this name is rarely found (being mainly popular in North American criminological literature), and "compensation" or "damages" are the more usual names by which it is known.

In support of the expression "restitution," it may be urged that this institution aims at the restoration of the state of affairs existing before the commission of the crime. Against the use of the term "restitution," on the one hand, it may be said that this complete restoration of the state of affairs existing before the commission of the crime is far from possible in every case. No amount of money could raise a murdered man from the dead, nor could any sum restore vitality to a permanently disabled limb. At best, only if the criminal offence resulted in financial loss alone can we speak of a true restoration of the position. Even in such a case the possibility of restoring the original position is not certain, as in the intervening period between the occurrence of the financial loss and the payment of restitution the victim may have had chances of increasing his assets to an immeasurable extent had he been in possession of his lost money, and these lost chances cannot be covered by interest.

For this reason it would seem that there is more to be said for the use of the term "compensation," as this does not mean the restoration of the position existing before the commission of the crime but only the making of some recompense to the victim, and indicates a more modest purpose for indemnification. Against the use of the term "compensation," however, similar arguments to those used against the term "restitution," can be advanced, such as the frequent impossibility of counterbalancing the injury by even the most generous award of compensation. An annuity for life payable to the dependants of a murdered man may not equal the murdered man's potential earning power, and no sum of money can compensate the victim of a rape for the psychical shock she has suffered.

The use of the expression " damages " can be supported by its use since Roman times, and by its general acceptance as meaning the making of amends to another person for the damage he has been caused. Also, it does not necessarily refer to complete restitution for the actual loss. The disadvantage of the use of the term " damages," however, is that it is essentially a concept of the civil law, associated only to a lesser extent with punishment or the compensatory activity of the state.

Legal systems can be found, where two of the three expressions are in use. The term " damages," for example, is understood as the compensation to be paid by the offender himself, while " compensation " refers to when the state contributes to the restitution to be made to the victim; or, to take another example, " restitution " means only the return of things unlawfully appropriated, while any other form of restitution is known as " compensation."

A philological or terminological discussion of the terms variously employed is, however, not the purpose of this work, nor is it by any means certain that such a discussion would be of any practical value.

In this work the term " restitution " is used to indicate compensation for injury to victims of crime, paid by the offender, and the term " compensation " is used to indicate compensation offered on the part of the state or with which the state concerns itself for the victim's benefit.

There are roughly five different systems for restitution or compensation to the victims of crime. They may be classified as follows:

1. damages—civil in character and awarded in civil proceedings;
2. restitution—civil in character but awarded in criminal proceedings;
3. restitution—civil in character, but interwoven with penal characteristics, and awarded in criminal proceedings;
4. compensation—civil in character, awarded in criminal proceedings and backed by the resources of the state;
5. compensation—neutral in character and awarded through a special procedure.

1. In this case the penal law is not concerned with any damage which the victim may have suffered through the commission of the crime. Where the law takes this shape, crime is regarded as an offence exclusively against the state, and the interests of the victim play no part in the criminal procedure at all. This divorcing of the victim's restitutive claim from the penal proceedings may be regarded as an extreme manifestation of the segregation of civil and criminal wrong.

Where this segregation applies, the victim is obliged to seek a legal remedy for his injury through the civil courts, where the provisions of civil procedure apply.

Only a few legal systems thus completely separate restitution to victims of crime from the criminal law, leaving the question of restitution to be dealt with entirely as a problem of the civil law. Besides India, Pakistan and New Zealand, the federal law of the United States of America utilises this purely civil solution, though some state laws in the United States not only allow a claim for restitution to be entertained within the scope of the criminal procedure, but utilise the penal law in order to enforce the victim's claim.

2. The most usual treatment of the question of restitution to victims of crime today is to allow a civil claim for restitution to be made during the criminal trial. This treatment, while retaining the clear distinction between civil and criminal wrong, as in 1, allows a claim for restitution, unlike an ordinary civil claim, to be brought as part of a criminal hearing.

In the German legal system, the civil character of the victim's claim for restitution is emphasised, the hearing of such a claim in criminal proceedings being termed an *Adhäsionsprozess*. The criminal trial predominates in the procedure, and takes precedence over the hearing of the victim's claim. The victim's claim for restitution is, for convenience sake, heard at the same time as the criminal charge, but the two hearings are, in fact, independent of each other. In France, the victim's restitutive claim is known as *l'action civile* and at the criminal trial the victim is merely a *civil partie*. In Hungarian law, the damage caused to the victim by a crime, though it can be sued for during a criminal trial, is sued for by means of a " civil claim " only. In general, all legal systems that apply this solution to the problem of restitution to victims of crime, emphasise the civil character of the victim's claim, although allowing it to be brought during criminal proceedings.

Where, moreover, in spite of this concept of the separation of the criminal trial from the civil remedy, a legal system allows the civil claim of the victim closer legal connection with the criminal proceedings, the predominance of the criminal case is ensured by various restrictions. In some legal systems (*e.g.*, those of England, Holland or Israel) there is a limitation on the amount which a victim may claim during criminal procedure. It is thus thought to prevent the diversion of the court's attention from the criminal case by reason of the considerable sum of money in issue in the civil claim, and to prevent the judge of the criminal charge from being overburdened with work of a civil (restitutory) nature, which is not considered his proper function. In addition, in almost all of these legal systems it is provided that in cases where the victim's restitutive civil claim is going to cause inconvenience (for example, where it would disturb the clear consideration of the criminal case, or the hearing of evidence in connection with it might greatly postpone the decision of the criminal case, etc.), the criminal court is allowed not to decide the victim's civil claim and to direct the civil claim to be heard in a civil court through civil procedure.

Furthermore, in none of these legal systems *must* the injured victim bring his claim against the wrongdoer before a criminal court. He is merely allowed to do so as an alternative to bringing his claim through the ordinary civil channels. Even in those legal systems (such as the French, Norwegian, Swedish or Dominican), where the law to a certain extent encourages the submission of the victim's restitutive claim before the criminal courts, provision is made for the criminal court to remit the civil claim to the civil courts.

Even where the criminal court has not considered the victim's claim suitable for transfer to civil procedure, the criminal court seems to decide the civil claim in a similar way to a civil court. Its decision on the civil claim has only a formal connection with the criminal proceedings, and is, in fact, an independent decision on the civil claim. Even the execution of this kind of decision is by means of civil procedural provisions.

3. Where restitution is of a civil character but interwoven with penal characteristics, and is sought in criminal procedure, it appears as an institution strikingly different from that previously mentioned. Whereas in that case the victim has a right to choose between the civil and criminal courts when claiming restitution for damage or injury caused by a criminal offence, in this case his restitutive claim must be decided by the criminal court. And whereas in the second case the criminal court may, in certain cases, decline to deal with or to decide the victim's claim for restitution and remit it to the jurisdiction of a civil court, in this case the criminal court must decide the victim's claim under any circumstances. While even here the institution of restitution to victims of crime may retain some civil characteristics, there can be no doubt of its general punitive nature.

This system of restitution takes three different forms.

One of these is the fine-like restitution, or compensatory fine, generally known as *Busse*, which appears mainly in the German and

Swiss legal systems, as well as in the laws of some of the United States of America and the law of Mexico. It is, essentially, in the nature of a monetary obligation imposed upon the offender as an indemnity to the victim, and which is in addition to the ordinary punishment imposed by the criminal court.

Another shape which this form of restitution takes is similar to the previous procedure, but with the difference that the court need not restrict its award to the actual damage suffered by the victim, and may require the offender to pay a greater sum of money, up to double or treble the value of the injury caused by the offender's crime. This again can be found in the laws of some of the United States of America: its punitive nature is evident from the extent to which the award is not restricted to the actual loss but may exceed it for the victim's benefit.

The third form is where it is substituted for criminal proceedings, or at any rate for punishment. It appears in this guise in the laws of some of the United States of America. Where the offender performs his obligation to indemnify his victim, the criminal proceedings may be closed and the offender discharged without punishment. By allowing restitution in lieu of punishment, the criminal law here becomes closely interwoven with the claim of the victim of crime to restitution.

4. Compensation, civil in character and awarded in criminal proceedings, but ensuring payment to the victim through the backing of the resources of the state, appears in Cuba. There, compensation has no penal character whatsoever, and though it is awarded in criminal proceedings, it remains a purely civil institution.

When an award of restitution has been made to a victim of crime by a Cuban court, the state, as it were, steps into the legal shoes of the offender and undertakes to fulfil all the indemnificatory obligations imposed upon him by the court. A fund, specially set up and drawn from various sources, endeavours to perform, in the offender's stead, his compensatory obligations, and the victim is thus freed from the trouble of deciding how to enforce his claim against the offender. Having satisfied the victim's claim, the state endeavours to reimburse itself from the offender. When it is successful in this, the money it recovers goes to the aforementioned special fund. It should be emphasised that the payment by the fund to the victim is quite independent of the wrongdoer's power to reimburse it subsequently.

While the indemnification itself displays civil characteristics, and the claim is submitted in criminal proceedings, the participation of the state is enshrined in the constitutional law of the country, and is administered by the State Treasury. It would not, perhaps, be going too far to say that this not only shows concern on the part of the state for the victim's interests, but may imply a recognition by the state that it has failed in its duty to protect the victim, and to prevent the commission of the crime.

5. Compensation which is neither civil nor criminal in character and is awarded in an independent procedure, appears in the Swiss legal system, and applies where the victim is in need and the offender appears to be insolvent and unable to satisfy the victim's claim for damages for the injury caused by his criminal offence. Neither the civil nor the criminal courts are competent to exercise jurisdiction, but a separate and independent procedure may lead to the intervention of the state, on the application of the victim. Where the victim is successful in his application, the state compensates him for the injury or damage caused by the crime.

As the injured person appears here neither as victim nor as plaintiff, but merely as an applicant, neither the procedure nor the nature of indemnification can be termed either civil or criminal. It can even be argued whether this is restitution or compensation performed by the state, or merely state assistance offered to a person whose need was caused by a criminal offence.

As can be seen from these five different approaches to restitution to the injured victim of crime, state contribution to the victim's claim is not widespread: the Swiss system has not yet been much applied in practice, while the Cuban method is inadequate because of the lack of sufficient funds. The adhesive procedure, the civil action and similar other systems are widely accepted, though, for example, in German court practice even the *Adhäsionsprozess* does not gain ground, and elsewhere the criminal courts seem often to prefer to transfer or direct the victim's restitutive claim to civil procedure. Obviously the adhesive and similar methods are consonant with those legal systems where punishment and restitution are considered as separate problems, and where the injury or loss suffered by the victim is considered purely civil in character. Thus, with rare exceptions, the victim's indemnification, whether awarded by a civil or a criminal court, is an award of a civil nature.

In the result, even where an award takes sufficient account of the injury or damage caused to the victim by an offence, its execution is very often extremely difficult. The imprisoned offender's work and income in the prison seldom offer any satisfactory solution. There can be found prison systems (Dutch, Finnish, Norwegian, Indian or New Zealand), where it is even prohibited for the victim or his dependants to enforce their claims for restitution against the prisoner's earnings, or where (as in Pakistan) there is no such possibility at all. In other prison systems (German, Austrian) though the victim is not authorised to enforce a claim against the offender's prison income, the offender is allowed voluntarily to pay from his earnings during his imprisonment. Most states, however (Canada, Denmark, Israel, Italy, Sweden, Hungary, Turkey, United States of America, etc.), allow the victim, at least in principle, the right to enforce his restitutive claim against the prisoner's earnings. Moreover, some legislations even provide encouraging rules for the victim (for example in the French prison system), or order the prisoner to pay out from his prison earnings for the victim in cases where the victim is in need (Finnish prison system), or even compel the offender to pay restitution to the victim of his crime by means of the threat of additional imprisonment (Dominican system).

Whatever provisions assist the execution of the victim's claim against the offender's earnings in prison, they are only of symbolic importance, since the prisoner's income is nowhere worth attaching.

This general situation involves the victim of crime in a more or less hopeless position with regard to his claim for restitution. It has been found in practice,[1] that the injured party has very little success in recovering damages because of the lack of means of the ordinary criminal and the opportunity which the criminal has to hide or transfer his property before attachment. Frequently the victim despairs of turning to the civil procedure or wants to save additional costs. Victims know that most offenders tend to be impecunious and a civil action alone or an award having merely a civil character will probably be worthless to them. For this reason it can be presumed that there are not a few victims of crime who do not seek satisfaction by civil procedure and employ the criminal law solely in order to obtain restitution. This may easily lead to the misuse of the criminal courts.

In only two ways, with very limited scope, does restitution play a role of somewhat greater importance in penal legislation: when it is used as a condition for suspending a sentence or awarding probation (in the Finnish, German, English, Hungarian, New Zealand, Norwegian, American, etc., legal systems), and when it affects the sentence in cases of voluntary restitution (this applies in nearly all legal systems, but not,

---

[1] Sutherland, *op. cit.* p. 576.

perhaps, in all, for example, the Indian legal system). In some legal systems to make restitution is regarded as an essential condition for the suspension of a sentence or the award of probation; and almost everywhere restitution, performed before sentence, is considered as a mitigating circumstance.

Apart from criminological literature and some voices in a few countries (for example, in the North European states and India), the general impression to be gained, mainly from official sources, is that the institution of restitution, as it stands at present, works satisfactorily. In other words, the various legislations do not think it necessary to improve the position of the victim as outlined and have no immediate intention of offering more guarantees for his claim for restitution for injury or damage caused by crime.

PART THREE

UNITED KINGDOM

18

DEVELOPMENTS TO 1960

THE foregoing brief survey of foreign legislation on the problem of restitution to victims of crime may be compared with the position in England, where restitution tends to be embodied in the sphere of civil law.

The Probation of Offenders Act, 1907, empowered the Bench to order compensation up to the sum of £10. This limit was subsequently raised by the Criminal Justice Act, 1948. According to subsection (2) of section 11 of the latter Act, a court, on making a probation order or an order for the conditional or absolute discharge of an offender, may order the offender to pay such damages for injury or compensation for loss, as the court thinks reasonable; this compensation is without limit if ordered by a superior court, but in the case of an order made by a court of summary jurisdiction, the damages and compensation together must not exceed £100.

This seems to be the total extent to which restitution to victims of crime is dealt with in England within the scope of criminal procedure. In all other respects it retains its civil character.

As compensation and punishment are dealt with separately, various proposals have been put forward for improving the system of restitution to victims of crime in England. In recent years even the idea of state compensation has been urged in Great Britain, it being suggested that the state should pay compensation to the victims of personal violence on a scale similar to that under the Industrial Injuries Scheme.[1] In urging the acceptance of this scheme, popular attention was drawn to the case of a man who was blinded as the consequence of a criminal offence and because of the injury was awarded compensation of £11,500. Considering the fact that the two assailants of this man were ordered to pay him five shillings weekly, " the victim will need to live another 442 years to collect the last instalment." Asking for " better help " for the victims of crime is, like so many other modern ideas in criminal law and criminology, not a new notion at all. Nevertheless, when the idea was recently raised, under the impressive title of " justice for victims," it met with

[1] Margery Fry, " Justice for Victims " (*The Observer*, London, July 7, 1957).

111

a favourable reception, and on several occasions was discussed in the House of Commons. The House appeared to be sympathetic to the idea of greater compensation to victims of crime, and such objections as were raised arose from the nature of the practical difficulties in the way of such a proposal rather than from objections to the idea in principle.

This revival of the idea of state compensation prompted a recent American " Round Table " article [2] in which several individual reactions were published containing not only practical criticism of the proposal, but also objections to the principle of state compensation.

Inter alia, concern was expressed about the abandonment of individual responsibility through the introduction of a system of state compensation, and " the sociological decadence that could come from that kind of thinking might be far worse than the economic consequences." Nevertheless, the practical benefits were also mentioned, and the " greater interest on the part of the public in the matter of law enforcement " if the institution of state compensation were to be adopted,[3] was pointed out.

Another commentator " in casting about to find something helpful to say " about the proposal of the state compensation system found that " the history of the methods we have used to take care of unfortunates " might be a helpful background.[4] The same writer suggested relating the punishment of criminals to their making reparation for the harm done by them, believing this might serve the rehabilitation of the criminals.[5]

Among other practical difficulties raised was that it would be hard to protect the public from fraudulent claims. Another argument against this form of state insurance was that: " the insured victim hardly fits the picture of the unfortunate object of pity . . . he simply calls up his insurance company and lets them worry about it." [6]

The question was also raised as to whether it might not be true that " insurance robs the insured of a good deal of the otherwise present vigilance toward the danger," and reference was made to " nonchalant victims " who take risks confident that their insurance will make good any resulting loss. It can be equally well argued that to restrict compensation to " violent " crime, as the late Margery Fry suggested, is to make an arbitrary and unnecessary distinction.[7]

---

[2] " Compensation for Victims of Criminal Violence, A Round Table," *Journal of Public Law*, Vol. 8, No. 1, pp. 191–253, Atlanta, 1959.
[3] *Ibid.* p. 202, Fred E. Inbau.
[4] *Ibid.* p. 204, Frank W. Miller.
[5] *Ibid.* p. 209, Frank W. Miller.   [6] *Ibid.* pp. 209–210, Henry Weihofen.
[7] *Ibid.* pp. 229–230, Gerhard O. W. Mueller.

Other difficulties raised were, *inter alia*, the possible reluctance of the victim to testify against his assailant in a criminal trial, the difficulty of establishing new criteria to determine when a victim or his survivors should be eligible for state compensation, the practice of accepting pleas of guilty to a lesser offence than that originally charged, and the measure of damages for non-material injuries.[8]

Nevertheless, these or similar technical difficulties should not prove insuperable ones. While the possibility of " sociological decadence " cannot be ignored, the penal reform should not be made dependent upon the question of insurance interests. It is more reasonable to ask how far the state compensation system might be able to help the fight against crime and the reform of the criminal.

In England, the Home Secretary's White Paper on " Penal Practice in a Changing Society," presented to Parliament in February 1959, drew attention to the fact that " the assumption that the claims of the victim are sufficiently satisfied if the offender is punished by society becomes less persuasive " and " suggests . . . a reconsideration of the position of the victims of crime."

Thereafter, a Private Member's Bill was presented to the House of Commons, entitled " The Criminal Injuries (Compensation) Bill," [9] " to compensate those injured by certain criminal offences against the person; to provide for their dependants and for the dependants of those killed by criminal acts; and for the purposes connected therewith."

According to this Bill, where a person suffers personal injury or death as a result of being the victim of an offence, then such person and the dependants of such person shall be entitled to the same benefits as are provided for insured persons and the dependants of insured persons in the National Insurance (Industrial Injuries) Act, 1946. Where, however, an injured or deceased person through his own misconduct was partly responsible for his personal injury or death the whole or part of any benefit due to the injured person or to his dependants may be withheld.

The Bill proposed that any question as to whether an injured or deceased person was the victim of an offence, or as to whether the injured or deceased person was partly responsible for his personal injury or death through his own misconduct, should be determined by the insurance officer. The Bill gave a list of the offences concerned, these included capital murder, murder, manslaughter, assault occasioning

8 *Journal of Public Law, op. cit.*
9 R. E. Prentice, M.P., Bill 33, November 11, 1959.

actual bodily harm, and certain offences under the Malicious Damage Act (1861), the Offences against the Person Act (1861), the Explosive Substances Act (1883), the Larceny Act (1916), the Firearms Act (1937), and the Sexual Offences Act (1956).

Some general theoretical considerations against a state compensation system, can be found in Parts 4 and 5 of this book. The acceptance by the state of a certain degree of responsibility for damage or injuries suffered by victims of crime might have unfortunate consequences in so far as it would relieve criminals of some of their financial obligations, and lead to carelessness on the part of their potential victims. It would also perhaps be unwise to abandon the possibility of awarding punitive damages against criminals. In practice, however, there is but slight danger of the prospect of compensation inducing undue carelessness on the part of potential victims, who would be unlikely to be complacent victims of crime through the prospect of receiving state compensation for any harm they might undergo. State compensation would merely redress the balance, at present so heavily tilted against the victim.

Before inaugurating any state compensation system, it would be necessary to hold an investigation into the relationship between criminals and their victims. The author of this work submitted a proposal for such a type of research, which is under consideration, though we still lack " victim statistics." " Vulnerability components " and " categoric risks " [10] seem to be applicable even more to victims than criminals. " Individuals display a wide variety of weakness components," especially people who fall into categories prone to be victims of crime. " There are risks of being a victim of aggressions or being injured by criminal behaviour," but we have little knowledge of these risks. There seems to exist a close relationship between the doer and the sufferer,[11] though this belief is based only on uncorrelated statistics. It is difficult to devise a scheme of insurance against crime, such as a system of state compensation, without reliable statistics as to the various sorts of risks different sorts of people are likely to be.

It should be noted that the proposed Bill allows the causal connection between crime and injury, and between criminal and victim, to be decided by the insurance officer. Both are difficult problems requiring specialised legal and criminological knowledge, and the proposed insurance officer ought therefore to be armed with the proper experience.

---

[10] Walter C. Reckless, *The Crime Problem*, pp. 2–4, 26–27 (New York, 1955).
[11] Hans von Hentig, *The Criminal and His Victim* (New Haven, 1948).

PART FOUR

PUNISHMENT AND RESTITUTION

19

THE RESTITUTIVE CONCEPT OF PUNISHMENT

IF one looks at the legal systems of different countries, one seeks in vain a country where a victim of crime enjoys a certain expectation of full restitution for his injury. In the rare cases where there is state compensation the system is either not fully effective, or does not work at all; where there is no system of state compensation, the victim is, in general, faced with the insufficient remedies offered by civil procedure and civil execution. While the punishment of crime is regarded as the concern of the state, the injurious result of the crime, that is to say, the damage to the victim, is regarded almost as a private matter. It recalls man in the early days of social development, when, left alone in his struggle for existence, he had himself to meet attacks from outside and fight alone against fellow-creatures who caused him harm. The victim of today cannot even himself seek satisfaction, since the law of the state forbids him to take the law into his own hands. In the days of his forefathers, restitution was a living practice, and " it is perhaps worth noting, that our barbarian ancestors were wiser and more just than we are today, for they adopted the theory of restitution to the injured, whereas we have abandoned this practice, to the detriment of all concerned." [1] " And this was wiser in principle, more reformatory in its influence, more deterrent in its tendency, and more economic to the community, than the modern practice." [2]

The number of victims may be assumed to have increased at the same rate as criminals,[3] but there has been no improvement in the victim's lot to compare with the advances which have been made in criminology, and certainly not to compare with the amelioration of the lot of the criminal which has taken place. Criminal law, among people living at a low cultural level, is considered primitive, not because

---

[1] Barnes and Teeters, *op. cit.* p. 401.
[2] Tallack, *op. cit.* pp. 6–7.
[3] In England and Wales, in 1958, in certain offence groups, the number of indictable offences known to the police was 626,509, but offences cleared up were 285,462. (Criminal Statistics, England and Wales, 1958; H.M. Stationery Office, London, 1959, p. 8.) " Nothing is known statistically of those who are victimised by larceny, burglary, robbery, or even the confidence game " (Hans von Hentig, *The Criminal and His Victim*, New Haven, 1948, p. 399).

117

criminal justice is practised by the victim himself as a recompense for
his injury, but because the state takes no part in it and no agency of
social control against crime is in existence. Since, however, the time
when the state took over from the victim the task of preserving law and
order and keeping the peace, concern for the previous performer of this
task (*i.e.*, the victim), with regard to restitution for injuries received from
a criminal act, has been lacking. " It is rather absurd, that the state
undertakes to protect the public against crime and then, when a loss
occurs, takes the entire payment and offers no effective remedy to the
individual victim." [4]

Crime, against which the state undertakes and endeavours to protect
the public, is a disturbance of some legally protected interest, usually an
interest which the state protects because current thought considers such
an interest to be worthy of protection. Almost all the ancient crimes,
apart from political ones, involve the injury of one individual by another,
though more recently created crimes frequently injure no person directly.
This disturbance of a legally protected interest is regarded as crime,
that is to say as a violation of law and order, whenever the violator of
public security is necessarily also an offender against an individual victim.
Crime gives rise to legal nexa not only between the violator and society,
but between the violator and his victim. Crime upsets the balance not
only between the criminal and society, but between the criminal and the
individual victim.

Material damage may be *lucrum cessans* or *damnum emergens*; non-
material damage comprises degradation, physical suffering and grief.
While the state soon visits punishment on the breaker of its criminal
laws, the individual victim of a crime is, as a result of the distinction
between civil and criminal wrong, left to seek redress as best he may
through the usually inadequate civil channels. Even where the law
allows civil redress to be awarded to the victim concurrently with the
passing of sentence for the crime, it lays down that the criminal trial is
to take precedence over and in no way to be impeded by the *Adhäsionsprozess* or similar proceedings.[5]

The intention of the present survey is not to give an account of the
centuries-old dispute about the difference between criminal and civil
wrongs; still less to argue this much-disputed question, which is one of

---

[4] Sutherland, *op. cit.*
[5] Würtemberger, *op. cit.* p. 205.

those problems of the legal sciences in which the spectacular multitude of opinions have for so long failed to agree. The problem of restitution is concerned with how far legal systems try to separate criminal and civil wrong, both theoretically and practically. The overwhelming majority of provisions concerning restitution are based on the principle of distinguishing between criminal and civil wrong. Such systems reject the unitary view of wrong, according to which wrong is simply a breach of the law, it being immaterial what sort of law is transgressed.

Not only does the law treat criminal and civil wrongs separately in a quantitative sense but also qualitatively. This would mean not only to the " contempt of law " (*Missachtung*), but also the disturbance of the general sense of justice (*Sicherheitsgefühl*),[6] but as an addition only and not as a qualitative difference.

It is obvious that claims for damages may result not only from illegal acts regarded as criminal offences, but also from many other acts which, while giving rise to an action for damages, according to contemporary thought are not considered by the state as being sufficiently undesirable to merit penal prosecution. For such non-penal actions the civil law remedies are sufficient. The law, however, makes no distinction in awarding damages for torts which are also crimes and torts which are not. The present general view concerning restitution is that, no matter what the cause of damage may be, the claim for restitution, even if it was caused by crime, is a civil matter only and not to be connected with the fate of the criminal case. The fact that a tort may also be a crime is recognised only to the extent that some legal systems allow suit for restitution for injuries caused by crime to be brought within the scope of the criminal procedure. No distinction is made, however, between penal and civil damages; there is but a single concept of damages. This may be why the victim's claim for restitution is regarded as something intruding into the criminal procedure, if it can be found there at all.

At present, the only satisfaction the victim can get from criminal justice is the punishment inflicted upon the criminal. Criminal justice applies punishment not only to maintain law and order in society and to protect the interests of the community, but, in addition, to conciliate the victim by the state's " bloodless " punishment of the guilty party.[7] Even though it may not be quite true that " in present society the demand

---

[6] A. Merkel, " Zur Lehre v.d. Grundeinteilungen des Unrechts und seiner rechtl. Folgen " (*Kriminalistische Abhandlungen*, 1), pp. 1–75.

[7] Hentig, *op. cit.* p. 217.

for vengeance is, to be sure, somewhat general," [8] there is probably no one who would not demand vengeance in certain circumstances.[9]

It was not inappropriate when classic Roman jurists described punishment as " satisfaction." Indeed, the victim not only expects the indemnification of the damage caused to him, but tends to think of criminal justice as nationalised vengeance and so claim satisfaction as well. The victim expects moral reproach of the crime, and in addition he expects a certain degree of injury to be inflicted upon the offender in order to satisfy his desire for revenge. Moreover, because it is believed that there is an unalterable demand for vengeance which, if it cannot be satisfied by legal, will be satisfied by illegal means, it is asserted that if the criminal is not punished, the victim will take the law into his own hands in the form of either self-redress or lynch-law.[10] This is rendered, if anything, more likely by the victim's realisation that the only satisfaction he is likely to get for his injury is the punishment inflicted upon the criminal.

Different theorists assign irreconcilable aims and purposes to punishment, viewing as they do the problem from different angles. When it comes to the question of how to satisfy the victim, however, almost all theorists hold essentially the same views. Among theories of the purpose and legal ground of punishment hardly one would omit counterbalancing the effect of the crime on the victim. Punishment satisfies our feelings of revenge against those who attack us,[11] and, *inter alia*, seems to be the expression of an instinct for vengeance. The evil visited on the wrong-doer in punishment is intended not only to make the power of moral and legal order felt by the criminal, but at the same time, to endeavour to compensate the victim for his encroached or destroyed right by offering him some spiritual satisfaction. Amid the involved and interminable discussion of the purpose of punishment it is generally accepted that one of the tasks of punishment is what might be called " idealistic damages " or " spiritual restitution."

This task of punishment was prominent in the golden age of classic criminal law, when criminal justice throughout the world adjusted the punishment roughly to the quality and quantity of the victim's injury.

---

[8] Sutherland, *op. cit.* p. 375.
[9] F. C. Sharp and M. C. Otto, " A Study of the Popular Attitude towards Retributive Punishment " (*Intern. Jour. Ethics*, 20: 341–357, 438–453, April–July 1910).
[10] Sutherland, *op. cit.* p. 375.
[11] Nathaniel F. Cantor, *Crime and Society* (New York, 1939), p. 393.

More recent criminology, however, directed attention away from the gravity of the injury towards the personality of the criminal. The German *Täterstrafrecht* (criminal law of the criminal) aimed at complete disregard of the crime and adjusted the punishment only to the personality of the criminal. This somewhat distorted revival of Lombroso's extreme and unacceptable theory wished entirely to separate punishment from satisfaction to the victim. Even constructive criminology, however, may lead to the failure of vengeance or reprisal. The tendency of modern criminology, after considering the importance of the crime itself, is to allow an increasingly dominant part to the possible reform and rehabilitation of the offender. In accordance with this development the victim's injury may lose importance, and on top of his lack of material restitution, spiritual restitution to the victim may also show a tendency to decrease.

It is in any case arguable whether satisfaction to the victim would accord with society's present moral and cultural level, if it consisted only of vengeance in some form or other. The question also arises as to whether harm to the criminal in fact involves restitution to the victim for his injury. The basis of criminal responsibility is the causing of harm. There fall on the criminal, as the causer of harm, certain consequences which are destined to destroy, to weaken or to direct in the right way the power to cause harm, and in that way to endeavour to prevent the recurrence of crime or at least to try to restrain the likelihood of it. The criminal is, however, often also the causer of injury and damage to an individual victim; this can hardly be compensated by mere revenge or satisfaction exacted by punishment, whether or not such punishment be restrained by the tenets of modern criminology.

The state, when dispensing criminal justice, does not fight against abstract legal phantoms but against the acts of living human beings. The object of punishment is not merely to grant citizens the pleasure of participating in a ritual restoration of law and order. The modern criminological approach to punishment will not tolerate retribution, but it must not neglect the victim's interests: the *tout comprendre* does not necessarily mean the *tout pardonner*. Punishment must lose its retributive character and lean towards giving the criminal a chance to work his passage back to society. One way of doing so would be to make the criminal's sentence in some way beneficial to his victim.

A thoughtful consideration of the place of restitution in criminal law calls for more than speculation about the elusive boundary between criminal and civil wrongs. It would be well to begin by abandoning traditional concepts concerning the " state's interest " in the suppression of crime.[12] In spite of theoretical distinctions, criminal law and civil law seem to be more integrated than ever before. It is unnecessary to distinguish between civil damages and punishment in effecting restitution. Restitution is not intended for the recovery of a debt but for the reparation of a criminal injury.

The state enforces criminal justice in order to maintain law and order, in the collective interests of its citizens. The individual victim is a part of the community, and for that reason criminal proceedings are, in the last analysis, applied in the interests of this individual victim as well as in the interests of the community as a whole. It therefore seems senseless to exclude the victim from the settlement of a criminal case, and to regard him merely as the cause of, or reason for, the criminal case. Besides the abstract protection of law and order, and the reform of the criminal, the victim's claim to restitution is the third element of punishment. In the retributive sense restitution exists in punishment even at present, but true restitution could develop if spiritual satisfaction were replaced by material.

---

[12] *Columbia Law Review, op. cit.* Vol. XXXIX, No. 7, pp. 1186–1187.

20

THE PUNITIVE CONCEPT OF RESTITUTION

IF it were realised that spiritual satisfaction is implicit in any system of punishment, a new conception of the purpose of punishment might arise, causing a strengthening of the restitutive character of punishment on the one hand, and imbuing restitution with a punitive character on the other.

Most modern criminological literature urges that a greater part be allotted to restitution in the operation of the criminal law. If the state sets a norm of conduct, it should, besides punishing breaches of this norm, see that where it is transgressed, any injury caused is repaired. That restitution deserves a place in criminal procedure should be evident if only because, without the crime which is being tried, the victim would not have suffered the damage for which he seeks restitution. Another reason for allowing claims for restitution to victims of crime a place in criminal procedure is that it would save time, expense and the unnecessary repetition of evidence. It would also avoid the possibility that a criminal and civil court might reach different decisions on the same facts. Against the argument that a criminal court may not be versed in the niceties of civil law, so as to be able to decide the civil question of restitution, it may be argued that criminal law is the most complex of all legal sciences, and is becoming increasingly even more and more complex, and today a good criminal judge is required to be well versed in criminology, penology, and in many other aspects of the law than just the criminal law.

Voices raised against the appearance of restitution in criminal procedure would be less effective if restitution were provided with punitive character and were in this guise to take its place within the scope of criminal procedure. To require the offender to pay money as a punishment is not something new and, in this sense, would not be strange to the judge of the criminal case: the origin of the present-day fine is restitution; the only difference is that while the main point of compensation was based on the enrichment of the victim and the community, which interposed itself between the wrongdoer and the vengeance of the victim, fines serve as a source of income for the state. The judge of the criminal case would not deal with civil damages, but, if punitive restitution were allowed to be imposed as a sentence, with an institution

123

of the criminal law. Similarly, " to the offender's pocket it makes no difference whether what he has to pay is a fine, costs, or compensation. But to his understanding of the nature of justice it may make a great deal." [1]

This or similar considerations have led to the idea of state compensation based on fines. This has achieved concrete form mainly in Cuban legislation. In criminological literature it has been proposed more than once to set up a central state fund to which fines should go, and out of which the state should pay restitution to victims of crime. There was as early as the Brussels Congress a proposal to set up a *caisse d'amendes*, into which fines imposed should be paid by the state, and from which should come relief for the loss sustained by the injured party in a crime. [2] Similar ideas appeared even earlier, in the Draft Criminal Code of Mexico of 1871, [3] later in Ferri's draft code of 1921, [4] and in the French Draft Criminal Code of 1934. [5] In this way the state would return to the victim the restitution which, in the shape of fines, was taken from him in the course of penal development several hundred years ago. It would also accord with modern sociological thinking, according to which the state is responsible for the welfare of its citizens. The point was raised, however, that this might imply some kind of admission that the state could be blamed for the commission of crime; but very early on it was pointed out that " it is not to be admitted that the State is responsible for damages caused by a malefactor." [6]

The ultimate aim of state compensation would be to guarantee that the victim should get his restitution. [7] This would close a vast lacuna in legislation. It is, however, all that state compensation can achieve, and it does not utilise the further possibility implicit in the institution of restitution: it would not aid at the same time the possible reform of the criminal, moreover it would perhaps exempt him beforehand and at state expense from an obligation which he ought to discharge. [8] The offender should, moreover, understand that he injured not only the state and law and order, but also the victim; in fact primarily the victim and

---

[1] Fry, *op. cit.* p. 124.

[2] Brussels Congress, *op. cit.* Report, p. 52.

[3] Art. 361.

[4] Enrico Ferri, *Relazione sul progretto preliminare di Codice Penale Italiano*, 1921, Art. 100.

[5] Art. 104.

[6] Brussels Congress, *op. cit.* U.S. Report, p. 21.

[7] Margery Fry, " Justice for Victims " (*The Observer*, July 7, London, 1957).

[8] " Compensation for Victims of Criminal Violence, A Round Table " (*Journal of Public Law*, Vol. 8, No. 1, Atlanta, 1959).

through this injury the abstract values of society. The institution of restitution is able not only within limits to make good the injury or loss of the victim, but, at the same time, to help the task of punishment. " Compensation cannot undo the wrong, but it will often assuage the injury, and it has a real educative value for the offender, whether adult or child." [9] " What is required, is an evaluation in terms of the deterrent and reformative potentialities of the requirements of restitution." [10] " In many cases payment to the injured party will have a stronger inner punishment value than the payment of a sum to the neutral state." [11]

Although penal methods have changed and are changing, there has for a long time been no change in the concept of the purpose of punishment, which has crystallised as the reform of the offender and in efforts to bring the criminal to ways of social conformity. Whatever might be thought of the different methods of realising this task, they hardly differ in their aims, which are, *inter alia*, to make the criminal aware that he has done wrong, and to bring this about with the least possible suffering. Punishment, however, without the assistance of punitive restitution, can aim only at making the criminal aware of the wrong he has done against the state and law and order; his awareness of having wronged an individual victim will become dull or disappear. Restitution, imbued with a punitive character, however, " would have a much better reformative effect on many offenders than would other methods, because the result of the offences would be more clearly recognised." [12]

Few systems of reforming criminals do not include among their aims to arouse understanding and the expiation of a sense of guilt on the part of the criminal. This is the sort of psychological process, which, while it can be initiated and assisted by others, cannot be done on behalf of the criminal, and must in the last resort be done by the criminal himself. Restitution, again, is something an offender does, not something done for him or to him, and as it requires effort on his part, it may be especially useful in strengthening his feelings of responsibility. Being related to the offence, creative restitution may redirect in a constructive way those same conscious or unconscious thoughts, emotions or conflicts, which motivated the offence.[13]

9 Fry, *Arms of the Law*, p. 126.   10 *Columbia Law Review, op. cit.* p. 1187.
11 Hentig, *op. cit.* p. 217.
12 Sutherland, *op. cit.* p. 576.
13 Albert Eglash, " Creative Restitution, Some Suggestions for Prison Rehabilitation Programs " (*American Journal of Correction*, Vol. 20:6, Nov.-Dec. 1958, New York), pp. 20–34; similarly August Aichhorn, *Wayward Youth* (New York, 1948), Chap. 10.

Besides reports that " rectification " or " making good " is an effective disciplinary technique with children, preventing repetition of mis-behaviour and creating little resentment,[14] there are grounds for believing that even with grown-up criminals the relationship between offender and restitution to his victim may, in addition to recompensing the victim, be reformative as well. Punitive restitution [15] may be one of the penal instruments, through which guilt can be felt, understood and alleviated. It ties up with the rehabilitation technique, in which an offender is directed to find some way to make amends to those he has hurt by his offence.[16]

Some hold the view that punitive restitution should, in certain cases, completely replace punishment as we understand it today. One reason for this is that it would relieve the state of the great burden of supporting in penal or reformatory institutions those guilty of minor offences, and because a reduction in the number of inmates would enable individual methods to be used to better advantage on those committed to these institutions.[17] To relieve the overcrowded state of prisons by substituting punitive restitution for punishment, however, may lead to evading the problem of criminality; in addition, in the present stage of development even punitive restitution cannot be substituted for punishment, and can at best be its accessory. While it appears to be reasonable to use punitive restitution as one method of dealing with criminals, if it were to be the only sentence available for any crime it might weaken the sense of wrongdoing attached to that crime, besides reducing the terror which potential wrongdoers might feel of committing the crime. It might expose criminal justice to the danger of the criminal's escaping punish-ment, and could lead to social injustice in that while the wealthy, possibly professional, criminal could buy off his liberty, the poor casual criminal might eventually serve a longer punishment for a minor crime. If resti-tution could be substituted for punishment, or in any way make it possible to buy off punishment with money, it might well have a reverse effect from that intended. A man ought not to be permitted " to buy his way out " of criminal liability. Some earlier proposals took note of this danger, objected to the wrongdoer buying off vengeance by

---

[14] Norma E. Cutts and Nicholas Moseley, *Better Home Discipline* (New York, 1952).
[15] In Eglash's concept (which is without punitive elements this is called " creative " or " guided " restitution.
[16] Similarly Eglash, *op. cit.* p. 20.
[17] Sutherland, *op. cit.* pp. 576–577; similarly, but in order " to re-establish the equation between the punishment inflicted and the evil done to the individual," Prins (Paris Congress, *op. cit.* Report, p. 8).

agreement with his victim, and insisted on an official trial.[18] " The extent to which these potentialities are enhanced or diminished when restitution is exacted by private parties "[19] gives a warning to avoid replacing punishment by restitution. The social and penal value of punitive restitution may be destroyed if individuals were permitted to compromise crimes by making restitution.

Punitive restitution may be distinguished from civil damages on this very point, that, while the latter are subject to compromise and are not in every case satisfied by the wrongdoer or injuror himself, restitution, like punishment, must always be the subject of judicial consideration. Without exception it must be carried out by personal performance by the wrongdoer, and should even then be equally burdensome and just for all criminals, irrespective of their means, whether they be millionaires or labourers.

The proposal that the offender should compensate, by his own work, for the damage he has caused has been made more than once. Where the punitive aspect of restitution has been most emphasised, it has been suggested that prison work and the prisoner's income should be the means of making restitution, keeping the offender in prison until the damage was repaired.[20] Another suggestion was that, where the offender was solvent, his property should be confiscated and restitution made therefrom by order of the court; while, if he were insolvent, he should be made a state workman.[21]

Yet another proposal tried to balance the burden of fines and restitution between the rich and poor. According to this proposal, a poor man would pay in days of work, a rich man by an equal number of days' income or salary. If two shillings represented the value of a day's work, and the poor man were sentenced to pay two shillings, he would be discharged by giving one day's labour to the victim. The rich man, instead of being sentenced to give so many days of labour, would pay an equal number of days' income or salary, and if this represented £5 a day, he would have to pay £5.[22] A similar idea emerged after the

18 Ferri, *op. cit.* Art. 95.
19 *Columbia Law Review, op. cit.* p. 1187.
20 Herbert Spencer, *Essais de morale de science et d'esthétique*, II. Essais de politique. VIII. Morale de la prison (4th ed., Paris, 1898), p. 352.
21 Raffaele Garofalo. *Criminology* (tr. by R. W. Millar, Boston, 1914), pp. 419–435; this is a somewhat changed presentation of his proposal submitted to the Paris Congress, where he suggested that instead of going to prison, the man should work for the state, retaining for himself only enough wages to keep him from starving and the rest should go into a " caisse d'épargne " for the reparation for the wrong done (Paris Congress, *op. cit.* Report, p. 9).
22 Brussels Congress, *op. cit.* Report, p. 52, proposal favoured by Garofalo and Prins.

Second World War, that the victim should be compensated from wages for the offender's labour.[23]

The " noble way " to care for the victim is to make it possible for the offender to fulfil his obligation by way of the income of his free work.[24] This noble way may at the same time be very effective, provided that it be not forgotten that the punitive side of restitution is a great aid in reforming the criminal. If restitution be unconnected with the offender's personal work, and can be performed from his property or by others, this would help the victim, but would minimise restitution's punitive-reformative character. On the other hand, if the performance of the restitutive obligation affected the freedom of work of the offender, or even his personal liberty, this would mean the extension of his punishment.

If, however, the offender were at liberty after he had served his punishment, but had to make restitution through his personal work, restitution would retain its punitive-reformative character, while, at the same time, the state would be relieved to a certain extent of the need to solve the problem of restitution to victims of crime.

This system of restitution could be operated in the following way :

1

Restitution to the victim of crime should be entertained within the scope of the criminal procedure by the same criminal court which deals with the criminal case, and the sentence should be a combined one, of which restitution should be a part.

2

Restitution may be claimed by the victim; but in default thereof, the court should deal with restitution as part of its duties.

3

If the question of restitution may cause considerable delay in deciding the sentence so far as ordinary punishment goes, the court should pass a part-sentence concerning this latter, and should postpone the decision of restitution. In such a case, the criminal court should entertain the question of restitution after passing this part-sentence but without delay, and should couple the previously passed part-sentence with the decision concerning restitution.

23 Georgio Del Vecchio, *The Problem of Penal Justice,* 27 Revista Juridica de la Universidad de Puerto Rico (from *op. cit. Journal of Public Law*).
24 Waeckerling, *op. cit.* p. 130.

4

A decision on restitution should state the amount of restitution and order the instalments as a percentage of the offender's earnings, to be paid by the offender after his release from the penal institute, or after he has paid the fine if this be the only penalty. This decision should be based on a consideration of the offender's social position, personal circumstances, and reasonable but minimum standard of living.

5

Restitution should be collected in the same way as taxes, and should be deducted from earnings by the criminal's employer, or collected by the tax office from the criminal's income and paid to the victim by the latter. If restitution is not recoverable because the offender has insufficient means, it should not be able to be commuted to any other kind of penalty.

6

With the aid of fines or other sources of revenue, the state should set up a Compensation Fund, and victims should be compensated from that where the total amount of restitution turns out to be irrecoverable, or if the offender is not known. In such cases a mixed committee of members of the court, the Home Office and the Treasury should decide, on application by the victim, whether his damage was caused by crime, and if so, what sum should be paid him by the Compensation Fund, to complete his restitution.

21

THE JUSTIFICATION OF COMPENSATION
AND CORRECTIONAL RESTITUTION

THE movement for the satisfaction of claims of victims of crime, which by 1970 seems to have slowed, might gather force and even inevitability if more public and official attention were given to the sound social, moral, and political reasons justifying at least state compensation to victims of violent crimes—a principle that may be understood as the shifting of the offender's original responsibility to society or the state. Almost all proponents of state compensation in the universities and legislatures have rested their support for promoting the victim's interests on one or more of six widely employed arguments analyzed by Massachusetts' Special Commission on the Compensation of Victims of Violent Crime under the title "The Case for Compensation."[1] These points are as follows.

(1) Perhaps the most popular and forceful argument bases compensation on the state's "failure to protect" the members of society or the so-called "legal obligation" theory. "The king usurped the right of the citizen to restore equilibrium after a crime had been committed"[2] thereby assuming responsibility for the protection of the citizen. As Marvin Wolfgang has stated, this idea "is neither new nor a radical departure from prevailing political and legal norms in Western Culture."[3] Indeed, since the state forbids a victim to take the law into his own hands, it falls to the state to recover damages for him when the state has failed in its protection.

(2) Another standard argument for victim compensation embraces the "social welfare" concept. Just as modern democracy dictates public assistance for the disabled veteran, the sick, the unemployed, or the aged, so the suffering victim of crime should also be assisted by the public. The argument does not rest on the inherent obligation of the

---

[1] *Report,* The Special Commission on the Compensation of Victims of Violent Crimes, The Commonwealth of Massachusetts, House, No. 5151 (Boston, July 1967), pp. 10–14.
[2] *Ibid.,* p. 11.
[3] Marvin E. Wolfgang, "Victim Compensation in Crimes of Personal Violence," in Walter C. Reckless and Charles L. Newman, eds., *Interdisciplinary Problems in Criminology* (Columbus, Ohio, 1965), p. 169.

state but rather on the conscience of twentieth-century man who cannot tolerate the misery of the helpless.

(3) Closely related to this theory is the argument for victim compensation "by the grace of the Government." While the one plan may reflect whole classes or categories of people, the latter mirrors the merciful intervention of the state in individual cases. Some need of the victim is acknowledged in both arguments.

(4) "Crime prevention" is sometimes invoked as a reason for victim compensation schemes which include (as most proposals do) compensation for "Good Samaritans" injured in attempting to aid victims or the police. (In 1964 much public notice was given to the Catherine Genovese case in New York City, in which thirty-eight citizens witnessed a murder without assisting the victim, exemplifying the apparent disappearance of the Good Samaritan from the streets.) The existence of a compensation plan for those injured while attempting to help enforce the law might encourage citizen assistance and prevent certain crimes, according to this argument.

(5) "Political" reasons are also given as justification of victim compensation plans. As the Massachusetts report has pointed out, "the articulators of political opinion at all points on the political spectrum enthusiastically endorse the concept of compensation."[4] It is emphasized that this is "what the people want."

(6) Finally, the "anti-alienation" argument is often cited to support the case for victim compensation. It points to the disillusionment of victimized individuals who have suffered the hardships of a crime plus the loss of time and income through cooperating in the criminal prosecution. While inflicting punishment upon the offender may express "spiritual restitution" or "idealistic damages" this may not sufficiently meet the expectation of the victim, so the argument runs, and thus he may conceivably become alienated from society unless compensation for his loss or injury is adequate to remove cause for complaint.

While these arguments support the idea of compensation to victims of crime they do not fully present the case for restitution by the offender, a principle employing the offender's personal obligation on a correctional basis. The persistent legislative apathy with which the effort to establish meaningful victim-compensation schemes has been faced has hindered the development of the broader concept of victim indemnification embracing the principle of restitution. All victim compensation

---

[4] *Report, op. cit.,* p. 12.

systems of the last decade are similar in that they are governed by the spirit of damages, without aiming at any restitutive goals. Even in this narrower context however, the eventual inclusion of any compensation program in the criminal law codes or in state-operated schemes would be regarded as an achievement. Among current proposals the usual suggestion for placing compensation (but not restitution) within the framework of criminal law, or under the jurisdiction of a state commission, is to make compensation proceedings parallel with civil law practice, or, in other words, having the criminal law or state board provide a platform for a formalistic recording of a civil law performance. Such suggestions are little more than sophisticated tort or insurance-law propositions which, while conceivably helping the victim of a criminal act receive compensation, could result only in the civil law provisions becoming mummified within the apparatus of criminology, criminal law, or social welfare institutions.

Despite the common principle of compensation without restitution which pervades the victim compensation systems of the last decade, each system has a different rationale which distinguishes its pattern of operation. If public assistance to the sufferer, the recognition of a social obligation of the state to indemnify the injured victim of crime, and the determination of loss to the victim through judicial process, are the central arguments in justifying the idea of compensation, then perhaps the systems of England, California, and Massachusetts might be cited as the most characteristic.

England's compensation scheme has developed out of a sense of social obligation to provide for victims of crimes of violence and not because the state considered itself to be legally obligated to pay. R. E. Prentice criticized the English scheme stating that although it represented a good beginning, it did not go far enough, probably referring to the fact that the British government has undertaken a program based on common law damages.

Considerations of flexibility and experimentation prompted the English lawmakers to place the compensation program under the jurisdiction of a Criminal Injuries Compensation Board, which is appointed by the Home Secretary and is regarded as a judicial or quasi-judicial body.

The "need of the victim" is the crucial issue in the "social welfare" approach to the understanding of victim compensation, and apparently this has been the guiding idea of the California system, in which the operation of indemnification was initially placed in the hands of the

State Welfare Department.[5] The California statute does not even use the terms "compensation" or "restitution" but "aid." The family of any person killed and any victim who is incapacitated as the result of a crime of violence, and his family (if any), receive "aid" but only if financial need can be established. Such a program is subject to criticism through its implication that only people in need suffer the pains and disadvantages of a physical injury and that violent crimes affecting persons in an income group above the poverty level do not establish the justification of remedy. Furthermore, as Gilbert Geis has pointed out, the "need of the victim" principle tends to identify such law "in the public mind with charity rather than with legitimate payment of one's due."[6] Indeed, this approach to victim compensation is far removed from the original concept of "composition."

The Commonwealth of Massachusetts, in its "Act to Provide for the Compensation of Victims of Violent Crimes,"[7] ruled that cases of compensation should be determined by the district courts, thereby acknowledging the responsibility of the state. The moral and historical justification for making the courts responsible for the operation of the compensation system is found in the spirit of the statement of Massachusetts' founding fathers in the Declaration of Rights in the state's constitution, which makes clear the right of every subject of the Commonwealth "to find a certain remedy by having recourse to the laws for all injuries or wrongs." It has been asserted that questions of victim compensation "involve a broad consideration of more intangible social and ethical factors," and that "the courts are most expert" here[8]—an expertness derived from years of training in the traditions of the common law which has served so well whenever fundamentals of fact-finding and adjudication are involved. The common law courts of today, it was argued, attune themselves more closely to the convictions of the present than to the convictions of the past, and recognize the necessity

---

[5] Cal. Stat. Ch. 1549, An act to add Section 1500.02 to the Welfare and Institutions Code and to add Section 11211 to Division 9 of the Welfare and Institutions Code as proposed by Assembly Bill No. 1682, relating to aid to families with dependent children (passed by the Assembly, June 17, 1965); *Department Bulletin,* State of California, Health and Welfare Agency, No. 648 (Sacramento, December 8, 1965), Ch. I.

[6] Gilbert Geis, "Experimental Design and the Law: A Prospectus for Research on Victim-Compensation in California," *California Western Law Review,* Spring 1966, 2:85.

[7] The Commonwealth of Massachusetts, *Acts and Resolves, 1967,* Chap. 852 (approved January 2, 1968), General Laws, Chap. 258A; also see *Report* (Mass.), *op. cit.,* pp. 15–32.

[8] *Report* (Mass.), *op. cit.,* p. 16.

of considering contemporary social, industrial, and political conditions. As the Massachusetts Special Commission stated, "law as developed in our common law courts today is something created with the interests of society in mind, through which the individual can find a means of securing his interest, so far as society recognizes them."[9] Unlike California law the Massachusetts statute allows all citizens protection regardless of class or need.

It is clearly seen that the present general view and the American trend is leaning toward what is meant by "compensation": no matter what the cause of the loss or the injury may be, the claim for compensation, even though the result of a crime, is considered a civil matter only and is divorced from the disposition of the criminal case and correctional action against the offender. At present the majority of legal provisions in force (even those born in the era of newly developed understanding for the victim and his loss) and almost all planning for future law calls for compensation based on the principle of distinguishing between criminal and civil wrong. However, a proper consideration of the place of compensation or restitution in our norm-system calls for more than speculation about the elusive boundary between criminal and civil law: it demands an understanding of how the functional relationship between the offender and the restitution to his victim may activate reformative, corrective, and rehabilitative goals in penal law.

The proposal that the offender should, by his own work, compensate for the damage he has caused—which is the essential idea of correctional restitution—has a long history. As early as the sixteenth century Sir Thomas More, in *Utopia,* proposed restitution "to the right owner, and not, as they do in other lands, to the king." Herbert Spencer's suggestion of restitution through prison work,[10] Raffaele Garofalo's idea of confiscating the offender's property,[11] Prins and Garofalo's effort to balance the burden of fines and restitution between the rich and the poor,[12] Kathleen Smith's recommendation of the "self-determinate prison sentence,"[13] and others, are well known in literature. In fact however

[9] *Ibid.,* pp. 16–17.
[10] Herbert Spencer, *Essais de morale de science et d'esthétique: Essais de politique, II.* (4th ed., Paris, 1898), VIII, "Morale de la prison," p. 352.
[11] Raffaele Garofalo, *Criminology,* trans. R. W. Millar (Boston, 1914), pp. 419–435.
[12] *The Paris Prison Congress, 1895,* Summary Report (London, n.d.); Samuel J. Barrows, *The Sixth International Congress. Brussels, 1900. Report of Its Proceedings and Conclusions* (Washington, 1903), p. 52.
[13] Kathleen J. Smith, *A Cure for Crime: The Case for the Self-Determinate Prison Sentence* (London, 1965).

it is something to debate and work for. As an extended concept of compensation, correctional restitution is something the offender must perform himself and not something done for or to him. In this respect it goes a significant step further than compensation, for while both compensation and restitution involve a payment of some kind to the victim, correctional restitution requires the offender to maintain a relationship with the person whom he made his victim until such time after the crime as the victim's condition has been restored to the fullest extent possible. It is during this act of restitution by the wrong-doer to his victim that reformative and rehabilitative goals can hopefully be achieved. Our modern understanding of the criminal-victim relationship demands new programs. Correctional restitution holds a threefold promise in that it compensates the victim, relieves the state of some burden of responsibility, and permits the offender to pay his debt to society and to his victim. As such it makes a contribution to the reformative and corrective goals of criminal law.

PART FIVE

DEVELOPMENTS IN VICTIM COMPENSATION TO 1970

22

NEW ZEALAND

"THE South Pacific country of New Zealand has since the end of the nineteenth century enjoyed a reputation for advanced legislation in social matters."[1] One of the examples of this distinctive legislative trend is the New Zealand Act "to provide for the compensation of persons injured by certain criminal acts, and of dependents of persons killed by such acts,"[2] known as "Criminal Injuries Compensation Act 1963." This act which came into force on January 1, 1964 was based on the philosophy "rather the community's duty towards those who suffer misfortune than the liability of the state for failing to prevent crime."[3]

To implement this act a Crimes Compensation Tribunal, consisting of three members, was appointed for a term of five years by the Governor General (on the recommendation of the Minister of Justice). It is stipulated that the chairman of the tribunal be a lawyer of the supreme court with not less than seven years' practice.

The New Zealand tribunal is a "Commission of Inquiry" whose chairman is given the power to issue summonses requiring witnesses to appear before the tribunal or requiring the production of documents, or to take any other action preliminary or incidental to the hearing of any matter of compensation. When an application is made, the tribunal fixes a time and place for the hearing, receives the evidence, and concludes the hearing with an "order." There is no appeal against any decision by the tribunal. The tribunal has power to award compensation in cases in which a person is injured or killed by any of the following criminal acts:

> completed or attempted rape
> sexual intercourse or indecency with a girl under 12
> indecent assault on a girl between 12 and 16, or on a woman,
>> or on a boy, or on a man
> completed or attempted murder or manslaughter

---

[1] Bruce J. Cameron, "Compensation for Victims of Crime: The New Zealand Experiment," *Journal of Public Law*, 12 (1963), p. 367.
[2] Criminal Injuries Compensation Act, 1963. No. 134, October 25, 1963.
[3] New Zealand Parliamentary Debate, 1865; as quoted in Cameron, *op. cit.* p. 370.

wounding with intent
injuring with intent or by unlawful act
aggravated assault, wounding, or injury
assault with intent to injure
assault on a child or by a male on a female
common assault
disabling
discharging a firearm or doing a dangerous act with intent
acid throwing
poisoning with intent
infecting with disease
endangering transport
abduction of a woman or a girl
kidnapping

In determining whether to order compensation for a victim or his dependents, the tribunal concerns itself with all matters that it considers relevant in any particular case, such as the offender's age, mental capacity, sobriety, or statutory competence, and any behavior on the part of the victim that directly or indirectly contributed to his injury or death. In taking into account the victim's behavior, the New Zealand legislation opened the way to the legal consideration of victim-precipitated crimes. The law defines "injury" as actual bodily harm, pregnancy, and mental or nervous shock.[4]

Compensation under the New Zealand Act can be awarded for expenses, pecuniary loss, and pain and suffering of the victim. The amount of compensation is left entirely to the discretion of the tribunal and may be made either as a lump-sum payment or periodic payments. The orders of the tribunal are restricted to personal injuries; no compensation can be made for loss or damage to property.

In the first four and a half years after the law's enactment the number of claims filed was small (57) and the sum of the awards did not exceed the amount allocated for the program for the first year. The following table shows the nature of offenses involved for the first two years and the amounts of the awards (in New Zealand pounds):[5]

[4] Criminal Injuries Compensation Act, 1963, Arts. 2, 4, 10–16, 17 and Sched. 18–19.
[5] *Report on Operation of the Criminal Injuries Compensation Act 1963, to December 31, 1965;* in personal communication from J. I. Robson, Secretary for Justice, Wellington, January 20, 1966.

First year, 1964 (seven awards)

Rape of elderly woman by intruder in home	£ 240
Assault against elderly woman in home	96
Assault with intent to rob elderly woman in home	88
Compensation to mother of victim killed in assault by a group of youths	56
Common assault	37
Provoked assault resulting in serious injury	482
Assault on taxi driver	43
	£ 1,042

Second year, 1965 (nine awards)

Common assault in street	£ 12
Boy shot with airgun by another boy, resulting in loss of sight in one eye	674
Assault and robbery of elderly man in public toilet	71
Common assault in street	119
Assault with indecent intent on young woman in street	64
Common assault	147
Common assault	85
Common assault	300
Common assault	127
	£ 1,599

In many of these cases the question of provocation had to be considered, often requiring the examination of public and court documents.[6]

The New Zealand Act provides for recovery from the offender of amounts paid to the victim. In effect, the state compensates the latter and endeavors to collect from the former, taking into account his income and family responsibilities.[7] During the first two years the tribunal issued five orders for repayment, but collection has yet to be effected.

As the Ministry of Justice of New Zealand reported, the act has not been used as much as had been expected. Its cost to the taxpayer has therefore been small. No unexpected difficulties have been encountered in the operation of the law, and the government is considering the extension of the compensation scheme, first of all to cases in which

---

[6] *Ibid.,* p. 1.
[7] Criminal Injuries Compensation Act, 1963, Arts. 23–26.

escaped prisoners cause harm or injury.[8]

In 1967 the so-called Woodhouse Report[9] challenged the merit of the compensation program then in force in New Zealand and proposed a unified program whereby all injured persons, regardless of cause of injury and regardless of fault, would receive benefits. The proposals of the Report have been debated, with no action taken on it to date.

[8] *Report, op. cit.,* p. 2.
[9] Royal Compensation for Personal Injury in New Zealand. Report of the Commission of Inquiry (Arthur Oliver Woodhouse, Herbert Bockett and Geoffrey Parsons, members).

23

UNITED KINGDOM

In England the concept of restitution to victims of crime has been recognized as an old one, yet "the idea that the victims of crimes should be compensated by state action is comparatively recent."[1] Although other countries had preceded England in taking legislative action on victim compensation, England (together with Wales and Scotland) will no doubt·be remembered as the pioneer in emphasizing the idea in our present-day penal systems. England's compensation scheme has developed "not because the state is under a legal liability to pay," but because it was felt "that provision should be made for victims of crimes of violence"[2]—a sort of social obligation arising from considerations of public policy and perhaps regarded as an extension of the welfare system.

The English scheme is based on two fundamental points. The first is that claims for compensation "should be determined by a judicial or quasi-judicial body." The second is that claims should be "payable only in deserving cases"—"the victim of a crime of violence should not be entitled automatically to compensation." The latter point takes into account whether "the victim himself was partly to blame."[3]

The British government has "decided on a scheme based on common law damages rather than on the Industrial Injuries Scheme."[4] The program "represents a hesitant step in the right direction."[5] Only *ex gratia* payments are designated, it being considered "best to start with a flexible scheme which can be altered in the light of experience,"[6] in other words, in an experimental and non-statutory form. "While no one suggested that the State 'was' responsible for the victim's misfortune, it was generally agreed, that the State 'should' accept responsibility."[7]

[1] Henry Brooke, Home Secretary (in the debate in the House of Commons), *Hansard*, Vol. 694, No. 103, col. 1127.
[2] Lord Dilhorne, Lord Chancellor (in the debate in the House of Lords), *Hansard*, Vol. 257, No. 72, col. 1354.
[3] Brooke, *op. cit.*, col. 1128.
[4] *Ibid.*, col. 1132.
[5] Reg. E. Prentice (in the debate in the House of Commons), *Hansard*, Vol. 694, No. 103, col. 1187.
[6] Home Office, Compensation for Victims of Crimes of Violence, Cmnd. No. 2323 (1964).
[7] Bernard W. M. Downey, "Compensating Victims of Violent Crime," *British Journal of Criminology*, Vol. 5, No. 1 (July 1964).

Indeed, "if society, by its indifference to those things which inculcate proper behavior, continues to make its contribution to the breeding of criminals, it must accept a large measure of responsibility for the consequences of criminal acts."[8]

The British compensation scheme is administered by a body known as the Criminal Injuries Compensation Board, which is appointed by the Home Secretary (in Scotland by the Secretary of State for Scotland) after consultation with the Lord Chancellor. It is required that the chairman of the board be a person of wide legal experience and the other members also be legally qualified. The board is completely responsible for deciding how much compensation should be paid in individual cases, and its decisions are not subject to appeal or ministerial review.

The board entertains applications for *ex gratio* payments of compensation in cases where personal injury is directly attributable to:

a criminal offense

an arrest or an attempted arrest of an offender or a
        suspected offender

the prevention or attempted prevention of an offense

helping any constable who is engaged in arresting or
        attempting to arrest an offender or suspected offender,
        or who is engaged in preventing or attempting to
        prevent an offense

If the injury causes at least three weeks' loss of earnings, or if it is an injury for which not less than £50 (about $120) compensation would be awarded, the circumstances of the injury are reported to the police without delay or become the subject of criminal court proceedings, and the applicant submits himself to a medical examination.

In cases of rape or sexual assault, the board considers applications for compensation with respect to pain, suffering, and shock, and also with respect to loss of earnings due to pregnancy resulting from rape. But compensation is not payable for the maintenance of any child born as a result of a sexual offense. Also excluded from compensation are offenses committed against a member of the offender's family who is living with him, as well as motoring offenses (except where the motor vehicle has been used as a weapon).

The board considers whether, because of provocation or otherwise, the victim has any share in the responsibility for the crime. In accord-

---

[8] Bishop of Chester (in the debate in the House of Lords), *Hansard,* Vol. 245, col. 269. Cited in Downey, *op. cit.*

ance with its assessment of the degree of responsibility, the board will reduce the amount of compensation or reject the claim altogether.

The scheme excludes "double compensation." The criminally injured person is not permitted to have both compensation granted by the board and an award obtained through an ordinary common law claim.[9]

Although no traditional type of appeal is open to the applicant, the scheme provides for a special review of cases which can be initiated by either the applicant or a board member.

In the normal procedure an applicant who complains of the initial decision of one of the board members is given a hearing before the "Appellate Tribunal," which consists of three members of the board exclusive of the member who made the initial decision.

Similarly, if a board member feels that he cannot reach a "just and proper" decision on a case he too can refer the application to the Appellate Tribunal.[10]

The Criminal Injuries Compensation Board, after being in existence for only eight months, released its first interim report[11] without commenting on the cases before it. A later report of the Board[12] summarized some of the cases disposed of by the end of 1965. It noted that 2,216 applications were submitted to the Board in this seventeen-month period, of which only 1,184 were settled, for a total of £304,643 (about $731,150). A majority of the cases closed were settled by a single member of the Board; only thirty-two cases went to hearings before the Appellate Tribunal, of which only nineteen had been requested by applicants dissatisfied with the one-member decision.

Following are selected cases in brief:

A woman, 59, assaulted and hospitalized for two months, received compensation of £582 (about $1,340). A woman, 33, absent from work four months due to injuries sustained when attacked by her knife-wielding estranged husband was awarded £500 (about $1,200). A girl, 14, struck with a chopper by a boy, 12, received £225 (about $612). A woman, 67, who suffered permanent incapacitating effects

[9] *The Scheme,* official publication of the Home Office, amended in August 1965, paras. 1, 4–7, 12, 20.
[10] *Ibid.,* revised para. 17; "Notes on Procedure," Criminal Injuries Compensation Board, Hearings Before Three Members of the Board, C.I.C.B. 14, para. 1 (1) *et seq;* "Notes on Procedure," Criminal Injuries Compensation Board, letter of the Home Office, January 18, 1966.
[11] Home Office, Criminal Injuries Compensation Board, First Report and Accounts, Cmnd. No. 2782 (1965).
[12] Home Office, December 31, 1965. Mimeographed.

from an attack in which she was raped, was awarded £2,020 (about $4,850). A girl, 7, indecently assaulted, received £251 (about $602). A male bus conductor, 26, assaulted by youths refusing to pay the fare and incapacitated for ten weeks, received £368 (about $884).

In another case a male storehouse caretaker, 29, was deliberately run down by thieves whom he attempted to prevent from escaping after surprising them. He was awarded £225 (about $540.) A boy, 7, suffering permanent eye damage as a result of an airgun pellet fired by an older youth was awarded £2,250 (about $5,400). A boy, 17, kicked and stabbed by a gang of youths, suffered a permanently weakened grip of the right hand and an impaired function of the left hand. He received £773 (about $1,855). A woman, 60, was granted a retirement pension of £4.0.6d (about $10) a week as the widow of a man, 60, whose death from a skull fracture was directly attributed to an assault by a stranger.

In some other cases the awards sought were reduced or completely disallowed. A reduction by 50 percent of the compensation applied for was decided in a case in which the victim, under the influence of alcohol, provoked the person who struck him. In another case the responsibility of a victim who was shot in the face during a dispute over shooting rights on farmland was assessed at ten percent. No award was given to a man of 57 cut by glass from a shop window that had been broken by another man during a struggle to hold a suspect until the police arrived (the suspect was charged). In this case the Board was not satisfied that the injury was directly attributable to a criminal offense. No award was granted to a man, 24, who was stabbed by his mother-in-law, with whom he and his wife shared an apartment. The application was denied because an offense had been committed against a member of the assailant's family while all were living together. In another case the Appellate Tribunal dismissed the application because the circumstances of the injury had not been reported to the police as required by the regulations.[13]

The number of applications and awarded compensatory payments is proportionately much higher in the United Kingdom than in New Zealand. Only further research into comparative crime rates and other factors can explain this disparity, and future developments will be awaited with interest.

[13] *Ibid.,* pp. 1–9.

24

UNITED STATES

THE ACADEMIC FORUM

IN addition to legislative efforts and experiments in various parts of the world, the academic platform has been used to urge restitution or compensation to victims of crime. In December 1964, five years after the pioneering discussion of the "Round Table" symposium in the *Journal of Public Law,*[1] the American Society of Criminology devoted a full meeting in Montreal to the subject.[2] At this meeting Gerhard O. W. Mueller and John Edwards made general recommendations; Robert Childres discussed the question of personal injury; James Starrs suggested that compensation for victims of crime be considered as part of the general problem of insurance law. Marvin Wolfgang and Stephen Schafer presented their views as outlined below.

Wolfgang, supporting the principle that society has a responsibility to compensate the victim of a criminal assault, suggested that if state compensation to the victim is adopted as a logical extension of the concern of criminal law for both parties in a two-person crime of personal violence, then some system for measuring harm is required, and some standard of, and system for, judging the degree of harm must be established. His research with Thorsten Sellin on the measurement of delinquency was offered toward this end, whereby crimes against the person and against property could be reduced to a unidimensional base and a means provided for grading the seriousness of offenses. He states, "If there is a virtue in establishing a state system of victim compensation, there should be a virtue in exploring the dimensions of the relationship between money values and physical harm beyond the arbitrary notions of a legislative committee."

Schafer supported the concept of offender-liability or the idea that while compensation to the victim of crime should be the personal responsibility of the offender it is but one part of a two-fold correc-

---

[1] "Compensation for Victims of Criminal Violence, A Round Table," *Journal of Public Law,* 8, no. 1 (1959), pp. 191–253.
[2] Joint Congress of the American Academy for the Advancement of Sciences and the American and Canadian Societies of Criminology, A Panel Discussion, Montreal, December 1964.

tional process. In terms of correctional restitution to a victim of crime, the offender understands that he has done injury not only to the state but also to the victim. From this viewpoint restitution not only makes good the injury or loss to the victim but at the same time helps in the correction, reform and rehabilitation of the offender. Correctional restitution could be a part of a more comprehensive concept of punishment; a response of criminal justice to the functional responsibility of the criminal.

The efforts of the American Society of Criminology in renewing the interest in victim compensation were effective within and without the legal profession. The almost forgotten problem of restitution to victims of crime "made its appearance on the post-midnight radio talkathons, in the popular magazines and the Sunday supplements. The very question—why not pay the victim of crime?—seems appealing to anyone with a social conscience."[3]

In December, 1965 the *Minnesota Law Review* published "An Examination of the Scope of the Problem," a symposium which concerned itself with the subject of compensation to victims of crimes of personal violence. The editorial introduction put forward the hope that the contributions would stimulate "further study and eventual solution of this topical issue."[4]

Of the contributors, Gerhard O. W. Mueller stated that the primary purpose of the symposium was "to circumscribe the grand outlines of the problem in an attempt to direct subsequent research and ultimate sociopolitical action." He attempted to clarify the concept of victim compensation and seemed to accept "in the sense of payments by a government agency to persons injured by a criminal agency" as a clear statement. He wondered how much compensation would cost and suggested that "if the Government wants to parallel the operations of a private insurance enterprise," the total cost of the administration of criminal justice should be taken into account, the difficulty being to determine this figure. Aware of the great obstacles that stand in the way of victim compensation schemes, he still hoped for an advance "from

[3] Gerhard O. W. Mueller, "Compensation for Victims of Crime: Thought Before Action," *Minnesota Law Review* 50 (December, 1965), p. 213.

[4] Gerhard O. W. Mueller, Marvin E. Wolfgang, Stephen Schafer, Ralph W. Yarborough, Robert D. Childres, and James E. Starrs, "Compensation to Victims of Crimes of Personal Violence: An Examination of the Scope of the Problem, A Symposium," *Minnesota Law Review, op. cit.,* p. 212.

research thought to research action, and ultimately, to implementation."[5]

Marvin Wolfgang continued his earlier support of the principle that society has a responsibility to compensate the victims of violent crimes. He suggested that "the federal and various states workmen's compensation laws provide a useful analogy and contemporary precedent for the proposal of victim compensation." He also proposed "some system for measuring harm,"[6] and repeated his recommendation of the "measurement of delinquency." He viewed the victim as a contributing and supporting member of a society "which has failed to protect him against certain types of crime;" consequently .that society should "undertake the obligation to compensate the victim of a criminal assault."[7]

Stephen Schafer coupled his concern for the victim with an examination of the restitutive effect a compensation system can have on the offender. He proposed that the criminal be considered as a member of his cultural group, and that his crime be viewed in terms of his social relationships. He suggested that attention be directed to what he tentatively calls "the criminal's functional responsibility," rather than to the isolated criminal act. He recommended a scheme wherein the administrator of criminal justice would deal not with civil damages but with "correctional restitution" as a part of the sentence and thus a principle of the criminal law.

In developing his concept, Schafer pointed out that any modern system of correctional restitution should ideally make the offender aware that not only his victim but also the state and law and order have been injured by his act of violence. Schafer referred to his research on violent crimes: many offenders evidenced no guilt feelings and could neither understand nor accept their functional responsibility to society or to their victims. "Their understanding of incarceration seemed limited to what they viewed as merely a formal or normative wrong, which had to be paid for to the agencies of criminal justice, but to nobody else."[8]

Senator Ralph Yarborough analyzed his bill, S. 2155, which sought to provide victim compensation within Federal jurisdiction. He suggested that "the idea is so simple and just that its novelty makes less of

---

[5] Mueller, "Compensation for Victims of Crime: Thought Before Action, *op. cit.*, pp. 214, 215, 218, 221.

[6] Marvin E. Wolfgang, "Victim Compensation in Crimes of Personal Violence," *Minnesota Law Review, op. cit., pp.* 230, 234.

[7] *Ibid.*, pp. 240–241.

[8] Stephen Schafer, "Restitution to Victims of Crime—An Old Correctional Aim Modernized," *Minnesota Law Review, op. cit.,* pp. 245, 249, 251, 254.

a first impression than regret that the idea has not been previously adopted." He viewed the victim of crime as one neglected and recognized the duty of the state to award compensation. He stated that "in view of the many social welfare programs that are in operation, the failure to recognize the special claims of this group seems to be a gross oversight."[9]

Robert Childres commented upon the Yarborough bill as having "unfortunate omissions." Apropos the California legislation, he suggested that the state's welfare department would not be able to mold its statute into a workable program. He criticized Mueller's and Schafer's approach to restitution while avoiding a discussion of the underlying concept of the criminal-victim relationship. Concerning himself more with formalistic questions than with theoretical difficulties, he considered the matter of federal-state relationships and suggested that the proposed reform would not "provoke fears of bureaucratic monsters."[10] He regarded fraudulent claims as a marginal problem.

James Starrs discussed the possibility of a victim compensation program run by private insurance companies. Although he expressed little doubt about the necessity of state compensation programs, he believed more would be done if "insurance companies assumed a greater share of the cost of crime." He stated that since most compensation programs rarely paid full damages an insurance program would best achieve "payments more commensurate with the losses actually sustained by crime victims." In his thinking, "private insurance plans need no defenders," and although some persons would reject the advantages of the flexibility and variability of these policies "that is no reason for haste in governmental intervention." Starrs referred to the California legislation in supporting his contention that "the thrust of proposals for state compensation is predicated upon the indigency or irresponsibility of some crime victims."[11]

In addition to a great number of articles in professional journals the issue of victim compensation was placed on the program of the National Violence Commission and in Spring 1970, the *Southern California Law Review* published a Symposium[12] with Arthur J. Goldberg,

---

[9] Ralph W. Yarborough, "S. 2155 of the Eighty-Ninth Congress, The Criminal Injuries Compensation Act," *Minnesota Law Review, op. cit.,* pp. 255–256.
[10] Robert Childres, "Compensation for Criminally Inflicted Personal Injury," *Minnesota Law Review, op. cit.,* pp. 278, 281–282.
[11] James E. Starrs, "A Modest Proposal to Insure Justice for Victims of Crime," *Minnesota Law Review, op. cit.,* pp. 305, 309–310.
[12] "Symposium: Governmental Compensation for Victims of Violence," *Southern California Law Review,* 43, no. 1 (1970).

Marvin E. Wolfgang, LeRoy L. Lamborn, Stephen Schafer, Duncan Chappell, Willard A. Shank, Ralph W. Yarborough, and Kent M. Weeks the participants.

Arthur J. Goldberg, in the Preface to the Symposium, gave another emphasis to the justification of compensation by stating that treating victims of crime with the same consideration as victims of floods and hurricanes "is especially appropriate in the light of the responsibility which society must bear for the crime itself. Crime is, after all, a sociological and economic problem as well as a problem of individual criminality." He concluded "what the equal protection clause of the Constitution does not command it may still inspire." [13]

Marvin E. Wolfgang discussed the "societal responsibility for violent behavior." He traced the etiology of violence through the socialization process to the causes of riots in the streets and unrest on the campuses. Wolfgang contended that our youth learn and accept violence within our culture "as a concomitant of everyday social intercourse and an instrument of political action." [14] He discussed "legitimate violence," masculine images and mass advertising, and the forces that generate crime and riots in the ghettos: "in everyday life, men witness the display of violence in an abundance of styles" [15] which will encourage him to accept its use by others and to employ it himself.

LeRoy L. Lamborn examined the various remedies available to a victim of crime. Citing "absorption by the victim," whereby the victim ignores the possibility of compensation or restitution as a remedy "by default," [16] he proceeded to evaluate restitution by the criminal, civil action by the victim against the criminal, and compensation by society in the form of charity, insurance and welfare programs. He detailed the extent to which any of these programs are realistically able to meet the needs of those injured and concluded that all the programs suffer from some inherent defect which limits their effectiveness. Lamborn concluded by stating "a comparative evaluation of the various remedies has not been attempted," although "each at least partially fills a certain social need." [17]

---

[13] Arthur J. Goldberg, "Preface," *Southern California Law Review, op. cit.,* pp. 1–3.
[14] Marvin E. Wolfgang, "Social Responsibility for Violent Behavior," *Southern California Law Review, op. cit.,* p. 5.
[15] *Ibid.,* p. 21.
[16] LeRoy L. Lamborn, "Remedies for the Victims of Crime," *Southern California Law Review, op. cit.,* p. 26.
[17] *Ibid.,* p. 53.

Stephen Schafer discussed the problem of victim compensation both historically and from the point of view of the offender's responsibility. He reflected on the ancient origins of compensation and restitution which ordered restitution to the victim "as part of the obligation of the criminal"[18] and the genesis of modern compensation programs. By having the fine entirely appropriated by the state the corrective balance between the wrongdoer's debt to society and his responsibility to his victim is weakened. Schafer again called attention to the "case for correctional restitution"[19] which holds the promise of both restitution to the victim of crime and implementation of reformative and corrective goals in the criminal law.

Duncan Chappell gave an account of the emergence of various Australian schemes to compensate the victims of crime all of which gained impetus after New Zealand and the United Kingdom enacted compensation schemes in 1963 and 1964 respectively. Although there were existing statutory provisions in two Australian states providing for partial victim compensation, in 1967 New South Wales became the first state in Australia to introduce a comprehensive compensation system in its modern sense. In December 1968 Queensland followed suit and enacted a victim compensation scheme modeled after that of New South Wales.

Compensation under both systems is awarded for injuries listed in the New South Wales Crimes Act and the Queensland Criminal Code, including pregnancy, mental shock and nervous shock. Victim precipitation of crime is taken into consideration when compensation awards are made. Chappell suggested that in view of the limited experience not too many inferences could be drawn concerning the operational efficiency of these programs. He pointed out that by combining the criminal trial with a determination of the victim's compensation the Australian scheme resulted in a confusion that "not only jeopardizes the accused's right to a speedy and impartial trial, but also delays compensation to the victim, who may be in a poor position to absorb the loss, even temporarily."[20]

Willard Shank described the California compensation program and analyzed the difficulty of reconciling victim compensation with the phi-

---

[18] Stephen Schafer, "Victim Compensation and Responsibility," *Southern California Law Review, op. cit.,* p. 55.
[19] *Ibid.,* pp. 65–67.
[20] Duncan Chappell, "The Emergence of Australian Schemes to Compensate Victims of Crime," *Southern California Law Review, op. cit.,* p. 82.

losophy of welfare.[21] He recognized the California program was still evolving, and made only limited comments, speculative in nature, on the limited number of cases available for analysis. Yet, he suggested, some changes have to be made if the California law is to achieve its objectives.[22]

Ralph W. Yarborough described his effort to achieve the passage of a Federal violent crimes compensation act, and renewed his call for a national program. He claimed that "as long as society continues to assume the task of preventing anti-social behavior, society will continue to owe some obligation (be it moral or legal) to the victims of crime."[23]

Kent M. Weeks discussed the New Zealand Criminal Injuries Compensation Scheme, the first victim compensation legislation in our time. He examined the recommendations of the Royal Commission to Inquire Into and Report Upon Workers' Compensation, which was established to study the inadequacy of the workers' compensation benefits, to determine how the program interacts with other similar programs such as compensation to victims of crime.[24]

AMERICAN COMPENSATION SYSTEMS

California

During the 1965 session of the California legislature, a law was enacted which provided compensatory financial assistance to victims of crimes of violence.[25] This was the first such law of its kind in the United States and was unique in that no board was created to administer the program. Arthur J. Goldberg praised it as "beneficial legislation" and hoped the example would be followed "throughout the country."[26] Robert Childres felt "the quality of the reform fails to meet the spirit."[27]

---

[21] Willard Shank, "Aid to Victims of Violent Crimes in California," *Southern California Law Review, op. cit.,* p. 85.
[22] *Ibid.,* p. 92.
[23] Ralph W. Yarborough, "The Battle for a Federal Violent Crimes Compensation Act: The Genesis of S. 9," *Southern California Law Review, op cit.,* p. 99.
[24] Kent M. Weeks, "The New Zealand Criminal Injuries Compensation Scheme," *Southern California Law Review, op. cit.,* p. 116.
[25] Cal. Stat. Ch. 1549, An act to add Section 1500.02 to the Welfare and Institutions Code and to add Section 11211 to Division 9 of the Welfare and Institutions Code as proposed by Assembly Bill No. 1682, relating to aid to families with dependent children; passed by the Assembly June 17, 1965. (The full text of the present California statute and other state and federal statutes is given in the Appendix.)
[26] *The New York Times,* 24 July 1965.
[27] Childres, *op. cit.,* p. 279.

The law itself left a number of criteria open to later decisions, many of which found an answer in an interpretative bulletin,[28] issued a few months after Governor Brown signed the bill into law. Most importantly, it should be noted that neither the law nor the bulletin uses the terms "compensation" or "restitution;" rather "aid" is to be paid to the family of any person killed and to the victim and family, if any, of any person incapacitated as the result of a crime of violence," and then only "if there is need of such aid."[29] This may be the reason the State Welfare Department was initially responsible for the administration of the law. (The program was removed to the State Board of Control in 1967.) The criteria for payment was substantially the same as those established for families with dependent children with the exception that "aid" was paid regardless of whether or not the applicant met the property qualifications prescribed for families with dependent children. For the fiscal year 1965-1966 the maximum aid any one victim might receive was placed at $100,000.

In the California law the definition of "crime of violence" is given as an act intended to do bodily harm to another. A child of the victim is eligible for aid if the victim was a resident of California, the crime was committed in California, and if the application for aid is made within five years from the date of the crime.[30] A reinvestigation can be made not later than six months from the last investigation.[31]

As of the summer of 1969 the State Board of Control had received a total of 508 claims. Of these 70 had been allowed, 189 denied, and 249 were still pending. Two claimants filed suits challenging the Board's decision. Both cases were dismissed.

The limited number of claims thus far received makes generalizations about the program too speculative. The current statute provides for attorney's fees not in excess of ten percent of the compensation awarded the victim.

New York

New York legislators gave attention to the idea of victim compensation in apparant reaction to the rising rate of violent crime. The subway murder in 1965 of Arthur Collins was one of the cases that aroused

[28] *Department Bulletin,* State of California, Health and Welfare Agency No. 648, Sacramento, December 8, 1965, Chs. 2–8.
[29] Cal. Stat. Ch. 1549, *op. cit.,* Section I, Section 1500.02.
[30] *Department Bulletin, op. cit.,* Ch. 4.
[31] *Ibid.,* Ch. 6.

interest in a law to compensate victims of crime. While jurists argued the merits of one scheme or another, Governor Rockefeller remarked that "the victims of violent crime are the forgotten men in our society."

In 1966 a Crime Victims Compensation Board, composed of three members, was appointed by the Governor. Consideration for indemnification was restricted to cases involving physical injury or death and to crimes that had been reported to the police within forty-eight hours of their occurrence.

Since the New York law compensates a victim of crime only in a case of serious financial hardship this again indicates the "matter of grace," rather than an assumption by the state of legal responsibility for the criminal loss suffered by the victim. The act became effective as of October 1, 1966; the appropriation for the first fiscal year was $500,000. Thus New York became the second state to compensate victims of crime.

Massachusetts

In 1968 Massachusetts introduced a compensation system which, like California and New York, extended aid only to those victims who suffered injury or harm from crimes which involved "the application of force or violence, or the threat of force or violence by the offender," excluding acts involving the operation of a motor vehicle.[32] Eligible for compensation are the victim, and in case of his death (if his death is the direct result of the crime) a dependent of the victim. An offender or an accomplice of an offender, a member of the family of the offender, a person living with the offender or a person maintaining sexual relations with the offender is in no case eligible to receive compensation with respect to a crime committed by the offender. These provisions insure that no one may benefit from a crime in which he may be indirectly involved.

Claims for compensation must be filed in a district court of the district in which the claimant lives. A time limit is imposed. The Attorney General, as a permanent participant in the case, has the authority to investigate the claim. Should the claimant be represented by counsel, said counsel's fee cannot exceed fifteen percent of any compensation

---

[32] The Commonwealth of Massachusetts, *Acts and Resolves,* 1967, Ch. 852 approved January 2, 1968), General Laws, Ch. 258A; also see *Report,* The Special Commission on the Compensation of Victims of Violent Crimes, The Commonwealth of Massachusetts, House, No. 5151 (Boston, July 1967).

awarded. The Massachusetts law takes into account the extent and nature of the victim's contribution to the infliction of his injury. Additionally, no compensation is paid unless the claimant has lost two weeks of earnings or support or incurred a loss of one hundred dollars. Compensation cannot exceed ten thousand dollars, and has to be reduced by the sum of any payments received by the claimant as a result of the injury by the offender from insurance programs or public funds. Double compensation is not allowable. By awarding compensation, the state steps into the legal shoes of the victim of crime and has the right of action to recover payments for losses resulting from the crime for which compensation was granted.

How far the Massachusetts system will succeed remains to be seen. After approximately one year of operation only two of thirty-five claims filed were concluded (a robbery case and an assault and battery case, both resulting in compensation being award to the victims).

Hawaii

Hawaii, in 1967, introduced legislation on criminal injuries compensation.[33] A three-man commission board is placed within the department of social services for administrative purposes, with annual reports submitted to the governor and the director of finance. Payment to the commission members is on a *per diem* basis plus traveling and subsistence expenses.

The commission's powers are similar to those of its counterpart under the English compensation scheme. It arranges the hearing, has powers of subpoena and compulsion of attendance of witnesses, can order medical examinations, etc., and in general can do everything necessary in order to reach a fair decision. The commission's decision can be subject to judicial review through appeal by "any person aggrieved by a final order" to the Supreme Court.

Crimes for which compensation may be awarded are arson, intermediate and aggravated assault or battery, use of dangerous substances, murder, manslaughter, kidnapping, child-stealing, unlawful use of explosives, sexual intercourse with a female under sixteen, assault with intent to rape or ravish, indecent assault, carnal abuse of a female under twelve, rape, and attempted rape. No compensation is to be awarded in excess of $10,000. Attorney's fees may not exceed fifteen percent of the award.

[33] Criminal Injuries Compensation. Ch. 351, 1967, c. 226, pt. of para. 1.

Provisions are made for the recovery of compensation from the offender. Compensation is awarded primarily for pecuniary losses, but also for "pain and suffering to the victim."

Maryland

Maryland's "criminal injuries compensation act" was enacted in 1968.[34] Again, following the British example, a Criminal Injuries Compensation Board has been created for settling compensatory claims. The Board has three members, all appointed by the governor with the advice and consent of the Senate. One member must be a lawyer practicing for not less than five years. In the composition of the Board it is interesting to recognize a political aspect not seen in any other legislation on compensation to victims of crime: Maryland's law ordered that of the three members of the Board "no more than two (of whom) shall belong to the same political party."

The powers and duties of the Board are similar to those in other similar legislations: rather broad in order to reach all relevant facts for decision making. Not only direct victims of crime are eligible for awards, but also their dependents, and even those who are injured or killed while trying to prevent a crime. Decisions on claims can be made by a single Board member, or upon the application of the claimant by the full Board. After the final decision the Attorney General may commence a proceeding in the circuit court of the county or the Supreme Bench of Baltimore.

Prompt reporting of the crime to the police is a prerequisite of awarding compensation. Victim precipitation is considered, and the award can be reduced or rejected if the conduct of the victim contributed to the infliction of his injury.

The Yarborough Proposals

On June 17, 1965, Senator Ralph Yarborough, long an active advocate of legislation providing for a national victim-compensation program, introduced the first such legislation in Congress.[35] The bill cited the duty of the state to award compensation to the neglected victim of crime.[36]

---

[34] Criminal Injuries Compensation Act. Annotated Code, Article 26A, 1968, Ch. 455.   [35] S. 2155, 89th Cong., 1st Sess. (1965).
[36] Similar bills were subsequently introduced in the House of Representatives by Congresswoman Edith Green and Congressmen William D. Hathaway, Spark M. Matsugana, Jonathan B. Dingham and George E. Brown, Jr. *The New York Times,* 24 October 1965, p. 1.

(Coincidentally, the California Assembly passed its law on aid to victims of crime on the identical date.)

Senator Yarborough reintroduced comparable legislation in 1967[37] and again in 1969.[38] It is the present version of his bill, S. 9, which is pending before the Senate Committee on the Judiciary and the one examined here.

Yarborough's proposal would create a Federal Violent Crime Compensation Commission composed of three men appointed by the President, none of whom would be permitted to engage in any other business or employment, for terms of eight years. The necessary staff would be appointed by the Commission. Although the principal address of the Commission would be in or near the District of Columbia, it would be empowered to appoint a representative to act for it anywhere.

Compensation to a victim of a violent crime would not be dependent on the prosecution or conviction of the offender. Criminal intent on the part of the perpetrator would not be required for an award: it would be essential only that the violent crime complained of did occur and that death or injury did result. The Commission would be empowered to institute an action against the offender for the recovery of some or all of the compensation awarded. The maximum payment woud be $25,000, including attorney's fees set by the Commission. Double compensation would not be allowable. All orders and decisions of the Commission would be reviewable on appeal.

The Yarborough proposal, in part reminiscent of the New Zealand compensation scheme, limits the crime-range to offenses causing personal injury. It rejects an extension to property losses in view of its high cost and the probable protection by private insurance. Criminal acts compensable under this bill are listed by offenses, derived from the District of Columbia Code and the United States Code, and include every type of violent crime that might result in compensable injury.

On September 19, 1969, Senator Yarborough introduced in the 91st Congress a version of his bill which is to provide for the compensation of persons injured by certain criminal acts in the District of Columbia.[39] This Act (S. 2936) is cited as the District of Columbia Injuries Compensation Act and is substantially the same as S. 9 with some slight differences in the offenses to which it applies.

[37] S. 646, 90th Cong., 1st Sess. (1967).
[38] S. 9, 91st Cong., 1st Sess. (1969).
[39] S. 2936, 91st Cong., 1st Sess. (1969).

APPENDIX

SURVEY QUESTIONNAIRE

[This Questionnaire served only as a basic starting point for further investigation.]

1. Has the victim and/or his dependants a legal right to claim restitution and/or damages from the offender?

2. What are the offences to which this right applies?

3. What type of court has jurisdiction to entertain claims for restitution and/or damages and what are at least the essential points of this procedure? Is this type of court a criminal court and is the question of restitution and/or damages entertained within the scope of the criminal procedure, or is there an independent procedure?

4. What is the practice of the courts concerning a decision *in merito* and on what basis is the amount of damages ascertained?

5. Are damages restricted to compensation for financial loss, or do they also include compensation for moral damage?

6. Is the offender (a) allowed (b) compelled to work in prison? Is he paid for such work and if so, is he permitted to keep his earnings at his discretion? Are the prisoners' wages different from those paid to non-criminals and if so what is the difference?

7. Can the victim (or his dependants) have recourse to the prisoner's earnings? Against what assets can the victim (or his dependants) enforce his or their claim?

8. Has the performance or non-performance of restitution or damages any effect on the punishment awarded or on the earnings of the prisoner? If so, to what extent?

9. Are there any other rules concerning restitution?

10. In general, how does this institution work in practice?

UNITED STATES STATUTES
PROVIDING GOVERNMENTAL COMPENSATION
FOR VICTIMS OF VIOLENCE

California	*page*	164
Hawaii		170
Maryland		179
Massachusetts		187
New York		192
S.9 (Proposed Federal Bill)		200

STATE OF CALIFORNIA

CHAPTER 5

Government Code of California

INDEMNIFICATION OF PRIVATE CITIZENS[1]
ARTICLE 1. VICTIMS OF CRIME[2]

§ 13960.   Declaration of purpose

The Legislature hereby declares that it serves a public purpose, and is of benefit to the state, to indemnify those needy residents of the State of California who are victims of crimes committed in the State of California, and those needy domiciliaries of California who are injured as a consequence of an act committed while temporarily in another state or jurisdiction where such act, if committed in California, would have been a public offense, for the injuries suffered as a result of the commission of the crimes.
(Added Stats. 1967, c. 1546, p. 3707, § 1)

§ 13961.   Victim of crime defined

A victim of a crime as used in this chapter is any person who sustains injury to himself, or pecuniary loss as a result of physical injury or death of another person on whom he is financially dependent, and which is the consequence of an act considered to be a public offense, as defined by Penal Code Section 15, whether the actor is criminally liable or not.
(Added Stats. 1967, c. 1546, p. 3707, § 1.)

§ 13962.   Filing of claim; forms; time of presenting claim

(a)   The victim of a crime of violence, his family, or any persons dependent upon the victim for their support may file a claim with the State Board of Control, provided that the crime was committed in California and the applicant was a resident of California, or provided the claimant is a domiciliary of California who was injured while temporarily in another state or jurisdiction.

(b)   The State Board of Control shall provide indemnification claim forms for purposes of this section and shall specify the information to be included in such forms.

---

1.   This heading was amended by: Stats 1969, ch. 1431, § 1, ch. 1111, § 1. The original language was "Victims of Crime [New]".

2.   This article heading was added by: Stats 1969, ch. 1431, § 2, ch. 1111, § 2.

(c)   The claim must be presented by the claimant to the Board of Control within a period of one year after the date of death or injury and no claim not so presented shall be considered by the Board of Control.
(Added Stats. 1967, c. 1546, p. 3707, § 1)

§§ 13963.   Hearing; notice; report of attorney general; approval of claim; amount; attorney's fees; subrogation; intervention by state

Upon presentation of any such claim, the Board of Control shall fix a time and place for the hearing of the claim, and shall mail notices thereof to interested persons or agencies and to the Attorney General. Prior to the hearing, the Attorney General shall investigate the facts of each claim, including the claimant's financial condition, filed pursuant to this chapter, and prepare a report thereof. The Attorney General shall at the hearing submit to the board, and the board shall receive the report, together with any evidence which he may have obtained as a result of his investigation. At the hearing, the board shall receive evidence showing

(a)   The nature of the crime committed and the circumstances involved;

(b)   That as a direct consequence, the victim incurred personal injury;

(c)   The extent of such injury;

(d)   The need of the claimant;

(e)   Such other evidence as the board may require.

If the board determines, on the basis of a preponderance of such evidence, that the state should indemnify the claimant for the injury sustained, it shall approve the claim for payment. The board shall determine that the state should indemnify a person who files a claim pursuant to this chapter if there is need for such indemnification, except that such a claim may be denied if the claimant has not cooperated with the police in the apprehension and conviction of the criminal committing the crime.

The maximum amount for which the board may approve a claim pursuant to this section shall not exceed the amount necessary to indemnify or reimburse the claimant for necessary expenses incurred for hospitalization or medical treatment, loss of wages, loss of support, or other necessary expenses directly related to the injury. If continued hospitalization or medical treatment is necessary, a partial award may be made and the claim subsequently reconsidered for the purpose of recommending an additional award.

In addition the board may award, as attorney's fees, an amount representing the reasonable value of legal services rendered a claimant, but in no event to exceed 10 percent of the amount of the award.

A claim shall be reduced to the extent that the claimant has received indemnification from any other source. If a claim is paid under this chapter the state shall be subrogated to the rights of the claimant to whom such claim was paid against any person causing the damage or injury for which payment was made to the extent of the payment of the claim. The state may recover the amount of the claim paid in a separate action, or may intervene in an action brought by the claimant. In no event shall a claim be approved pursuant to this section in excess of five thousand dollars ($5,000).
(Added Stats. 1967, c. 1546, p. 3707, § 1.)

§ *13964. Fine imposed in addition to penalty for conviction of crime of violence; determination by court*

Upon conviction of a person of a crime of violence committed in the State of California resulting in the injury or death of another person who was a resident of the State of California at the time the crime was committed, the court shall take into consideration the defendant's economic condition, and unless it finds such action will cause the family of the defendant to be dependent on public welfare, may, in addition to any other penalty, order the defendant to pay a fine commensurate in amount with the offense committed. The fine shall be deposited in the Indemnity Fund in the State Treasury, which is hereby continued in existence, and the proceeds in such fund shall be available for appropriation by the Legislature to indemnify persons filing claims pursuant to this chapter.
(Added Stats. 1967, c. 1546, p. 3707, § 1)

§ *13965. District attorney; duty to inform persons eligible to file claim*

(a) The district attorney of each county shall inform each person in the county who may be eligible to file a claim pursuant to this chapter of such eligibility. The district attorney of each county shall obtain from the board any forms which may be necessary in the preparation and presentation of such claims.

(b) If a victim of a crime does not cooperate with a state or local law enforcement agency in the apprehension and conviction of the criminal committing the crime, the agency shall immediately notify the board of such lack of cooperation.

(Added Stats. 1967, c. 1546, p. 3707, § 1.)

§ 13966. *Payment of claims*

Claims under this chapter shall be paid from a separate appropriation made to the State Board of Control in the Budget Act and as such claims are approved by the board.
(Added Stats. 1967, c. 1546, p. 3707, § 1)

ARTICLE 2. CITIZENS BENEFITING THE PUBLIC[3]

§ 13970.

Direct action on the part of private citizens in preventing the commission of crimes against the person or property of others, or in apprehending criminals, or rescuing a person in immediate danger of injury or death as a result of fire, drowning, or other catastrophe, benefits the entire public. In recognition of the public purpose served, the state may indemnify such citizens, their widows, and their surviving children in appropriate cases for any injury, death, or damage sustained by such citizens, their widows or their surviving children as a direct consequence of such meritorious action to the extent that they are not compensated for the injury, death, or damage from any other source.

§ 13971.

As used in this article, "private citizen" means any natural person other than a peace office, fireman, lifeguard, or person whose employment includes the duty to protect the public safety acting within the course and scope of such employment.

§ 13972.

In the event a private citizen incurs personal injury or death or damage to his property in preventing the commission of a crime against the person or property of another, in apprehending a criminal, or in materially assisting a peace officer in prevention of a crime or apprehension of a criminal, or rescuing a person in immediate danger of injury or death as a result of fire, drowning, or other catastrophe, the private citizen, his widow, his surviving children, or a public safety agency acting on his or their behalf may file a claim with the State Board of Control for indemnification to the extent that the claimant

---

3. Article 2 was added by: Cal. Gov't Code § 13970 *et. seq.* (Deering Supp. 1970).

is not compensated from any other source for such injury, death, or damage. The claim shall generally show:

(a) The date, place and other circumstances of the occurrence or events which gave rise to the claim;

(b) A general description of the activities of the private citizen in prevention of a crime, apprehension of a criminal, or rescuing a person in immediate danger of injury or death as a result of fire, drowning, or other catastrophe;

(c) The amount or estimated amount of the injury, death, or damage sustained for which the claimant is not compensated from any other source, insofar as it may be known at the time of the presentation of the claim;

(d) Such other information as the Board of Control may require.

The claim shall be accompanied by a corroborating statement and recommendation from the appropriate state or local law enforcement agency.

§ 13973.

Upon presentation of any such claim, the Board of Control shall fix a time and place for the hearing of the claim, and shall mail notices thereof to interested persons or agencies and to the Attorney General. At the hearing, the board shall receive recommendations from the Attorney General and law enforcement agencies, and evidence showing:

(a) The nature of the crime committed by the apprehended criminal or prevented by the action of the private citizen, or the nature of the action of the private citizen in rescuing a person in immediate danger of injury or death as a result of fire, drowning, or other catastrophe, and the circumstances involved;

(b) That the actions of the private citizen substantially and materially contributed to the apprehension of a criminal, the prevention of a crime, or the rescuing of a person in immediate danger of injury or death as a result of fire, drowning, or other catastrophe;

(c) That as a direct consequence, the private citizen incurred personal injury or damage to property or died;

(d) The extent of such injury or damage for which the claimant is not compensated from any other source;

(e) Such other evidence as the board may require.

If the board determines, on the basis of such evidence, that the state should indemnify the claimant for the injury, death, or damage sustained, it shall submit a report of the facts and its conclusion to the

Legislature, and recommendation that an appropriation be made by the Legislature for the purposes of indemnifying the claimant. In no event shall a claim be approved by the board under this article in excess of five thousand dollars ($5,000).

§ *13974.*

The Board of Control is hereby authorized to make all needful rules and regulations consistent with the law for the purpose of carrying into effect the provisions of this act.

STATE OF HAWAII

Chapter 351

Criminal Injuries Compensation

Part I. Introductory

§ 351-1. Purpose. The purpose of this chapter is to aid victims of criminal acts, by providing compensation for victims of certain crimes or dependents of deceased victims, and for indemnification of private citizens for personal injury or property damage suffered in prevention of crime or apprehension of a criminal. [L 1967, c 226, pt of § 1]

§ 351-2. Definitions. As used in this chapter, unless the context otherwise requires:

"Child" means an unmarried person who is under twenty years of age and includes a stepchild or an adopted child;

"Commission" means the criminal injuries compensation commission established by this chapter;

"Dependents" mean such relatives of a deceased victim who were wholly or partially dependent upon his income at the time of his death or would have been so dependent but for the incapacity due to the injury from which the death resulted and includes the child of the victim born after his death;

"Injury" means actual bodily harm and, in respect of a victim, includes pregnancy and mental or nervous shock; and "Injured" has a corresponding meaning;

"Private citizen" means any natural person other than a peace officer of the State;

"Relative" means a victim's spouse, parent, grandparent, stepfather, stepmother, child, grandchild, brother, sister, half brother, half sister, or spouse's parents;

"Victim" means a person who is injured or killed by any act or omission of any other person coming within the criminal jurisdiction of the State which is within the description of any of the crimes specified in section 351-32 of this chapter. [L 1967, c 226, pt. of § 1]

Part II. Establishment of Commission

§ 351-11. Criminal injuries compensation commission. There shall be a criminal injuries compensation commission which shall be composed of three members to be appointed and be removable in the manner prescribed by section 26-34. One member of the commission shall be an attorney who has been admitted to practice before the supreme court of the State for at least five years. No officer or employee of the State or any political subdivision thereof shall be eligible for appointment to the commission. The commission is placed within the department of social services for administrative purposes. [L 1967, c 226, pt of § 1]

§ 351-12. Tenure and compensation of members. The term of office of each member of the criminal injuries compensation commission shall be four years or until his successor is appointed except that (1) the terms of office of the members first taking office shall expire as designated by the governor at the time of the appointment, one on December 31, 1968, one on December 31, 1969, and one on December 31, 1970; and (2) any member appointed to fill a vacancy occurring prior to the expiration of the term for which his predecessor was appointed, shall be appointed for the remainder of the term. Each member of the commission shall be eligible for reappointment, subject to section 26-34. A vacancy in the commission shall not affect its powers. If any member of the commission is unable to act because of absence, illness, or other sufficient cause, the governor may make a temporary appointment, and such appointee shall have all the powers and duties of a regular member of the commission for the period of his appointment.

Each member of the commission except the chairman shall be compensated at the rate of $50 per day for each day's actual attendance to his duties, provided such compensation shall not exceed a maximum of $6,600 per year. The chairman shall be compensated at the rate of $55 per day for each day's actual attendance to his duties, provided such compensation shall not exceed a maximum of $7,200 per year. The members of the commission shall be paid their necessary travelling and subsistence expenses incurred in the discharge of their duties. [L 1967, c 226, pt of § 1]

§ 351-13. Powers and procedures of commission. Upon an application made to the criminal injuries compensation commission under this chapter, the commission shall fix a time and place for a hearing on such application and shall cause notice thereof to be given to the applicant. The commission may hold such hearings, sit and act at such times and places, and take such testimony as the commission may deem advisable. The chairman and one other member of the commission shall constitute a quorum; and where opinion is divided and only one other member is present, the opinion of the chairman shall prevail. Any member of the commission may administer oaths or affirmations to witnesses appearing before the commission. The commission shall have such powers of subpoena and compulsion of attendance of witnesses and production of documents and of examination of witnesses as are conferred upon a circuit court. Subpoenas shall be issued under the signature of the chairman. The circuit court of any circuit in which a subpoena is issued or served or in which the attendance or production is required may, upon the application of the commission, enforce the attendance and testimony of any witness and the production of any document so subpoenaed. Subpoena and witness fees and mileage shall be the same as in criminal cases in the circuit courts, and shall be payable from funds appropriated for expenses of administration. [L 1967, c 226, pt of § 1]

§ 351-14. Hearings and evidence. Where any application is made to the criminal injuries compensation commission under this chapter, the applicant and the commission's legal adviser shall be entitled to appear and be heard. Any other person may appear and be heard who satisfied the commission that he has a substantial interest in the proceedings. In any case in which the person entitled to make an application is a child, the application may be made on his behalf by any person acting as his parent or guardian. In any case in which the person entitled to make an application is mentally defective, the application may be made on his behalf by his guardian or such other individual authorized to administer his estate.

Where under this chapter any person is entitled to appear and be heard by the commission, that person may appear in person or by his attorney. All hearings shall be open to the public unless in a particular case the commission determines that the hearing, or a portion thereof, should be held in private, having regard to the fact that the offender has not been convicted or to the interest of the victim of an alleged sexual offense.

Every person appearing under this section shall have the right to produce evidence and to cross-examine witnesses. The commission may receive in evidence any statement, document, information, or matter that may in the opinion of the commission contribute to its functions under this chapter, whether or not such statement, document, information, or matter would be admissible in a court of law.

If any person has been convicted of any offense with respect to an act or omission on which a claim under this chapter is based, proof of that conviction shall, unless an appeal against the conviction or a petition for a rehearing in respect of the charge is pending or a new trial or rehearing has been ordered, be taken as conclusive evidence that the offense has been committed. [L 1967, c 226, pt of § 1]

§ 351-15. Medical examination. The criminal injuries

compensation commission may appoint an impartial licensed physician to examine any person making application under this chapter, and the fees for the examination shall be paid from funds appropriated for expenses of administration. [L 1967, c 226, pt of § 1]

§ 351-16. Attorneys' fees. The criminal injuries compensation commission may, as a part of any order entered under this chapter, determine and allow reasonable attorneys' fees, which if the award of compensation is more than $1,000 shall not exceed fifteen percent of the award, to be paid out of but not in addition to the award, to the attorneys representing the applicant, provided that the amount of the attorneys' fees shall not, in any event, exceed the award of compensation remaining after deducting that portion thereof for expenses actually incurred by the claimant.

Any attorney who charges, demands, receives, or collects for services rendered in connection with any proceedings under this chapter any amount in excess of that allowed under this section, if any compensation is paid, shall be fined not more than $2,000. [L 1967, c 226, pt of § 1]

§ 351-17. Judicial review. Any person aggrieved by a final order or decision of the criminal injuries compensation commission on the sole ground that the order or decision was in excess of the commission's authority or jurisdiction, shall have a right of appeal to the Supreme Court, provided the appeal is filed within thirty days after service of a certified copy of the order or decision. Except as provided in the preceding sentence, orders and decisions of the commission shall be conclusive and not subject to judicial review. [L 1967, c 226, pt of § 1]

PART III.   COMPENSATION TO VICTIMS OR DEPENDENTS

§ 351-31. Eligibility for compensation. (a)   In the event any person is injured or killed by any act or omission of any other person coming within the criminal jurisdiction of the State after June 6, 1967, which act or omission is within the description of the crimes enumerated in section 351-32, the criminal injuries compensation commission may, in its discretion, upon an application, order the payment of compensation in accordance with this chapter:

(1)   To or for the benefit of the victim; or
(2)   To any person responsible for the maintenance of the victim, where that person has suffered pecuniary loss or incurred expenses as a result of the victim's injury; or

(3)   In the case of the death of the victim, to or for the benefit of any one or more of the dependents of the deceased victim.

(b)   For the purposes of this chapter, a person shall be deemed to have intentionally committed an act or omission notwithstanding that by reason of age, insanity, drunkenness, or otherwise he was legally incapable of forming a criminal intent.

(c)   In determining whether to make an order under this section, the commission may consider any circumstances it determines to be relevant, and the commission shall consider the behavior of the victim, and whether, because of provocation or otherwise, the victim bears any share of responsibility for the crime that caused his injury or death and the commission shall reduce the amount of compensation in accordance with its assessment of the degree of such responsibility attributable to the victim.

(d)   An order may be made under this section whether or not any person is prosecuted for or convicted of a crime arising out of an act or omission described in subsection (a), provided an arrest has been made or such act or omission has been reported to the police without undue delay. No order may be made under this section unless the commission finds that:

(1)   The act or omission did occur; and

(2)   The injury or death of the victim resulted from the act or omission. Upon application from the prosecuting attorney of the appropriate county, the commission may suspend proceedings under this chapter for such period as it deems desirable on the ground that a prosecution for a crime arising out of the act or omission has been commenced or is imminent. [L 1967, c 226, pt of § 1]

§ 351-32.   Violent crimes. The crimes to which part III of this chapter applies are the following enumerated offenses and all other offenses in which any enumerated offense is necessarily included:

(1)   Arson—Sec. 723-2;

(2)   Intermediate Assault or Battery—Sec. 724-5;

(3)   Aggravated Assault or Battery—Sec. 724-3 or any other aggravated assault offense enacted by law;

(4)   Use of dangerous substances—Sec. 724-4;

(5)   Murder—Sec. 748-1;

(6)   Manslaughter—Sec. 748-6;

(7)   Kidnapping—Sec. 749-1;

(8)   Child-stealing—Sec. 749-4;

(9)   Unlawful use of explosives—Sec. 753-3;

(10)   Sexual intercourse with female under sixteen—Sec. 768-21;

(11)   Assault with intent to rape or ravish—Sec. 768-26;
(12)   Indecent Assault—Sec. 768-31;
(13)   Carnal abuse of female under twelve—Sec. 768-36;
(14)   Rape—Sec. 768-61;
(15)   Attempted Rape—Sec. 702-1, 768-61. [L 1967, c 226, pt of § 1]

§ 351-33.   Award of compensation.   The criminal injuries compensation commission may order the payment of compensation under this part for:

(1)   Expenses actually and reasonably incurred as a result of the injury or death of the victim;
(2)   Loss to the victim of earning power as a result of total or partial incapacity;
(3)   Pecuniary loss to the dependents of the deceased victim;
(4)   Pain and suffering to the victim; and
(5)   Any other pecuniary loss directly resulting from the injury or death of the victim which the commission determines to be reasonable and proper. [L 1967, c 226, pt of § 1]

§ 351-34.   Relationship to offender.   No compensation shall be awarded, except for expenses specified in section 351-33(1), if the victim:

(1)   Is a relative of the offender; or
(2)   Was at the time of his injury or death living with the offender as spouse or as a member of the offender's household. [L 1967, c 226, pt of § 1]

§ 351-35.   Recovery from offender.   Whenever any person is convicted of an offense that includes any crime enumerated in section 351-32 and an order or the payment of compensation is or has been made under this part for injury or death resulting from the act or omission constituting such offense, the criminal injuries compensation commission may institute a derivative action against the person and against any person liable at law on his behalf, in the name of the victim or such of his dependents as have been awarded compensation under this part in the circuit court of the circuit in which any such person resides or is found, for such damages as may be recoverable at common law by the victim or such dependents without reference to the payment of compensation under this part. The court shall have jurisdiction to hear, determine, and render judgment in any such action. The time from the occurence of the act or omission until conviction of the offense and, thereafter, as long as the offender is in confinement for conviction of the offense, shall not constitute any part of the time limited for the commencement of the action by the commission under the applicable statute of limitations. Any recovery in the action shall belong to the State, provided that the commission shall amend its order of compensation to provide for the payment of any portion of the recovery in excess of the amount of compensation prescribed in the order to any of the persons entitled to receive compensation under section 351-31 in such proportions and upon such terms as the commission shall deem appropriate. If the legislature fails to appropriate funds to pay all or any part of the award of payment made by the commission and there is a recovery of the money from the offender, the commission shall pay all of such recovery to the claimant or such portion thereof, to the claimant as to the commission appears just and equitable, but in no case shall any claimant be given an award in excess of both the recovery and the award. [L 1967, c 226, pt of § 1]

PART IV. COMPENSATION TO PRIVATE CITIZENS

§ 351-51.   Eligibility for compensation. In the event a private citizen incurs injury or property damage in preventing the commission of a crime within the State, in apprehending a person who has commited a crime within the State, or in materially assisting a peace officer who is engaged in the prevention or attempted prevention of such a crime or the apprehension or attempted apprehension of such a person, the criminal injuries compensation commission may, in its discretion, upon an application, order the payment of compensation in accordance with this chapter:

(1)   To or for the benefit of the private citizen; or

(2)   To any person responsible for the maintenance of the private citizen, where that person has suffered pecuniary loss or incurred expenses as a result of the private citizen's injury. [L 1967, c 226, pt of § 1]

§ 351-52.   Award of compensation. The criminal injuries compensation commission may order the payment of compensation under this part for:

(1)   Expenses actually and reasonably incurred as a result of the injury of the private citizen;

(2)   Pain and suffering to the private citizen;

(3)   Loss to the private citizen of earning power as a result of total or partial incapacity; and

(4)   Pecuniary loss to the private citizen directly resulting from damage to his property. [L 1967, c 226, pt of § 1]

PART V. GENERAL PROVISIONS

§ 351-61. Terms of order. Except as otherwise provided in this chapter, any order for the payment of compensation under this chapter may be made on such terms as the criminal injuries compensation commission deems appropriate. Without limiting the generality of the preceding sentence, the order may provide for apportionment of the compensation, for the holding of the compensation or any part thereof in trust, and for the payment of the compensation in a lump sum or periodic installments. All such orders shall contain words clearly informing the claimant that all awards and orders for payments under this chapter are subject to the making of an appropriation by the legislature to pay the claim. [L 1967, c 226, pt of § 1]

§ 351-62 Limitations upon award of compensation. (a) No order for the payment of compensation shall be made under this chapter unless the application has been made within eighteen months after the date of injury, death or property damage.

(b) No compensation shall be awarded under this chapter in an amount in excess of $10,000. [L 1967, c 226, pt of § 1]

§ 351-63. Recovery from collateral source. (a) The criminal injuries compensation commission shall deduct from any compensation awarded under this chapter any payments received from the offender or from any person on behalf of the offender, or from the United States, a state, or any of its subdivisions, or any agency of any of the foregoing, for injury or death compensable under this chapter.

(b) Where compensation is awarded under this chapter and the person receiving same also receives any sum required to be, and that has not been deducted under subsection (a), he shall refund to the State the lesser of the sum or the amount of the compensation paid to him under this chapter. [L 1967, c 226, pt of § 1]

§ 351-64. No double recovery. Application may be made by any eligible person for compensation under both parts III and IV of this chapter, but no order shall have the effect of compensating any person more than once for any loss, expense, or other matter compensable under this chapter. [L 1967, c 226, pt of § 1]

§ 351-65. Legal adviser. The attorney general shall serve as legal adviser to the criminal injuries compensation commission. [L 1967, c 226, pt of § 1]

§ 351-66. Exemption from execution. No compensation payable under this chapter shall, prior to actual receipt thereof by the person or beneficiary entitled thereto, or their legal representatives, be assignable or subject to execution, garnishment, attachment, or other process whatsoever, including process to satisfy an order or judgment for support or alimony. [L 1967, c 226, pt of § 1]

§ 351-67.   Survival and abatement. The rights to compensation created by this chapter are personal and shall not survive the death of the person or beneficiary entitled thereto, provided that if such death occurs after an application for compensation has been filed with the criminal injuries compensation· commission, the proceeding shall not abate, but may be continued by the legal representative of the decedent's estate. [L 1967, c 226, pt of § 1]

§ 351-68.   Rule-making powers. In the performance of its functions, the criminal injuries compensation commission may adopt, amend, and repeal rules and regulations, not inconsistent with this chapter, prescribing the procedures to be followed in the filing of applications and the proceedings under this chapter and such other matters as the commission deems appropriate. [L 1967, c 226, pt of § 1]

§ 351-69.   Commission staff. Supervisory, administrative, and clerical personnel necessary for the efficient functioning of the criminal injuries compensation commission shall be appointed as provided in section 26-35. [L 1967, c 226, pt of § 1]

§ 351-70.   Annual Report. The criminal injuries compensation commission shall transmit annually to the governor and to the director of finance, at least thirty days prior to the convening of legislature a report of its activities under this chapter including the name of each applicant, a brief description of the facts in each case, and the amount, if any, of compensation awarded. The director of finance shall, within five days after the opening of the legislative session, transmit the report, together with a tabulation of the total amount of compensation awarded, to the Committee on Ways and Means of the Senate and the Committee on Appropriations of the House of Representatives (or any successor committee). The funds necessary to pay the compensation awarded shall be appropriated in the same manner as payment of other claims for legislative relief sought pursuant to section 37-6. Compliance with this section shall be deemed compliance with section 37-6. [L 1967, c 226, pt of § 1]

STATE OF MARYLAND

Annotated Code, Article 26A

CRIMINAL INJURIES COMPENSATION ACT.

§ *1. Declaration of policy and legislative intent.*

The legislature recognizes that many innocent persons suffer personal physical injury or death as a result of criminal acts or in their efforts to prevent crime or apprehend persons committing or attempting to commit crimes. Such persons or their dependents may thereby suffer disability, incur financial hardships or become dependent upon public assistance. The legislature finds and determines that there is a need for government financial assistance for such victims of crime. Accordingly, it is the legislature's intent that aid, care and support be provided by the State, as a matter of moral responsibility, for such victims of crime. (1968, ch. 455, § 1.)

§ *2. Definitions.*

For the purpose of this article:

(a) *"Board"* shall mean the Criminal Injuries Compensation Board.

(b) *"Claimant"* shall mean the person filing a claim pursuant to this article.

(c) *"Crime"* shall mean an act committed by any person in the State of Maryland which would constitute a crime as defined in Article 27 of the Annotated Code of Maryland (1967 Replacement Volume) or at common law, provided, however, that no act involving the operation of a motor vehicle which results in injury shall constitute a crime for the purpose of this article unless the injuries were intentionally inflicted through the use of a vehicle.

(d) *"Family"* when used with reference to a person, shall mean (1) any person related to such person within the third degree of consanguinity or affinity, (2) any person maintaining a sexual relationship with such person, or (3) any person residing in the same household with such person.

(e) *"Victim"* shall mean a person who suffers personal physical injury or death as a direct result of a cime. (1968, ch. 455 § 1.)

§ *3. Criminal Injuries Compensation Board—Creation; composition; appointment, qualifications and terms of members; chairman; salaries.*

(a) There is hereby created in the executive department a Board, to be known as the Criminal Injuries Compensation Board, to consist of three members, no more than two of whom shall belong to the same political party. The members of the Board shall be appointed by the Governor, with the advice and consent of the Senate. One member of the Board shall have been admitted to practice law in the State of Maryland for not less than five years next preceding his appointment.

(b) The term of office of each such members shall be five years, except that the members first appointed shall serve for terms of five years, four years and three years respectively. Any member appointed to fill a vacancy occurring otherwise than by expiration of a term shall be appointed for the remainder of the unexpired term.

(c) The Governor shall designate one member of the Board as chairman, to serve at the pleasure of the Governor.

(d) The members of the Board shall devote such time as is necessary to perform the duties imposed upon them. They shall receive an annual salary as may be provided in the annual budget. (1968, ch. 455, § 1.)

§ 4.   *Same—Powers and duties.*

The Board shall have the following powers and duties:

(a) To establish and maintain an office and appoint a secretary, clerks and such other employees and agents as may be necessary, such employees to be subject to the provisions of Article 64A, titled Merit System, and prescribe their duties.

(b) To adopt, promulgate, amend and rescind suitable rules and regulations to carry out the provisions and purposes of this article, including rules for the approval of attorneys' fees for representation before the Board or before the court upon judicial review as hereinafter provided.

(c) To request from the State's Attorney, State Police, county or municipal police departments such investigation and data as will enable the Board to determine if, in fact, a crime was committed or attempted, and the extent, if any, to which the victim or claimant was responsible for his own injury.

(d) To hear and determine all claims for awards filed with the Board pursuant to this article, and to reinvestigate or reopen cases as the Board deems necessary.

(e) To direct medical examination of victims.

(f) To hold hearings, administer oaths or affirmations, examine any person under oath or affirmation and to issue summons requiring the attendance and giving of testimony of witnesses and require the production of any books, papers, documentary or other evidence. The powers provided in this subsection may be delegated by the Board to any member or employee thereof. A summons issued under this subsection shall be regulated by the Maryland Rules of Procedure.

(g)   To take or cause to be taken affidavits or depositions within or without the State.

(h)   To render each year to the Governor and to the legislative council a written report of its activities. (1968, ch. 455, § 1.)

§ 5.   *Eligibility for awards.*

(a)   Except as provided in subsection (b) of this section, the following persons shall be eligible for awards pursuant to this article.

(1)   A victim of a crime;

(2)   A surviving spouse or child of a victim of a crime who died as a direct result of such crime; and

(3)   Any other person dependent for his principal support upon a victim of a crime who died as a direct result of such crime.

(4)   Any person who is injured or killed while trying to prevent a crime or an attempted crime from occurring in his presence or trying to apprehend a person who had committed a crime in his presence or had, in fact, committed a felony.

(5)   A surviving spouse or child of any person who dies as a direct result of trying to prevent a crime or an attempted crime from occurring in his presence or trying to apprehend a person who had committed a crime in his presence or had, in fact, committed a felony.

(6)   Any other person dependent for his principal support upon any person who dies as a direct result of trying to prevent a crime or an attempted crime from occurring in his presence or trying to apprehend a person who had committed a crime in his presence or had, in fact, committed a felony.

(b)   A person who is criminally responsible for the crime upon which a claim is based or an accomplice of such person or a member of the family of such persons shall not be eligible to receive an award with respect to such claim. (1968, ch. 455, § 1.)

§ 6.   *Filing of claims.*

(a)   A claim may be filed by a person eligible to receive an award, as provided in § 5 of this article, or if such person is a minor, by his parent or guardian. In any case in which the person entitled to make a claim is mentally incompetent, the claim may be filed on his behalf by his guardian or such other individual authorized to administer his estate.

(b)   A claim must be filed by the claimant not later than ninety days after the occurrence of the crime upon which such claim is based, or not later than ninety days after the death of the victim, provided, however, that upon good cause shown, the Board may extend that time for filing for a period not exceeding one year after such occurrence.

(c)   Claims shall be filed in the office of the secretary of the Board in person or by mail. The secretary shall accept for filing all claims submitted by persons eligible under subsection (a) of this section and alleging the jurisdictional requirements set forth in this article and meeting the requirements as to form in the rules and regulations of the Board.

(d)   Upon filing of a claim pursuant to this article, the Board shall promptly notify the State's attorney of the county, or Baltimore City, as the case may be, wherein the crime is alleged to have occurred. If, within ten days after such notification, the State's attorney so notified advises the Board that a criminal prosecution is pending upon the same alleged crime, the Board shall defer all proceedings under this article until such time as such criminal prosecution has been concluded and shall so notify such State's attorney and the claimant. When such criminal prosecution has been concluded, the State's attorney shall promptly so notify the Board. Nothing in this section shall limit the authority of the Board to grant emergency awards as hereinafter provided. (1968, ch. 455, § 1.)

§ 7.   *Minimum allowable claim.*

No award shall be made on a claim unless the claimant has incurred a minimum out-of-pocket loss of one hundred dollars or has lost at least two continuous weeks' earnings or support. Out-of-pocket loss shall mean reimbursed and unreimbursable expenses or indebtedness reasonably incurred for medical care or other services necessary as a result of the injury upon which such claim is based. (1968, ch. 455, § 1.)

§ 8.   *Decisions on claims— By single Board member.*

(a)   A claim, when accepted for filing, shall be assigned by the chairman to himself or to another member of the Board. All claims arising from the death of an individual as a direct result of a crime, shall be considered together by a single Board member.

(b)   The Board member to whom such claim is assigned shall examine the papers filed in support of the claim and shall thereupon cause an investigation to be conducted into the validity of the claim.

The investigation shall include, but not be limited to, an examination of police, court and official records and reports concerning the crime and an examination of medical and hospital reports relating to the injury upon which the claim is based.

(c) Claims shall be investigated and determined, regardless of whether the alleged criminal has been apprehended or prosecuted for or convicted of any crime based upon the same incident, or has been acquitted, or found not guilty of the crime in question owing to criminal responsibility or other legal exemption.

(d) The Board member to whom a claim is assigned may decide the claim in favor of a claimant on the basis of the papers filed in support thereof and the report of the investigation of the claim. If the Board member is unable to decide the claim upon the basis of the said papers and report, he shall order a hearing. At the hearing any relevant evidence, not legally privileged, shall be admissible.

(e) After examining the papers filed in support of the claim and the report of investigation, and after a hearing, if any, the Board member to whom the claim was assigned shall make a decision either granting an award pursuant to § 12 of this article or deny the claim.

(f) The Board member making a decision shall file with the secretary a written report setting forth such decision and his reasons therefore. The secretary shall thereupon notify the claimant and furnish him a copy of such report upon request. (1968, ch. 455, § 1.)

§ 9. Same—By full Board.

(a) The claimant may, within thirty days after receipt of the report of the Board member to whom his claim was assigned, make an application in writing to the Board for consideration of the decision by the full Board.

(b) Upon receipt of an application pursuant to subsection (a) of this section or upon its own motion, the Board shall review the record and affirm or modify the decision of the Board member to whom the claim was assigned. The action of the Board in affirming or modifying such decision shall be final. If the Board receives no application pursuant to subsection (a) of this section or takes no action upon its own motion the decision of the Board member to whom the claim was assigned shall become the final decision of the Board.

(c) The secretary of the Board shall promptly notify the claimant, the Attorney General and the Comptroller of the final decision of the Board and furnish each with a copy of the report setting forth the decision. (1968, ch. 455, § 1.)

§ 10. Same—Judicial review.

(a) Within thirty days after receipt of the copy of the report containing the final decision of the Board, the Attorney General may, if in his judgment the award is improper, commence a proceeding in the circuit court of the county or the Supreme Bench of Baltimore City, as the case may be, to review the decision of the Board. Any such proceeding shall be heard in a summary manner and shall have precedence over all other civil cases in such court. The court may, however, take additional testimony, if it so desires. There shall be no other judicial review of any decision made or action taken by the Board, by a member of the Board or by the secretary of the Board with respect to any claim.

(b) Any such proceeding shall be commenced by the service of notice thereof upon the claimant and the Board in person or by mail. (1968, ch. 455, § 1.)

§ 11. Emergency awards

Notwithstanding the provisions of §§ 6 and 8 of this article, if it appears to the Board member to whom a claim is assigned, prior to taking action upon such claim, that (a) such claim is one with respect to which an award probably will be made and (b) undue hardship will result to the claimant if immediate payment is not made, the Board member may make an emergency award to the claimant pending a final decision in the case, provided, however, that (1) the amount of such emergency award shall not exceed five hundred dollars, (2) the amount of such emergency award shall be deducted from any final award made to the claimant, and (3) the excess of the amount of such emergency award over the final award, or the full amount of the emergency award if not final award is made, shall be repaid by the claimant to the Board. (1968, ch. 455, § 1.)

§ 12. Prerequisites to award; amount; apportionment; reduction or denial.

(a) No award shall be made unless the Board or Board member, as the case may be, finds that (1) a crime was committed, (2) such crime directly resulted in personal physical injury to, or death of the victim, and (3) police records show that such crime was promptly reported to the proper authorities; and in no case may an award be made where the police records show that such report was made more than forty-eight hours after the occurrence of such crime unless the

Board, for good cause shown, finds the delay to have been justified. The Board, upon finding that any claimant or award recipient has not fully cooperated with all law enforcement agencies, may deny or withdraw any award, as the case may be.

(b) Any award made pursuant to this article shall be made in accordance with the schedule of benefits and degree of disability as specified in § 36 of Article 101 of the Code, excluding § 66 entitled "Subsequent Injury Fund."

(c) If there are two or more persons entitled to an award as a result of the death of a person which is the direct result of a crime, the award shall be apportioned among the claimants.

(d) Any award made pursuant to this article shall be reduced by the amount of any payments received or to be received as a result of the injury (1) from or on behalf of the person who committed the crime, (2) from any other public or private source, including an award of the Workmen's Compensation Commission under Article 101, (3) as an emergency award pursuant to § 11 of this article.

(e) In determining the amount of an award, the Board or Board members, as the case may be, shall determine whether, because of his conduct, the victim of such crime contributed to the infliction of his injury, and the Board or Board member shall reduce the amount of the award or reject the claim altogether, in accordance with such determination; provided, however, that the Board or Board member, as the case may be, may disregard for this purpose the responsibility of the victim for his own injury where the record shows that such responsibility was attributable to efforts by the victim to prevent a crime or an attempted crime from occurring in his presence or to apprehend a person who had committed a crime in his presence or had, in fact, committed a felony.

(f) If the Board or Board member, as the case may be, finds that the claimant will not suffer serious financial hardship, as a result of the loss of earnings or support and the out-of-pocket expenses incurred as a result of the injury, if not granted financial assistance pursuant to this article to meet such loss of earnings, support or out-of-pocket expenses, the Board or Board members shall deny an award. In determining such serious financial hardship, the Board or Board member shall consider all of the financial resources of the claimant. (1968, ch. 455, § 1.)

§ 13.   *Manner of Payment of Award; execution or attachment.*

Any award made under this article shall be paid in accordance with the provisions of § 36 and other applicable sections of Article 101 of this Code, excluding § 66 of that article entitled "Subsequent Injury Fund." No award made pursuant to this article shall be subject to execution or attachment other than for expenses resulting from the injury which is the basis for the claim. (1968, ch. 455, § 1.)

§ 14.   Confidentiality of records.

The record of a proceeding before the Board or a Board member shall be a public record; provided, however, that any record or report obtained by the Board, the confidentiality of which is protected by any other law or regulation, shall remain confidential subject to such law or regulation. (1968, ch. 455, § 1.)

§ 15.   Subrogation.

Acceptance of an award made pursuant to this article shall subrogate the State, to the extent of such award, to any right or right of action occurring to the claimant or the victim to recover payments on account of losses resulting from the crime with respect to which the award is made. (1968, ch. 455, § 1.)

§ 16.   Penalty.

Any person who asserts a false claim under the provisions of this article shall be guilty of a misdemeanor, and upon conviction thereof, shall be subject to a fine of not less than $500 or one year imprisonment or both, and shall further forfeit any benefit received and shall reimburse and repay the State for payments received or paid on his behalf pursuant to any of the provisions hereunder. (1968, ch. 455, § 1.)

§ 17.   Additional cost to be imposed in criminal cases.

Where any person is convicted after July 1, 1968, of any crime by any judge, or trial magistrate, with criminal jurisdiction, there shall be imposed as additional cost, in the case, in addition to any other costs required to be imposed by law, the sum of five dollars ($5). All such sums shall be paid over to the Comptroller of the State to be deposited in the general funds of the State. Under no condition shall a political subdivision be held liable for the payment of this sum of five dollars ($5). Crime as used in this section does include violations of Articles 66½ (Motor Vehicles) or 66c (Natural Resources) of this Code. (1968, ch. 455, § 1; 1969, ch. 286.)

STATE OF MASSACHUSETTS

The General Laws, Chapter 258A

COMPENSATION OF VICTIMS OF VIOLENT CRIMES

Section 1. The following words as used in this chapter shall have the following meaning, unless the context requires otherwise:

"Crime", an act committed in the commonwealth which, if committed by a mentally competent, criminally responsible adult, who had no legal exemption or defense, would constitute a crime; provided that such act involves the application of force or violence or the threat of force or violence by the offender upon the victim; and provided, further, that no act involving the operation of a motor vehicle which results in injury to another shall constitute a crime for the purpose of this chapter unless such injury was intentionally inflicted through the use of a motor vehicle.

"Dependent", mother, father, spouse, spouse's mother, spouse's father, child, grandchild, adopted child, illegitimate child, niece or nephew, who is wholly or partially dependent for support upon and living with the victim at the time of his injury or death due to a crime alleged in a claim pursuant to this chapter.

"Family", the spouse, parent, grandparent, step-mother, step-father, child, grandchild, brother, sister, half-brother, half-sister, adopted children of parent, or spouse's parents of the offender.

"Offender", a person who commits a crime.

"Victim", a person who suffers personal injury or death as a direct result of a crime.

Section 2. The district courts of the commonwealth shall, pursuant to the provisions of this chapter, have jurisdiction to determine and award compensation to victims of crimes.

Such claims shall be brought in a district court within the territorial jurisdiction in which the claimant lives. A judge who has heard a criminal case in which the crime alleged as the basis of such claim shall not sit in determination of such claim. A judge who has heard such a claim shall not sit in a criminal case arising from a crime alleged in such claim. Failure to prosecute, or to prosecute successfully an offender in a criminal case, shall not in any way prejudice the claim of an eligible claimant unless such failure is due to the provocation of the offender by the victim.

Section 3. Except as hereinafter provided, the following persons shall be eligible for compensation pursuant to this chapter:

(a)   a victim of crime;

(b)   in the case of the death of the victim as a direct result of the crime, a dependent of the victim.

An offender or an accomplice of an offender, a member of the family of the offender, a person living with the offender or a person maintaining sexual relations with the offender shall in no case be eligible to receive compensation with respect to a crime committed by the offender.

Section 4.   A claim for compensation may be filed by a person eligible for compensation or if he is a minor or is incompetent, by his parent or guardian.

A claim shall be filed not later than one year after the occurrence of the crime upon which it is based, or not later than ninety days after the death of the victim whichever is ·earlier; provided, however, that upon good cause, the court may either before or after the expiration of said filing period extend the time for filing such claim.

Each claim shall be filed in the office of the clerk of the district court in person or by mail, and shall be accompanied by an entry fee of five dollars. Said clerk shall immediately notify the attorney general of the claim. Such notification shall be in writing, with copies of such material as is included in the claim or in support thereof. The attorney general shall investigate such claim, prior to the opening of formal court proceedings. Said clerk of court shall notify the claimant and the attorney general of the date and time of any hearing on such claim.

The attorney general shall present any information he may have in support of or in opposition to the claim. The claimant may present evidence and testimony on his own behalf or may retain counsel. The court may, as part of any order entered under this chapter, determine and allow reasonable attorney's fees, which shall not exceed fifteen per cent of the amount awarded as compensation under this chapter, which fee shall be paid out of, but not in addition to, the amount of compensation, to the attorney representing the claimant. No attorney for the claimant shall ask for, contract for or receive any larger sum than the amount so allowed.

The person filing a claim shall, prior to any hearing thereon, submit reports, if available, from all hospitals, physicians or surgeons who treated or examined the victim for the injury for which compensation is sought. If, in the opinion of the court, an examination of the injured victim and a report thereon, or a report on the cause of death of the victim, would be of material aid, the court may appoint a duly qualified impartial physician to make such examination and report.

Section 5. No compensation shall be paid unless the claimant has incurred an out-of-pocket loss of at least one hundred dollars or has lost two continuous weeks of earnings or support. Out-of-pocket loss shall mean unreimbursed or unreimbursable expenses or indebtedness reasonably incurred for medical care or other services necessary as a result of the injury upon which such claim is based. One hundred dollars shall be deducted from any award granted under this chapter.

No compensation shall be paid unless the court finds that a crime was committed, that such crime directly resulted in personal physicial injury to, or the death of, the victim, and that police records show that such crime was promptly reported to the proper authorities. In no case may compensation be paid if the police records show that such report was made more than forty-eight hours after the occurrence of such crime unless the court finds said report to the police to have been delayed for good cause.

Any compensation paid under this chapter shall be in an amount not exceeding out-of-pocket loss, together with loss of earnings or support resulting from such injury.

Any compensation for loss of earnings or support shall be in an amount equal to the actual loss sustained; provided, however, that no award under this chapter shall exceed ten thousand dollars. If two or more persons are entitled to compensation as a result of a death of a person which is the direct result of a crime, the compensation shall be apportioned by the court among the claimants in proportion to their loss.

Section 6. For the purpose of determining the amount of compensation payable pursuant to this chapter, the chief justice of the district court and the chief justice of the municipal court of the city of Boston shall, insofar as practicable, formulate standards for the uniform application of this chapter. The court shall take into consideration the provisions of this chapter, the rates and amounts of compensation payable for injuries and death under other laws of the commonwealth and of the United States, excluding pain and suffering, and the availability of funds appropriated for the purpose of this chapter. All decisions of the court on claims heard under this chapter shall be in writing, setting forth the name of the claimant, the amount of compensation and the reasons for the decision. The clerk of the court shall immediately notify the claimant in writing of the decision and shall forward to the state treasurer a certified copy of the decision. The state treasurer without further authorization shall, subject to appropriation, pay the claimant the amount determined by the court.

Any compensation paid pursuant to this chapter shall be reduced by the amount of any payments received or to be received as a result of the injury (a) from or on behalf of the offender, (b) under insurance programs, or (c) from public funds.

In determining the amount of compensation payable, the court shall determine whether because of his conduct the victim contributed to the infliction of his injury; and the court shall reduce the amount of the compensation or deny the claim altogether, in accordance with such determination; provided, however, that the court may disregard the responsibility of the victim for his own injury where such responsibility was attributable to efforts by the victim to aid a victim, or to prevent a crime or an attempted crime from occurring in his presence or to apprehend a person who had committed a crime in his presence or had in fact committed a felony.

Section 7. Acceptance of any compensation under this chapter shall subrogate the commonwealth, to the extent of such compensation paid, to any right or right of action accruing to the claimant or to the victim to recover payments on account of losses resulting from the crime with respect to which the compensation has been paid. The attorney general may enforce the subrogation, and he shall bring suit to recover from any person to whom compensation is paid, to the extent of the compensation actually paid under this chapter, any amount received by the claimant from any source exceeding the actual loss to the victim.

Section 2. The first paragraph of section 108 of chapter 231 of the General Laws is hereby amended by striking out the first sentence and inserting in place thereof the following sentence:—there shall be an appellate division of each district court for the rehearing of matters of law arising in civil cases therein and in claims for compensation of victims of violent crimes.

Section 3. Chapter 218 of the General Laws is hereby amended by inserting after section 43c the following section:

Section 43D. The chief justice of the district courts shall make uniform rules applicable to all the district courts except the municipal court of the city of Boston, and the chief justice of the municipal court of the city of Boston shall make rules applicable to that court, providing for a simple, informal and inexpensive procedure for the determination of claims for compensation of victims of violent crimes, as provided under chapter two hundred and fifty-eight A.

Section 4.   Section three of this act shall take effect conformably with law, and sections one and two shall take effect on July first, nineteen hundred and sixty-eight, and shall apply only to victims of crimes committed on or after said date.

Approved January 2, 1968.

STATE OF NEW YORK

Article 22

Executive Law of New York

CRIME VICTIMS COMPENSATION BOARD

§ 620 Declaration of policy and legislative intent. The legislature recognizes that many innocent persons suffer personal physical injury or death as a result of criminal acts. Such persons or their dependents may thereby suffer disability, incur financial hardships, or become dependent upon public assistance. The legislature finds and determines that there is a need for government financial assistance for such victims of crime. Accordingly, it is the legislature's intent that aid, care and support be provided by the state, as a matter of grace, for such victims of crime.

§ 621 Definitions. For the purposes of this article:

1. "Board" shall mean the crime victims compensation board.

2. "Claimant" shall mean the person filing a claim pursuant to this article.

3. "Crime" shall mean an act committed in New York state which would, if committed by a mentally competent criminally responsible adult, who has no legal exemption or defense, constitute a crime as defined in and proscribed by the penal law, provided, however, that no act involving the operation of a motor vehicle which results in injury shall constitute a crime for the purposes of this article unless the injuries were intentionally inflicted through the use of a vehicle.

4. "Family" when used with reference to a person, shall mean (a) any person related to such person within the third degree of consanguinity or affinity, (b) any person maintaining a sexual relationship with such person, or (c) any person residing in the same household with such person.

5. "Victim" shall mean a person who suffers personal physical injury as a direct result of a crime.

§ 622 Crime victims compensation board. 1. There is hereby created in the executive department a board, to be known as the crime victims compensation board. Such board shall consist of three members, no more than two of whom shall belong to the same political party, who shall be appointed by the governor by and with the advice and consent of the senate. The members of the board shall have been admitted to practice law in the state of New York for not less than ten years next preceding their appointment. 2. The term of office of each such member shall be seven years, except that the members first appointed shall serve for terms of seven years, five years and three years, respectively. Any member appointed to fill a vacancy occurring otherwise than by expiration of a term shall be appointed for the remainder of the unexpired term. 3. The governor shall designate one member of the board as chairman thereof, to serve as such at the pleasure of the governor. 4. The members of the board shall devote their whole time and capacity to their duties, and shall not engage in any other occupation, profession or employment, and shall receive an annual salary to be fixed by the governor within the amount made available therefor by appropriation.

§ 623 Powers and duties of the board. The board shall have the following powers and duties:

1. To establish and maintain a principal office and such other offices within the state as it may deem necessary.

2. To appoint a secretary, counsel, clerks and such other employees and agents as it may deem necessary, fix their compensation within the limitations provided by law, and prescribe their duties.

3. To adopt, promulgate, amend and rescind suitable rules and regulations to carry out the provisions and purposes of this article, including rules for the approval of attorneys' fees for representation before the board or before the appellate division upon judicial review as provided for in section six hundred twenty-nine of this article.

4. To request from the division of state police, from county or municipal police departments and agencies and from any other state or municpal department or agency, or public authority, and the same are hereby authorized to provide, such assistance and data as will enable the board to carry out its functions and duties.

5. To hear and determine all claims for awards filed with the board pursuant to this article, and to reinvestigate or reopen cases as the board deems necessary.

6. To direct medical examination of victims.

7. To hold hearings, administer oaths or affirmations, examine any person under oath or affirmation and to issue subpoenas requiring the attendance and giving of testimony of witnesses and require the production of any books, papers, documentary or other evidence. The powers provided in this subdivision may be delegated by the board to any member or employee thereof. A subpoena issued under this subdivision shall be regulated by the civil practice law and rules.

8. To take or cause to be taken affidavits or depositions within or without the state.

9. To render each year to the governor and to the legislature a written report of its activities.

§ 624 Eligibility. 1. Except as provided in subdivision two of this section, the following persons shall be eligible for awards pursuant to this article:

(a) a victim of a crime;

(b) a surviving spouse, parent[1] or child of a victim of a crime who died as a direct result of such crime; and

(c) any other person dependent for his principal support upon a victim of a crime who died as a direct result of such crime.

2. A person who is criminally responsible for the crime upon which a claim is based or an accomplice of such person or a member of the family of such persons shall not be eligible to receive an award with respect to such claims.

§ 625 Filing of claims. 1. A claim may be filed by a person eligible to receive an award, as provided in section six hundred twenty-four of this article, or, if such person is a minor, by his parent or guardian. 2. A claim must be filed by the claimant not later than ninety days after the occurrence of the crime upon which such claim is based, or not later than ninety days after the death of the victim, provided, however, that upon good cause shown, the board may extend the time for filing for a period not exceeding one year after such occurrence. 3. Claims shall be filed in the office of the secretary of the board in person or by mail. The secretary of the board shall accept for filing all claims submitted by persons eligible under subdivision one of this section and alleging the jurisdictional requirements set forth in this article and meeting the requirements as to form in the rules and regulations of the board. 4. Upon filing of a claim pursuant to this article, the board shall promptly notify the district attorney of the county wherein the crime is alleged to have occurred. If, within ten days after such notification, such district attorney advises the board that a criminal prosecution is pending upon the same alleged crime and requests that action by the board be deferred, the board shall defer all proceedings under this article until such time as such criminal prosecution has been concluded and shall so notify such district attorney and claimant. When such criminal prosecution has been concluded, such district attorney shall promptly so notify the board. Nothing in this section shall limit the authority of the board to grant

---

1. The word "parent" was added by: N.Y. Exec. Law § 624 (4 CLS Supp. 1969).

emergency awards pursuant to section six hundred thirty[2] of this article.

§ 626   Minimum allowable claim.   No award shall be made on a claim unless the claimant has incurred a minimum out-of-pocket loss of one hundred dollars or has lost at least two continuous weeks earnings or support. Out-of-pocket loss shall mean unreimbursed and unreimbursable expenses or indebtedness reasonably incurred for medical care or other services necessary as a result of the injury upon which such claim is based.

§ 627   Determination of claims.   1.   A claim, when accepted for filing, shall be assigned by the chairman to himself or to another member of the board. All claims arising from the death of an individual as a direct result of a crime, shall be considered together by a single board member.   2.   The board member to whom such claim is assigned shall examine the papers filed in support of such claim. The board member shall thereupon cause an investigation to be conducted into the validity of such claim. Such investigation shall include, but not be limited to, an examination of police, court and official records and reports concerning the crime and an examination of medical and hospital reports relating to the injury upon which such claim is based.   3.   Claims shall be investigated and determined, regardless of whether the alleged criminal has been apprehended or prosecuted for or convicted of any crime based upon the same incident, or has been acquitted, or found not guilty of the crime in question owing to criminal irresponsibility or other legal exemption.   4.   The board member to whom a claim is assigned may decide such claim in favor of a claimant in the amount claimed on the basis of the papers filed in support thereof and the report of the investigation of such claim. If the board member is unable to decide such claim upon the basis of such papers and such report, he shall order a hearing. At such hearing any relevant evidence, not legally privileged, shall be admissible.   5. After examining the papers filed in support of such claim and the report of investigation, and after a hearing, if any, the board member to whom such claim was assigned shall make a decision either granting an award pursuant to section six hundred thirty-one of this article or deny the claim.   6.   The board member making a decision shall file with the secretary a written report setting forth such decision and his reasons therefor. The secretary shall thereupon notify the claimant and furnish him a copy of such report.

---

2.   The section number "six hundred thirty" was added by: N.Y. Exec. Law § 625 (4 CLS Supp. 1969). The original language was: "six hundred twenty-nine."

§ 628   Consideration of decisions by full board.   1.   The claimant may, within thirty days after receipt of the report of the decision of the board member to whom his claim was assigned, make an application in writing to the board for consideration of such decision by the full board.   2.   Any member of the board may, within thirty days after the filing of such report, make an application in writing to the board for consideration of such decision by the full board.   3.   Upon receipt of an application pursuant to subdivision one or two of this section, the board shall review the record and affirm or modify the decision of the board member to whom the claim was assigned. The action of the board in affirming or modifying such decision shall be final. The board shall file with the secretary of the board a written report setting forth its decision, and if such decision varies in any respect from the report of the board member to whom the claim was assigned setting forth its reasons for such decision. If the board receives no application pursuant to subdivision one or two of this section the decision of the board member to whom the claim was assigned shall become the final decision of the board.   4.   The secretary of the board shall promptly notify the claimant, the attorney general and the comptroller of the final decision of the board and furnish each with a copy of the report setting forth such decision.

§ 629   Judicial review.   1.   Within thirty days after receipt of the copy of the report containing the final decision of the board, the attorney general may, if in his judgment the award is improper or excessive, commence a proceeding in the appellate division of the supreme court, third department, to review the decision of the board. Within thirty days after receipt of the copy of such report, the comptroller may, if in his judgment the award is improper or excessive, request the attorney general to commence a proceeding in the appellate division of the supreme court, third department, to review the decision of the board in which event the attorney general shall commence such a proceeding. Such proceeding shall be heard in a summary manner and shall have precedence over all other civil cases in such court. There shall be no other judicial review of any decision made or action taken by the board, by a member of the board or by the secretary of the board with respect to any claim.   2.   Any such proceeding shall be commenced by the service of notice thereof upon the claimant and the board in person or by mail.

§ 630   Emergency awards.   Notwithstanding the provisions of section six hundred twenty-seven of this article, if it appears to the board member to whom a claim is assigned, prior to taking action upon such claim, that (a) such claim is one with respect to which an award probably will be made, and (b) undue hardship will result to the claimant if immediate payment is not made, such board member may make an emergency award to the claimant pending a final decision in the case, provided, however, that (a) the amount of such emergency award shall not exceed five hundred dollars, (b) the amount of such emergency award shall be deducted from any final award made to the claimant, and (c) the excess of the amount of such emergency award over the amount of the final award, or the full amount of the emergency award if no final award is made, shall be repaid by the claimant to the board.

§ 631   Awards.   1.   No award shall be made unless the board or board member, as the case may be, finds that (a) a crime was committed, (b) such crime directly resulted in personal physical injury to, or death of, the victim, and (c) police records show that such crime was promptly reported to the proper authorities; and in no case may an award be made where the police records show that such report was made more than forty-eight hours after the occurrence of such crime unless the board, for good cause shown, finds the delay to have been justified.   2.   Any award made pursuant to this article shall be in an amount not exceeding out-of-pocket expenses, including indebtedness reasonably incurred for medical or other services necessary as a result of the injury upon which the claim is based, together with loss of earnings or support resulting from such injury.   3.   Any award made for loss of earnings or support shall, unless reduced pursuant to other provisions of this article, be in an amount equal to the actual loss sustained, provided, however, that no such award shall exceed one hundred dollars for each week of lost earnings or support, and provided further that the aggregate award for such loss shall not exceed fifteen thousand dollars. If there are two or more persons entitled to an award as a result of the death of a person which is the direct result of a crime, the award shall be apportioned by the board among the claimants.   4.   Any award made pursuant to this article shall be reduced by the amount of any payments received or to be received as a result of the injury (a) from or on behalf of the person who committed the crime, (b) under insurance programs mandated by law, (c) from public funds, (d) as an emergency award pursuant to section six hundred thirty of this article.   5.   In determining the amount of an award, the board or board member, as the case may be, shall determine whether, because of his conduct, the victim of such crime contributed to the infliction of his injury, and the board or board member shall reduce the amount of the award or reject the claim altogether, in accordance with such determination; provided, however, that the board or board member, as the case may be, may disregard for this purpose the responsibility of the victim for his own injury where the record shows that such responsibility was attributable to efforts by the victim to prevent a crime or an attempted crime from occurring in his presence or to apprehend a person who had committed a crime in his presence or had in fact committed a felony. 6. If the board or board member, as the case may be, finds that the claimant will not suffer serious financial hardship, as a result of the loss of earnings or support and the out-of-pocket expense incurred as a result of the injury, if not granted financial assistance pursuant to this article to meet such loss of earnings, support or out-of-pocket expenses, the board or board members shall deny an award. In determining such serious financial hardship, the board or board member shall consider all of the financial resources of the claimant. The board shall establish specific standards by rule for determining such serious financial hardship.

§ 632 Manner of payment. The award shall be paid in a lump sum, except that in the case of death or protracted disability the award shall provide for periodic payments to compensate for loss of earnings or support. No award made pursuant to this article shall be subject to execution or attachment other than for expenses resulting from the injury which is the basis for the claim.

§ 633 Confidentiality of records. The record of a proceeding before the board or a board member shall be a public record; provided, however, that any record or report obtained by the board, the confidentiality of which is protected by any other law or regulation, shall remain confidential subject to such law or regulation.

§ 634 Subrogation. Acceptance of an award made pursuant to this article shall subrogate the state, to the extent of such award, to any right or right of action accruing to the claimant or the victim to recover payments on account of losses resulting from the crime with respect to which the award is made.

§ 635 Severability of provisions. If any provision of this article or the application thereof to any person or circumstances is held invalid, the remainder of this article and the application of such provision to other persons or circumstances shall not be affected thereby.

§ 2 The sum of five hundred thousand dollars ($500,000), or so much thereof as may be necessary, is hereby appropriated to the crime victims compensation board in the executive department out of any moneys in the state treasury in the general fund to the credit of the state purposes fund, and not otherwise appropriated, for the purposes of such board pursuant to article twenty-two of the executive law. Such sums shall be payable on audit and warrant of the comptroller on vouchers certified by the chairman or secretary of such board, in the manner provided by law.

§ 3   This act shall take effect immediately, but the provisions of article twenty-two of the executive law, as added by this act, shall apply only to claims resulting from crimes committed on or after October first, nineteen hundred sixty-six.

S. 9

IN THE SENATE OF THE UNITED STATES

January 15 (legislative day, January 10), 1969
Mr. Yarborough introduced the following bill; which was read twice
and referred to the Committee on the Judiciary

A BILL

To provide for the compensation of persons injured by certain criminal
acts.

*Be it enacted by the Senate and House of Representatives of the
United States of America in Congress assembled,*

TITLE I—SHORT TITLE AND DEFINITIONS

SHORT TITLE

Sec. 101. This Act may be cited as the "Criminal Injuries
Compensation Act of 1969".

DEFINITIONS

Sec. 102. As used in this Act—

(1) The term "child" means an unmarried person who is under
eighteen years of age and includes a stepchild or an adopted child;

(2) The term "Commission" means the Violent Crimes
Compensation Commission established by this Act;

(3) The term "dependents" means those who were wholly or
partially dependent upon his income at the time of his death or would
have been so dependent but for the incapacity due to the injury from
which the death resulted and shall include the child of such victim born
after his death;

(4) The term "personal injury" means actual bodily harm and
includes pregnancy and mental or nervous shock;

(5) The term "relative" means his spouse, parent, grandparent,
stepfather, stepmother, child, grandchild, brother, sister, half brother,
half sister, or spouse's parents;

(6) The term "victim" means a person who is injured or killed
by any act or omission of any other person which is within the
description of any of the offenses specified in section 302 of this Act.

TITLE II—ESTABLISHMENT OF VIOLENT CRIMES COMPENSATION COMMISSION

VIOLENT CRIMES COMPENSATION COMMISSION

SEC. 201. (a) There is established a Violent Crimes Compensation Commission which shall be composed of three members to be appointed by the President, by and with the advice and consent of the Senate, solely on the grounds of fitness to perform the duties of the office. The President shall designate one of the members of the Commission who has been a member of the bar of a Federal court or of the highest court of a State for at least eight years as Chairman.

(b) No member of the Commission shall engage in any other business, vocation, or employment.

(c) The Chairman and one other member of the Commission shall constitute a quorum, except as provided in section 205(b); and where opinion is divided and only one other member is present, the opinion of the Chairman shall prevail.

(d) The Commission shall have an official seal.

TERMS AND COMPENSATION OF MEMBERS

SEC. 202. (a) The term of office of each member of the Commission taking office after December 31, 1969, shall be eight years, except that (1) the terms of office of the members first taking office after December 31, 1969, shall expire as designated by the President at the time of the appointment, one at the end of four years, one at the end of six years, and one at the end of eight years, after December 31, 1969; and (2) any member appointed to fill a vacancy occurring prior to the expiration of the terms for which his predecessor was appointed shall be appointed for the remainder of such term.

(b) Each member of the Commission shall be eligible for reappointment.

(c) A vacancy in the Commission shall not affect its powers.

(d) Any member of the Commission may be removed by the President for inefficiency, neglect of duty, or malfeasance in office.

(e) Each member of the Commission shall be compensated at the rate prescribed for level IV of the Federal Executive Salary Schedule of the Federal Executive Salary Act of 1964 except the Chairman who shall be compensated at the rate prescribed for level III of such schedule.

ATTORNEYS, EXAMINERS, AND EMPLOYEES OF THE COMMISSION; EXPENSES

SEC. 203. (a) The Commission is authorized to appoint such officers, attorneys, examiners, and other experts as may be necessary for carrying out its functions under this Act, and the Commission may, subject to the civil service laws, appoint such other officers and employees as are necessary and fix their compensation in accordance with the Classification Act of 1949.

(b) All expenses of the Commission, including all necessary traveling and subsistence expenses of the Commission outside the District of Columbia incurred by the members or employees of the Commission under its orders, shall be allowed and paid on the presentation of itemized vouchers therefor approved by the Commission or by any individual it designates for that purpose.

PRINCIPAL OFFICE

SEC. 204. (a) The principal office of the Commission shall be in or near the District of Columbia, but the Commission or any duly authorized representative may exercise any or all of its powers in any place.

(b) The Commission shall maintain an office for the service of process and papers within the District of Columbia.

POWERS AND PROCEDURES OF THE COMMISSION

SEC. 205. (a) Upon request made to the Commission after the filing of an application under the provisions of this Act, the Commission or its duly authorized representative shall have a hearing on such application, shall fix a time and place for such hearing, and shall cause notice thereof to be given to the applicant.

(b) For the purpose of carrying out the provisions of this Act, the Commission, or any member thereof, or its duly authorized representative, may hold such hearings, sit and act at such times and places, and take such testimony as the Commission or such member may deem advisable. Any member of the Commission may administer oaths, or affirmations to witnesses appearing before the Commission or before such member. The Commission shall have such powers of subpoena and compulsion of attendance and production of documents as are conferred upon the Securities and Exchange Commission by subsection (c) of section 18 of the Act of August 26, 1935, and the provisions of subsection (d) of such section shall be applicable to all persons summoned by subpoena or otherwise to attend or testify or produce such documents as are described therein before the Commission, except that no subpena shall be issued except under the signature of the Chairman, and application to any court for aid in enforcing such subpena may be made only by said Chairman. Subpenas shall be served by any person designated by the said Chairman.

(c) In any case in which the person entitled to make an application is a child, the application may be made on his behalf by any person acting as his parent or guardian. In any case in which the person entitled to make an application is mentally defective, the application may be made on his behalf by his guardian or such other individual authorized to administer his estate.

(d) Where any application is made to the Commission under this Act, the applicant, and any attorney assisting the Commission, shall be entitled to appear and be heard.

(e) Any other person may appear and be heard who satisfies the Commission that he has a substantial interest in the proceedings.

(f) Where under this Act any person is entitled to appear and be heard by the Commission, that person may appear in person or by his attorney.

(g) Every person appearing under the preceding subsections of this section shall have the right to produce evidence and to cross-examine witnesses.

(h) The Commission or its duly authorized representative may receive in evidence any statement, document, information, or matter that may in the opinion of the Commission contribute to its functions under this Act, whether or not such statement, document, information, or matter would be admissible in a court of law, except that any evidence introduced by or on behalf of the person or persons charged with causing the injury or death of the victim, any request for a stay of the Commission's action, and the fact of any award granted by the Commission shall not be admissible against such person or persons in any prosecution for such injury or death.

(i) If any person has been convicted of any offense with respect to an act or omission on which a claim under this Act is based, proof of that conviction shall, unless an appeal against the conviction or a petition for a rehearing or certiorari in respect of the charge is pending or a new trial or rehearing has been ordered, be taken as conclusive evidence that the offense has been committed.

(j) Except as otherwise provided in this Act, the Administrative Procedure Act shall apply to the proceedings of the Commission.

ATTORNEYS' FEES

SEC. 206. (a) The Commission shall publish regulations providing that an attorney shall, at the conclusion of proceedings under this Act, file with the agency the amount of fee charged in connection with his services rendered in such proceedings.

(b) After the fee information is filed by an attorney under (a) above, the Commission may determine, in accordance with such published rules or regulations as it may provide, that such fee charged is excessive. If, after notice to the attorney of this determination, the Commission and the attorney fail to agree upon a fee, the Commission may, within ninety days after the receipt of the information required by (a) above, petition the United States district court in the district in which the attorney maintains an office, and the court shall determine a reasonable fee for the services rendered by the attorney.

(c) Any attorney who charges, demands, receives, or collects for services rendered in connection with any proceedings under this Act any amount in excess of that allowed under this section, if any compensation is paid, shall be fined not more than $2,000 or imprisoned not more than one year, or both.

FINALITY OF DECISION

SEC. 207. The orders and decisions of the Commission shall be reviewable on appeal, except that no trial de novo of the facts determined by the Commission shall be allowed.

REGULATIONS

SEC. 208. In the performance of its functions, the Commission is authorized to make, promulgate, issue, rescind, and amend rules and regulations prescribing the procedures to be followed in the filing of applications and the proceedings under this Act, and such other matters as the Commission deems appropriate.

TITLE III—AWARD AND PAYMENT OF COMPENSATION

AWARDING COMPENSATION

SEC. 301. (a) In any case in which a person is injured or killed by any act or omission of any other person which is within the description of the offenses listed in section 302 of this Act, the Commission may, in its discretion, upon an application, order the payment of compensation in accordance with the provisions of this Act, if such act or omission occurs—

(1)   within the "special maritime and territorial jurisdiction of the United States" as defined in section 7 of title 18 of the United States Code; or

(2)   within the District of Columbia.

(b)   The Commission may order the payment of compensation—

(1)   to or on behalf of the injured person; or

(2)   in the case of the personal injury of the victim, where the compensation is for pecuniary loss suffered or expenses incurred by any person responsible for the maintenance of the victim, to that person; or

(3)   in the case of the death of the victim, to or for the benefit of the dependents or closest relative of the deceased victim, or any one or more of such dependents.

(c)   For the purposes of this Act, a person shall be deemed to have intended an act or omission notwithstanding that by reason of age, insanity, drunkenness, or otherwise he was legally incapable of forming a criminal intent.

(d)   In determining whether to make an order under this section, or the amount of any award, the Commission may consider any circumstances it determines to be relevant, including the behavior of the victim which directly or indirectly contributed to his injury or death, unless such injury or death resulted from the victim's lawful attempt to prevent the commission of a crime or to apprehend an offender.

(e)   No order may be made under this section unless the Commission, supported by substantial evidence, finds that—

(1)   such an act or omission did occur; and

(2)   the injury or death resulted from such act or omission.

(f)   An order may be made under this section whether or not any person is prosecuted or convicted of any offense arising out of such act or omission, or if such act or omission is the subject of any other legal action. Upon application from the Attorney General or the person or persons alleged to have caused the injury or death, the Commission shall suspend proceedings under this Act until such application is withdrawn or until a prosecution for an offense arising out of such act or omission is no longer pending or imminent. The Commission may suspend proceedings in the interest of justice if a civil action arising from such act or omission is pending or imminent.

(g)   Upon certification by the Commission, the Secretary of the

Treasury shall pay to the person named in such order the amount specified therein.

OFFENSES TO WHICH THIS ACT APPLIES

SEC. 302. The Commission may order the payment of compensation in accordance with the provisions of this Act for personal injury or death which resulted from offenses in the following categories:

(1)   assault with intent to kill, rob, rape, or poison;
(2)   assault with intent to commit mayhem;
(3)   assault with a dangerous weapon;
(4)   assault;
(5)   mayhem;
(6)   malicious disfiguring;
(7)   threats to do bodily harm;
(8)   lewd, indecent, or obscene acts;
(9)   indecent act with children;
(10)   arson;
(11)   kidnapping;
(12)   robbery;
(13)   murder;
(14)   manslaughter, voluntary;
(15)   attempted murder;
(16)   rape;
(17)   attempted rape;
(18)   or other crimes involving force to the person.

NATURE OF THE COMPENSATION

SEC. 303. The Commission may order the payment of compensation under this Act for—

(a)   expenses actually and reasonably incurred as a result of the personal injury or death of the victim;
(b)   loss of earning power as a result of total or partial incapacity of such victim;
(c)   pecuniary loss to the dependents of the deceased victim;
(d)   pain and suffering of the victim; and
(e)   any other pecuniary loss resulting from the personal injury or death of the victim which the Commission determines to be reasonable.

LIMITATIONS UPON AWARDING COMPENSATION

SEC. 304. (a) No order for the payment of compensation shall be made under section 301 of this Act unless the application has been made within two years after the date of the personal injury or death.

(b)   No compensation shall be awarded under this Act to or on behalf of any victim in an amount in excess of $25,000.

(c)   No compensation shall be awarded if the victim was at the time of the personal injury or death of the victim living with the offender as his wife or her husband or in situations when the Commission at its discretion feels unjust enrichment to or on behalf of the offender would result.

TERMS OF THE ORDER

SEC. 305. (a) Except as otherwise provided in this section, any order for the payment of compensation under this Act may be made on such terms as the Commission deems appropriate.

(b)   The Commission shall deduct from any payments awarded under section 301 of this Act any payments received by the victim or by any of his dependents from the offender or from any person on behalf of the offender, or from the United States (except those received under this Act), a State or any of its subdivisions, for personal injury or death compensable under this Act, but only to the extent that the sum of such payments and any award under this Act are in excess of the total compensable injuries suffered by the victim as determined by the Commission.

(c)   The Commission may at any time, on its own motion or on the application of the Attorney General, or of the victim or his dependents, or of the offender, vary any order for the payment of compensation made under this Act in such manner as the Commission thinks fit, whether as to terms of the order or by increasing or decreasing the amount of the award or otherwise.

TITLE IV—RECOVERY OF COMPENSATION
RECOVERY FROM OFFENDER

SEC. 401. (a) Whenever any person is convicted of an offense and an order for the payment of compensation is or has been made under this Act for a personal injury or death resulting from the act or omission constituting such offense, the Commission may institute an action against such person for the recovery of the whole or any specified part of such compensation in the district court of the United States for any judicial district in which such person resides or is found. Such court shall have jurisdiction to hear, determine, and render judgment in any such action.

(b)   Process of the district court for any judicial district in any action under this section may be served in any other judicial district by the United States marshal thereof. Whenever it appears to the court in which any action under this section is pending that other parties should be brought before the court in such action, the court may cause such other parties to be summoned from any judicial district of the United States.

(c)   An order for the payment of compensation under this Act shall not affect the right of any person to recover damages from any other person by a civil action for the injury or death.

TITLE V—MISCELLANEOUS
REPORTS TO THE CONGRESS

SEC. 501. The Commission shall transmit to the President and to the Congress annually a report of its activities under this Act including the name of each applicant, a brief description of the facts in each case, and the amount, if any, of compensation awarded.

PENALTIES

SEC. 502. The provisions of section 1001 of title 18 of the United States Code shall apply to any application, statement, document, or information presented to the Commission under this Act.

APPROPRIATIONS

SEC. 503. There are hereby authorized to be appropriated such sums as may be necessary to carry out the provisions of this Act.

EFFECTIVE DATE

SEC. 504. This Act shall take effect on January 1, 1970.

INDEX

Accomplices, liability of, 69
Adhesive procedure, 9, 11, 30, 31, 36, 39, 42, 103, 106, 118
Africa, 94–97
American Society of Criminology, 147, 148
Anglo-Saxons, 6, 7
Argentina, 76–79
Arney, George, 9
Assault, 77
Associations, liability of, 69
Attorneys' fees, 154, 155–156, 158
Australia, xi, 89–92, 152
Austria, 30–31
Automobile accidents. *See* Motor-car accidents
Bail, 74
Barnes, Harry Elmer, 117n
Belgium, 18–21
Bonneville de Marsangy, Arnould, 9, 10
Books of the Digest, 4
Brown, Gov. Edmund G., 154
Busse, 7, 9, 11, 32, 38–40, 96, 104–105
California, 132–133, 150, 152–153, 154
Canada, xi, 60–61
Capital punishment, 55
Chappell, Duncan, 152
Children, 43, 68, 91, 94
Childres, Robert, 147, 150, 153
Civil law, 7, 18, 33, 46, 56, 59, 76, 77, 85, 87, 92, 98, 111, 118–119, 132, 134
Civil proceedings, 19, 20, 21, 22, 24, 25, 28, 30, 31, 35, 39, 41–42, 43, 44, 48, 50, 51, 53–54, 57–58, 60, 62, 73, 80, 81, 83, 86, 89, 91, 92, 93, 95, 96, 99, 102–107
Code Napoleon, 72
Code of Hammurabi, 4
Collins, Arthur, 154–155
Compensation. *See also* Damages; State compensation
  defined, ix–x, 101, 102
  double, 145, 156, 158

Composition, xii, 3, 5, 6–7, 8–9, 133
  community share, 6–7
  state power, 6
Congress of Nordic Criminologists, 42, 45
Corporations, liability of, 69, 71–72
Correctional restitution. *See* Punishment
Court fees, 31, 70, 81
Crime, 117n, 139–140, 156
  offense against state, 8, 11, 98
  preventing, 131, 144, 157
Criminal insult, 4, 25, 27, 33, 38, 39, 47, 48, 50, 67, 77–78, 85
Criminal law, 6, 7, 9, 76, 121, 132, 134
Criminal personality, 121
Criminal proceedings, 19–20, 21, 22, 26–27, 30, 31, 36, 39, 41–42, 43, 44, 47–48, 51, 53–54, 56, 60, 62, 63, 73, 80, 81, 83, 98, 99, 102–107, 128
  advantages, 26
  limitations, 26–27, 103
Cuba, ix, 66–72, 105, 106, 124
Damages, 18–19
  defined, 32, 102
Death compensated, 34, 41, 43, 46, 50, 56, 57, 77, 80
Debt, imprisonment for, 24, 28, 73, 84
Defamation. *See* Criminal insult
Delinquency, 147, 149
Denmark, 41–42
Doctors' fees, 50, 67
Dominica, 72–73
Earnings, loss of, 50, 66, 67, 144, 156
Edwards, John, 147
Egypt, 84
Embezzlement, 47, 63, 64, 78
Emerton, Ephraim, 6n
Employers, liability of, 19
England, ix–xi, 7, 111–114, 132, 143–146, 152
  House of Commons, 112, 113
Fines, 63, 74, 87, 88, 96, 97, 104–105, 123, 124, 134, 152

209

Finland, 43–45
Fonds de garantie automobile, 21–22
France, 21–24, 103, 124
Frankish Empire, 7
Fry, Elizabeth, x
Fry, Margery, x, 112, 124n, 125n
Garofalo, Raffaelo, xiii–xiv, 9, 10, 134
Geis, Gilbert, 133
Genovese, Catherine, 131
Germanic common laws, 3, 5, 6
Germany, 32–40, 103, 104–105, 106, 121
Goldberg, Arthur J., 151, 153
"Good Samaritans," 131
Graham-Harrison, Francis, ix
Greece, 57–59
    death fine, 3
Grünhut, Max, x
Hawaii, 156–157
Hebrews, 3
Hentig, Hans von, 114n, 125n
Hinduism, 3
Holland, 24–29
Homer, 3
Homicide. *See* Murder
Hungary, 98–99, 103
Iliad, 3
Imprisonment, 63, 97. *See also* Debt, imprisonment for; Prisoners; Punishment
Indemnity Fund, 69, 70, 71, 72
India, 85–86, 103
    Sutra period, 3
Injured party, 47. *See also* Victims
Inquisition, 9
Insurance companies, 150
International Prison Congresses, xii, 9–10
Islam, 4
Israel, 80–83
Italy, xi, 53–55, 124
Lamborn, LeRoy L., 151
Landlords, liability of, 19
Law of Moses, 4
Law of the Twelve Tables, 4
Legal expenses. *See* Attorneys' fees; Court fees
Liability, third party, 19, 47, 69
Libel. *See* Criminal insult
Lodge, Tom, ix
Lombroso, Cesare, 121
Manslaughter, 25, 27
Maryland, 157
Massachusetts, 130–131, 133–134, 155–156
Mexico, 74–75, 105, 124

Middle Ages, 3, 5, 11
Minnesota Law Review, 148
Misappropriation of money. *See* Embezzlement
Misdemeanors, 62–63
Moral injury, 18, 21, 24, 27, 30, 33, 38–39, 41, 43, 46–47, 50, 54, 56, 57, 59, 66, 67, 73, 74, 76, 81, 85, 87, 91, 99, 118, 140, 152, 156. *See also* Criminal insult
More, Sir Thomas, 134
Mosaic Dispensation, 3
Moslem faith, 80
Motor-car accidents, 21–22
Mueller, Gerhard O. W., 147, 148, 150
Murder, 3, 5, 77
New York, 154–155
New Zealand, xi, 92–93, 103, 139–142, 152, 153
Non-material damage. *See* Moral injury
Norway, 46–50
Offenders
    assets, 78, 84, 134. *See also* Prisoners, assets
    personal circumstances, 25, 43, 68, 74, 129, 140, 141
    rehabilitation, 148
    third party, 68, 69
    two or more, 43, 68
Ottoman law, 80
"Outlawry," 6
Owners, liability of, 69
Pakistan, 87–88, 103
Parents, liability of, 19
Persia, 83–84
Prentice, R. E., 132
Prins, Adolphe, xiii, 10, 11, 134
Prisoners
    accident victims, 70–71
    assets, 42, 44, 54, 59, 71, 73, 74–75
    dependents, 95
    earnings, 10, 20, 23–24, 28, 30–31, 32, 37–38, 42, 44–45, 49, 51–52, 54, 55, 57, 58–59, 60–61, 65, 70, 73, 74–75, 79, 82, 84, 86, 87, 90, 91, 92, 93, 95, 98, 99–100, 107, 127
    escaped, 142
    work required, in prison, 20, 23, 28, 30, 37, 42, 45, 49, 54, 56, 60, 65, 70, 82, 84, 86, 87, 90, 91, 93, 95, 134
    work required, outside prison, 52, 84, 99
Probation, 38, 49, 61, 62, 91, 93, 108, 111

Public officials, 35, 43, 68
Publishers, liability of, 47, 69
Punishment, x, xiv, 3, 4, 5, 7, 8, 11, 63, 72, 74, 119–128, 134–135, 147–148, 149, 150, 152
  restitution as mitigating factor, 10, 28, 30, 38, 41, 44, 49, 52, 55, 58, 64, 82, 83, 86, 87, 90, 91, 93, 95, 98
Punitive restitution. *See* Punishment
Rape, 77, 144
Restitution
  defined, ix–x, 101, 102
  without compensation, 132
Riots, 151
Rockefeller, Gov. Nelson A., 155
Roman law, 4
Ruggles-Brise, Evelyn, xiiin
Schafer, Stephen, 147–148, 149, 150, 152
Sellin, Thorsten, 147
Sentencing. *See* Punishment; Suspended sentence
Shank, Willard, 152–153
Slander. *See* Criminal insult
Smith, Kathleen, 134
Southern California Law Review, 150–151
Soviet Union, 99–100
Spencer, Herbert, 134
Starrs, James, 147, 150
State compensation, 24, 35, 43–44, 66, 105–106, 111–114, 124–125, 129, 130, 141, 143, 147, 148, 149, 150
  anti-alienation, 131
  boards, 144–145, 155, 156, 157
  claims, 140–141, 145–146, 154, 155–156, 157
  crime prevention, 131
  legal obligation, 130
  objections, 112–114

social welfare, 130–131, 132–133, 143, 150, 152–153, 154
tribunal, 139–140
Stolen property, 61, 82–83, 87, 92, 95–96
Suspended sentence, 38, 44, 49, 61, 62, 108
Sutherland, Edwin H., 118n, 125n
Sweden, 50–52
Switzerland, ix, 31–32, 105, 106
Tallack, William, 9, 117n
Teachers, liability of, 19
Teeters, Negley K., 117n
Theft, 4, 5, 20, 78, 87, 96–97
Thieves, negotiations with, 65
Torts, 5, 8, 25, 27, 80, 85, 119, 132
Treaty of Verdun, 7
Turkey, 56–57
Turkish Empire, 3
United States, xi, 5, 61–65, 103, 105, 130–131, 132–134, 150, 152–153, 154–158
Utopia, 134
Victims, xi
  personal circumstances, 6, 25, 73, 132–133, 143, 155
  provocative behavior, 140, 141, 143, 144–145, 146, 152, 156, 157
  right to restitution, 7, 8, 10
  third party, 34, 66, 77, 78, 157
Weeks, Kent M., 153
Whipping, 97n
Wilkins, Leslie T., ix
Wolfgang, Marvin E., 130, 147, 149, 151
Women, immoral crime against, 33
Woodhouse Report, 142
Workmen, liability of, 19
Yarborough, Ralph W., xi, 149–150, 153, 157–158
Yugoslavia, 59

PATTERSON SMITH REPRINT SERIES IN
CRIMINOLOGY, LAW ENFORCEMENT, AND SOCIAL PROBLEMS

1. Lewis: *The Development of American Prisons and Prison Customs, 1776-1845*
2. Carpenter: *Reformatory Prison Discipline*
3. Brace: *The Dangerous Classes of New York*
4. Dix: *Remarks on Prisons and Prison Discipline in the United States*
5. Bruce *et al: The Workings of the Indeterminate-Sentence Law and the Parole System in Illinois*
6. Wickersham Commission: *Complete Reports, Including the Mooney-Billings Report.* 14 Vols.
7. Livingston: *Complete Works on Criminal Jurisprudence.* 2 Vols.
8. Cleveland Foundation: *Criminal Justice in Cleveland*
9. Illinois Association for Criminal Justice: *The Illinois Crime Survey*
10. Missouri Association for Criminal Justice: *The Missouri Crime Survey*
11. Aschaffenburg: *Crime and Its Repression*
12. Garofalo: *Criminology*
13. Gross: *Criminal Psychology*
14. Lombroso: *Crime, Its Causes and Remedies*
15. Saleilles: *The Individualization of Punishment*
16. Tarde: *Penal Philosophy*
17. McKelvey: *American Prisons*
18. Sanders: *Negro Child Welfare in North Carolina*
19. Pike: *A History of Crime in England.* 2 Vols.
20. Herring: *Welfare Work in Mill Villages*
21. Barnes: *The Evolution of Penology in Pennsylvania*
22. Puckett: *Folk Beliefs of the Southern Negro*
23. Fernald *et al: A Study of Women Delinquents in New York State*
24. Wines: *The State of the Prisons and of Child-Saving Institutions*
25. Raper: *The Tragedy of Lynching*
26. Thomas: *The Unadjusted Girl*
27. Jorns: *The Quakers as Pioneers in Social Work*
28. Owings: *Women Police*
29. Woolston: *Prostitution in the United States*
30. Flexner: *Prostitution in Europe*
31. Kelso: *The History of Public Poor Relief in Massachusetts: 1820-1920*
32. Spivak: *Georgia Nigger*
33. Earle: *Curious Punishments of Bygone Days*
34. Bonger: *Race and Crime*
35. Fishman: *Crucibles of Crime*
36. Brearley: *Homicide in the United States*
37. Graper: *American Police Administration*
38. Hichborn: *"The System"*
39. Steiner & Brown: *The North Carolina Chain Gang*
40. Cherrington: *The Evolution of Prohibition in the United States of America*
41. Colquhoun: *A Treatise on the Commerce and Police of the River Thames*
42. Colquhoun: *A Treatise on the Police of the Metropolis*
43. Abrahamsen: *Crime and the Human Mind*
44. Schneider: *The History of Public Welfare in New York State: 1609-1866*
45. Schneider & Deutsch: *The History of Public Welfare in New York State: 1867-1940*
46. Crapsey: *The Nether Side of New York*
47. Young: *Social Treatment in Probation and Delinquency*
48. Quinn: *Gambling and Gambling Devices*
49. McCord & McCord: *Origins of Crime*
50. Worthington & Topping: *Specialized Courts Dealing with Sex Delinquency*

PATTERSON SMITH REPRINT SERIES IN
CRIMINOLOGY, LAW ENFORCEMENT, AND SOCIAL PROBLEMS

51. Asbury: *Sucker's Progress*
52. Kneeland: *Commercialized Prostitution in New York City*
53. Fosdick: *American Police Systems*
54. Fosdick: *European Police Systems*
55. Shay: *Judge Lynch: His First Hundred Years*
56. Barnes: *The Repression of Crime*
57. Cable: *The Silent South*
58. Kammerer: *The Unmarried Mother*
59. Doshay: *The Boy Sex Offender and His Later Career*
60. Spaulding: *An Experimental Study of Psychopathic Delinquent Women*
61. Brockway: *Fifty Years of Prison Service*
62. Lawes: *Man's Judgment of Death*
63. Healy & Healy: *Pathological Lying, Accusation, and Swindling*
64. Smith: *The State Police*
65. Adams: *Interracial Marriage in Hawaii*
66. Halpern: *A Decade of Probation*
67. Tappan: *Delinquent Girls in Court*
68. Alexander & Healy: *Roots of Crime*
69. Healy & Bronner: *Delinquents and Criminals*
70. Cutler: *Lynch-Law*
71. Gillin: *Taming the Criminal*
72. Osborne: *Within Prison Walls*
73. Ashton: *The History of Gambling in England*
74. Whitlock: *On the Enforcement of Law in Cities*
75. Goldberg: *Child Offenders*
76. Cressey: *The Taxi-Dance Hall*
77. Riis: *The Battle with the Slum*
78. Larson *et al: Lying and Its Detection*
79. Comstock: *Frauds Exposed*
80. Carpenter: *Our Convicts.* 2 Vols. in 1
81. Horn: *Invisible Empire: The Story of the Ku Klux Klan, 1866-1871*
82. Faris *et al: Intelligent Philanthropy*
83. Robinson: *History and Organization of Criminal Statistics in the United States*
84. Reckless: *Vice in Chicago*
85. Healy: *The Individual Delinquent*
86. Bogen: *Jewish Philanthropy*
87. Clinard: *The Black Market: A Study of White Collar Crime*
88. Healy: *Mental Conflicts and Misconduct*
89. Citizens' Police Committee: *Chicago Police Problems*
90. Clay: *The Prison Chaplain*
91. Peirce: *A Half Century with Juvenile Delinquents*
92. Richmond: *Friendly Visiting Among the Poor*
93. Brasol: *Elements of Crime*
94. Strong: *Public Welfare Administration in Canada*
95. Beard: *Juvenile Probation*
96. Steinmetz: *The Gaming Table.* 2 Vols.
97. Crawford: *Report on the Pentitentiaries of the United States*
98. Kuhlman: *A Guide to Material on Crime and Criminal Justice*
99. Culver: *Bibliography of Crime and Criminal Justice: 1927-1931*
100. Culver: *Bibliography of Crime and Criminal Justice: 1932-1937*

PATTERSON SMITH REPRINT SERIES IN
CRIMINOLOGY, LAW ENFORCEMENT, AND SOCIAL PROBLEMS

101. Tompkins: *Administration of Criminal Justice, 1938-1948*
102. Tompkins: *Administration of Criminal Justice, 1949-1956*
103. Cumming: *Bibliography Dealing with Crime and Cognate Subjects*
104. Addams *et al: Philanthropy and Social Progress*
105. Powell: *The American Siberia*
106. Carpenter: *Reformatory Schools*
107. Carpenter: *Juvenile Delinquents*
108. Montague: *Sixty Years in Waifdom*
109. Mannheim: *Juvenile Delinquency in an English Middletown*
110. Semmes: *Crime and Punishment in Early Maryland*
111. National Conference of Charities and Correction: *History of Child Saving in the United States*
112. Barnes: *The Story of Punishment.* 2d ed.
113. Phillipson: *Three Criminal Law Reformers*
114. Drähms: *The Criminal*
115. Terry & Pellens: *The Opium Problem*
116. Ewing: *The Morality of Punishment*
117. Mannheim: *Group Problems in Crime and Punishment*
118. Michael & Adler: *Crime, Law and Social Science*
119. Lee: *A History of Police in England*
120. Schafer: *Compensation and Restitution to Victims of Crime.* 2d ed.
121. Mannheim: *Pioneers in Criminology.* 2d ed.
122. Goebel & Naughton: *Law Enforcement in Colonial New York*
123. Savage: *Police Records and Recollections*
124. Ives: *A History of Penal Methods*
125. Bernard (Ed.): *The Americanization Studies*
    Thompson: *The Schooling of the Immigrant*
    Daniels: *America via the Neighborhood*
    Thomas *et al: Old World Traits Transplanted*
    Speek: *A Stake in the Land*
    Davis: *Immigrant Health and the Community*
    Breckinridge: *New Homes for Old*
    Park: *The Immigrant Press and Its Control*
    Gavit: *Americans by Choice*
    Claghorn: *The Immigrant's Day in Court*
    Leiserson: *Adjusting Immigrant and Industry*
126. Dai: *Opium Addiction in Chicago*
127. Costello: *Our Police Protectors*
128. Wade: *A Treatise on the Police and Crimes of the Metropolis*
129. Robison: *Can Delinquency Be Measured?*
130. Augustus: *A Report of the Labors of John Augustus*
131. Vollmer: *The Police and Modern Society*
132. Jessel: *A Bibliography of Works in English on Playing Cards and Gaming.* Enlarged
133. Walling: *Recollections of a New York Chief of Police*
134. Lombroso: *Criminal Man*
135. Howard: *Prisons and Lazarettos.* 2 vols.
136. Fitzgerald: *Chronicles of Bow Street Police-Office.* 2 vols. in 1
137. Goring: *The English Convict*
138. Ribton-Turner: *A History of Vagrants and Vagrancy*
139. Smith: *Justice and the Poor*
140. Willard: *Tramping with Tramps*